World Re

Approaches to
Hinduism

Robert Jackson
Senior Lecturer in Arts Education
University of Warwick

Dermot Killingley
Senior Lecturer in Religious Studies
University of Newcastle upon Tyne

John Murray

World Religions in Education
Series Editor: Robert Jackson

Approaching World Religions
Robert Jackson (editor)

Approaches to Islam
Richard Tames

Approaches to Hinduism
Robert Jackson and Dermot Killingley

© Robert Jackson and Dermot Killingley 1988

First published 1988
by John Murray (Publishers) Ltd
50 Albemarle Street
London W1X 4BD

Typeset by Inforum Ltd, Portsmouth
Printed in Great Britain by
The Bath Press, Avon

British Library Cataloguing in Publication Data

Jackson, Robert, *1945–*
   Approaches to Hinduism.
   1. Hinduism
   I. Title   II. Killingley, Dermot, *1935–*
   III. Series
   294.5

   ISBN 0-7195-4362-2

Contents

Acknowledgements

Many friends and colleagues have helped us directly or indirectly with the production of this book. We would like to thank the following especially: Ann Cochrane, Denise Cush, Chris Fuller, Babu Garala, Cherry Gould, Mary Hayward, Jacqueline Suthren Hirst, Carolyn Hoare, Rosemary Jewel-Clark, Siew-Yue Killingley, Lallubhai Lad, Anita Lipner, Julius Lipner, Madhu Lodhia, Penny Logan, Heather Meldrum, Carri Mercier, Eleanor Nesbitt, Manju Radia, Colin Talbot, Marilyn Thomas, the University of Newcastle upon Tyne First Year Religious Studies group 1986–1987, the University of Warwick First Year Religious Studies group 1985–1986, Simon Weightman and the editors at John Murray. However, any mistakes that appear are our own.

The cover illustration was drawn by Ed Dovey.

Introduction

This book is a guide to the Hindu tradition for teachers. It aims to provide a thorough introduction to Hinduism with discussions of educational issues and teaching methods. There are numerous teaching ideas – from infant to post-16 – and an eye has been kept on GCSE syllabuses which include Hinduism. A detailed review of a wide selection of currently available school books and audio-visual aids is also provided.

Part 1 introduces Hinduism and some of the issues involved in teaching about it. Chapter 1 begins by arguing that our perception of what Hinduism is can be partly shaped by our views about the nature of religion and of religious education. A particular philosophy of religious education is advanced, and reasons are given for teaching about Hinduism. Chapter 2 attempts an overview of the Hindu tradition including a discussion of the term 'Hinduism' and some principles for selecting material for use with children. Chapter 3 suggests teaching methods and children's activities for making a study of Hinduism lively, colourful and attractive. The subject of Hinduism in Britain is introduced in Chapter 4 and is linked with a guide to organising children's visits to Hindu temples.

Part 2 looks at various aspects of Hinduism under ten headings which will already be familiar to many teachers of RE, though Hinduism may put them in a new light. Each topic is introduced by a case study in which it is seen as far as possible through the eyes of an actual Hindu. Since no one person's experience could cover the whole of a topic, each case study is followed by a general outline. Some of the subjects are outstanding people; others would not have been known unless some anthropologist or some other observer had interviewed and written about them. The details of each case study are authentic, but real names appear only in Chapters 7, 10, 12, 13 and 14.

There is no standard Hindu, just as there is no standard Hinduism. Any Hindu is heir to the particular traditions of his or her region, caste and lineage, not to those of all Hindus, so that any example drawn from real life is bound to contrast with some other example that might have been chosen. We tried, therefore, to choose people from different parts of India, and of different castes, social positions and religious groups. We would have liked to include more female subjects, but few Hindu women have written autobiographies, and anthropologists have tended to look mainly at men. (The case study in Chapter 7, which features a Gujarati woman, born in East Africa but now living in England, was done specially for this book.) Most of the material was gathered fairly recently, so we have introduced most of the subjects in the present tense, although they may no longer be living. The reader is urged not to generalise from the details of each case study. We chose to run the risk of giving details of individual examples in the interests of bringing the Hindu tradition to life; for, as we argue in Chapter 2, it is in the individual Hindu that the tradition lives, though not the whole tradition in each Hindu (p. 20).

If one is writing a fictional account of a branch of experience, one can fill it with material about that branch and little else. But when one is taking material from real life, one finds that there are always other concerns that keep coming in. We will find that none of our subjects told us simply about Hindu society, or Hindu worship; each subject will provide material for some other topic besides the one in hand, and some concerns recur in several case studies. This is neither carelessness nor a deliberate attempt to make the book difficult. If we had written fictional accounts, however well informed, they would have been tidier, but they would merely have reflected our own concerns and presuppositions. In selecting and recasting our material, we have indeed been influenced by our own ideas, but we have also received some surprises from the material itself. Except for Chapter 7, the accounts are taken from books that are available for further reading.

A word should be said about the order in which we have placed the chapters of Part 2. Our intention is to start from people – as members of families, of wider society, as worshippers – and then to move to the gods and their mythology and other topics. Some readers may prefer to read the chapters in a different order, perhaps starting with mythology and the gods and then worship. The chapters are written for the teacher, and not for the pupil, although sixth formers should have no difficulties in reading them. Material from the chapters can be adapted for use with pupils; when appropriate, the teaching ideas which appear at the end of each chapter suggest possible uses for it.

The aim of the teaching ideas is to stimulate teachers into developing their own schemes of work, tailored to the needs of their own particular classes. They are a selection only, not an exhaustive list. Teachers of infant and junior children may wish to incorporate some of the ideas into general topic work which covers a range of curriculum areas in addition to religious education. Some adaptation of the ideas may be necessary according to the ethnic composition of classes, especially where Hindu children may be able to make a direct contribution of knowledge and experience. Teaching ideas are listed, as appropriate, under three general headings: early years; the middle years; adolescence and post-16. These headings are no more than a rough guide and teachers are encouraged to read through all the material; the appearance of an idea under one heading need not preclude its adaptation and use with children of a different age group. We hope that the case studies and general discussions will stimulate teachers to come up with their own ideas for the classroom.

The teaching ideas take into account the discussion of the nature of religious education and Hinduism's place in it, found earlier in the book on pp. 6–11. Thus, while the ideas present wide ranging topics from the Hindu tradition, some activities start from or draw on the children's own experience and pupils are encouraged to raise questions and relate material studied to their own concerns. Teachers should read Chapter 3 'Teaching About Hinduism' (especially pp. 23–6) before adapting or developing the ideas offered at the end of each chapter in Part 2. It is hoped that teachers will be flexible in using the teaching ideas, particularly in allowing opportunities and time for questions to be raised, shared and discussed.

A wide selection of school books and audio-visual materials on Hinduism for all age groups is reviewed in Part 3, in an attempt to help readers to select the best material available. There is also a list of religious artefacts and addresses of Hindu organisations and suppliers of educational materials.

How to use the book

The book has been planned so that it can be read straight through (Part 1 providing an introduction, and Part 2 a more detailed study) or used as a reference book. The sub-headings in each chapter, together with the frequent cross references, will help readers to locate material on particular themes and topics.

We usually give Indian words in their Sanskrit form, except where another form (e.g. *Diwālī*) is more likely to be familiar. Because Sanskrit is known, if only to a few, in all regions of India, the use of Sanskrit rather than vernacular forms avoids restricting a description to any particular region.

The -*a* at the end of Sanskrit word or name (*Rāma, prasāda*), and sometimes also in the middle (*āratī, Bhagavat*) is usually omitted in Gujarati, Hindi, and Panjabi (*Rām, prasād, ārtī, Bhagwat*). In Bengali and South Indian languages there may be further differences, and teachers should be prepared for variety in the spelling and pronunciation of Indian words. Variation between *s* and *sh*, or *v* and *w*, is particularly common.

In spelling Indian words we have aimed at simplicity, and have not tried to convey the exact pronunciation. In speaking Indian words and names, however, it is important to use an approximate pronunciation within the limits of the English sound system. A macron ($^-$) is used to mark long vowels (*ā* as in *father*, *ī* as in *machine*, *ū* as in *rule*). The vowels *e* and *o* are always long, and sound somewhat like the vowels in *vain*, *go*. The diphthongs *ai*, *au* are somewhat like the vowels in *mind*, *loud*. The unmarked vowels *a, i, u* are short, and sound like the vowels in *cut, bit, put*. For further information on languages and pronunciation, see Shackle (1985); Killingley (1984: 105–23). Modern place names and personal names are spelt in their commonly accepted forms; macrons are included in their first occurrence and in the Index.

The Index contains brief glosses on the Indian words used.

Quotations from Sanskrit texts are translated by Dermot Killingley; references are given to other translations where appropriate.

Part One

Introducing Hinduism

Religious Education and Hinduism

Hinduism in the development of religious education

Hinduism has appeared in religious education programmes since the publication of some of the earliest Agreed Syllabuses for Religious Instruction which followed in the wake of the 1944 Education Act. Although religious education has gone through several levels of philosophical development since the 1940s, relics of each stage are still around on the educational scene. Some of these are portions of old Agreed Syllabuses which have been incorporated into new or revised versions, while others are in the form of textbooks or books for teachers. Since the portrayal of Hinduism in these sources depends largely on their underlying assumptions about the nature of religious education, it would be as well to draw attention to some representative examples.

Early comparative religion in schools

The early Agreed Syllabuses, in the main, confined any study of religions other than Christianity to the sixth form. The approach was a type of religious instruction in which the truth of Christian revelation was taken as read. As this extract from the 1947 West Riding of Yorkshire syllabus shows, Christianity was regarded as the standard by which other faiths should be judged.

> The teacher should not only aim at describing the outstanding features of the great religions of the world but should also bear in mind that the study is to be a comparative one, i.e. resemblances and contrasts and the relations between the different religious systems should be emphasised. The pupil should be led to appreciate that, while each great religion has made its contribution at some period of

the world's history either to man's knowledge of God or to man's relations with God or to his fellow men, all these contributions are unified and on a higher plane in the Christian religion. (West Riding 1947: 73)

It may come as a surprise to learn that the section on comparative religion from which this passage is taken is in the current (at the time of writing) Agreed Syllabuses of at least two English Local Education Authorities. Specifically on Hinduism the syllabus makes serious factual errors, for example, equating khama (sic) ('karma' means 'action' – anything that a person has done) with transmigration of the soul. Other early syllabuses, such as the 1944 Sunderland document (adopted by several other local authorities), picture Hinduism through Christian spectacles. Hinduism is seen as a unified religion, not a loosely knit, pluralistic tradition, while Hindu concepts are not examined in relation to other Indian ideas but are rather judged from a position rooted in a Hebraic understanding of God and morality.

'Religion is life'

In the 1960s religious education retained its Christian ethos but, influenced by the work of researchers such as Ronald Goldman and Harold Loukes, became much less characterised by its subject content. At primary level the emphasis was on the exploration of Christian values and emotions through contemporary life-theme material, while secondary students were often encouraged to discuss in depth important issues of personal and social concern. Explicitly religious material did not figure prominently in such approaches, but when it did, the particular Christian view of religious experience that underpinned them not only influenced what was selected from a religion for presentation to children, but also determined what was regarded as religion. Hinduism received little attention and at primary level some of the earliest 'experiential' material to appear was in Elizabeth Wilson's contribution to *Hinduism* (ed. Hinnells and Sharpe: 1972). With hindsight, it is difficult to see how some of the modern Indian children's books recommended by this author (they explore themes such as joy and friendship) could be said to introduce the Hindu tradition in its own terms – valuable as they are as general educational resources. As far as secondary work was concerned, the emphasis on the discussion of Christian perspectives on social issues in one widely used Agreed Syllabus resulted in the relegation of a brief introduction to world religions to the tail end of a series of topics including 'mass media', 'world hunger', 'politics', 'gambling' and 'war' (West Riding, 1966).

Religious studies

The 1970s brought both a restoration of subject matter and a broadening of perspective to religious education. Under the joint influences of the rise of religious studies in universities and colleges and a growing awareness of the presence in Britain of substantial numbers of followers of religions other than Christianity, religious education became concerned with an impartial study of religions. The City of Birmingham's Agreed Syllabus for Religious Instruction (1975) was the first in Britain to reject unequivocally the view that religious education should nurture pupils in the Christian faith. It prepared the ground for later syllabuses which adopt this view (e.g. Hampshire 1978; Berkshire 1982; ILEA 1984; Warwickshire 1985) and its dissemination encouraged publishers to commission more material on world religions. The Birmingham syllabus asserts that religious education should be directed towards 'developing a critical understanding of the religious and moral dimensions of human experience and away from attempting to foster the claims of particular religious standpoints'. Hinduism is specifically mentioned as offering appropriate material for the religious education of children at all school ages, including the three to eight age range. Teaching material designed to resource the ideas suggested in the syllabus is to be found in *Living Together, A Handbook of Suggestions for Religious Education*, also published by the City of Birmingham Education Authority in 1975. This handbook includes a basic course in Hinduism drawn up by Eric Rolls together with a panel of practising Hindus and Birmingham teachers. Many other school books and teaching materials on Hinduism have been published since this time which, with varying degrees of success, attempt to give an impartial treatment of Hinduism.

Personal development and spirituality

The 1980s response to what some saw as a knowledge explosion in RE has been, as in the 1960s, to become wary of an over-emphasis on 'content' at the expense of a reflective, pupil-centred approach to the subject. Terms like 'personal development' and 'spirituality' are as common in the current jargon as 'phenomenology' and 'explicit religion' were in the 1970s. Further, there is once again a drift away from the study of religions in some recently published curriculum material with attention, for example, to contemplation of abstract works of art as a means to gaining spiritual insight.

Which variety of religious education?

The position adopted in this book is that religious education requires *both* a study of religions and an opportunity for pupils to reflect on the significance of their studies. Without a study of religions, the subject is likely to attract idiosyncratic and tendentious interpretations of the nature of religion while at the same time tending to lose its identity – as it did in the 1960s. Without the opportunity for pupils to reflect on the responses of the religions to major human concerns and draw on and relate material to their own experience, the subject will have limited relevance to those who pursue it and will miss a vital source of data for religious education, namely the children themselves. This dual emphasis does not represent special pleading on religious education's part. In universities, for example, philosophy undergraduates study the writings of philosophers not simply to appreciate them, but to engage with them and to react to them in clarifying their own positions on whatever issues are under scrutiny. To take but one school subject: English, in British schools, has for many years been concerned with developing pupils' responses to the issues raised by literature as well as with its appreciation.

Religious studies and personal quest

Despite changing fashions in the subject, there is a thread running through the recent history of British religious education which supports the amalgamation of the study of religion with the pupils' quest for a coherent and personally satisfying set of beliefs and values. Both elements are there in the 1944 Education Act and they appear in some of the key documents in the development of the subject including the Anglican *Durham Report* (1970, para. 215) and the influential Schools Council Working Paper 36, *Religious Education in Secondary Schools* (1971: 43).

The two elements also appear in more recent writing on religious education, for example, in the section on personal development which appears in *Approaching World Religions*, the introductory volume to this series, and at a practical level in several newer Agreed Syllabuses such as those of Berkshire and Warwickshire. The aims of religious education, according to the Warwickshire document, are 'to promote in children and young people an understanding of religion' and yet 'to encourage children and young people to develop well-reasoned views and opinions about religion and about the basic questions of meaning and value with which religions and philosophies are concerned'.

The experience of children

What is perhaps under-emphasised in some of the documents already cited is a recognition of the dialectical nature of religious education. Some of RE's subject matter must come not from the teacher but from the children. Some children will belong to religious traditions. Others, while not practising believers, will have thought about the questions which are of perennial concern to the religions. The experiences, feelings and views of such children are relevant to, and may be the starting point for, activities which seek to promote an understanding of a religion. On the other hand, the sensitive introduction by the teacher of material from the religions should stimulate pupils to raise questions and make responses. Further, the understanding of a religion that a young person gets from its study is relevant to his or her understanding and assessment of currently held beliefs, opinions and attitudes. Again, this interplay between subject matter and pupil is not unique to religious education. The content and even the public examination of biology, for example, have been influenced by the moral and practical arguments advanced by some students against the dissection of animals.

Why teach about Hinduism?

Given this view of religious education, why should we include Hinduism in it? Wouldn't it be simpler to leave out such a complex and multi-faceted religion? The rest of this chapter argues that Hinduism has an important place, and that there are at least four reasons why material from Hinduism can enhance work done in religious education.

Understanding religion

If one of religious education's aims is to develop in students an understanding of religion, then different examples of the various phenomena of religion need to be studied. But to approach centrally important topics – such as worship, sacred literature, ideas of deity, sacred places, religious experience and ritual actions – without any reference to the Indian tradition can give only a partial image of religion. For just as Judaism's principal ideas can give access to 'Western' faiths, so Hinduism's concepts and emphases offer a key to 'Eastern' religion. Indeed, study of the Hindu tradition raises the question, 'What *is* religion?' We do not, however, wish to give the impression that Hinduism can only be approached with older students through an abstract study of its concepts. The following teaching example illustrates that something of the distinctiveness of Hinduism can be appreciated by younger pupils. In this case, Hindu ideas of sacred place and deity were explored during a fourth-year middle school topic on 'water'. The children saw slides of worshippers bathing in the Ganges, and two superb pictures of a *sādhu*, the first showing him plunging into the icy waters at the source of the Ganges in the Himalayas, the second showing him in prayer, facing the sun with water running through his cupped hands and the frost glistening on his beard in the morning sunlight. The slides and pictures generated a considerable amount of comment and discussion – about prayer, about the solitary life, and about the idea that divinity might be located in a place, such as a river. The last point in turn raised questions about images and the number of gods in Hinduism, and some comparisons and contrasts with Christian views of deity.

More teaching examples could be cited, but the point has been made. In order to elucidate what religion means, one needs to study the phenomena of religion, and Hinduism provides us with material that is unique and distinctive as well as engaging and thought-provoking.

Hundus in Britain

A second, crucial reason for studying Hinduism in school is the fact that we have substantial numbers of Hindus living and worshipping in our society and many of these are pupils in our schools, or their parents. To ignore their faith would be a great discourtesy, as well as a lost opportunity. Visits by children to Hindu temples, and by members of Hindu communities to schools have proved to be extremely effective both in motivating pupils and in giving them direct experience of faith and practice (see Chapter 4). This is not to imply that children who do not live in cities or large towns cannot learn about Hinduism in this country. There is an increasing number of readily available audio-visual resources and books for children about Hinduism in Britain (see pp. 206–30). Further, some enterprising schools and colleges have organised study-visits to parts of the country where Hindu communities reside. Many of the resources give information about Hindus in Britain and raise issues, the discussion of which will help prepare pupils for adult life in a multi-cultural society; it will be recalled that the Swann report emphasises the importance of multi-cultural education *for all*, not just for children from ethnic minorities or for pupils in multi-racial schools.

A special privilege afforded by the multi-faith school is the teacher's opportunity to talk to children and for children to talk to each other about their own religious faith and practice. Those who doubt whether students below the sixth form can understand Hinduism would do well to remember that there are Hindus of all school ages in our classrooms and they include junior children who are able to talk simply but deeply about their faith and in some detail about the performance of rituals and dances. During the collection of material for a radio programme on the Navaratri festival (p. 130) an eleven-year-old British Gujarati girl told of her prayers to the goddess whom she called Mātājī ('respected mother'): 'We ask to be kept safe and to be healthy, to be nice in the future'. She and her friend went on to give a detailed description of the steps and movements of the stick-dance performed for Mātājī at Navarātri

It should be remembered, however, that, unlike their counterparts in India, Hindu children in Britain have restricted access to their inherited tradition. They are exposed to non-Hindu influences through their schooling, through peer groups and through the media and they are likely to encounter hostility to their parental religion and culture from some elements within British society. Nevertheless, the available evidence, limited though it is, suggests that many Hindu youngsters are learning a good deal about their tradition (Jackson 1985; Jackson and Nesbitt 1986). Much religious culture is transmitted informally or semi-formally through participation in a range of rituals and practices. Even though Hindu communities are themselves evolving, this is how styles of Hinduism distinctive to particular regions, castes and sects are being perpetuated.

At the same time some of those communities which provide formal Hindu nurture for children (often language classes which include some introductory material on Hinduism) – whether they are conscious of it or not – seem to be presenting young people with a more conceptual and unitary view of Hinduism than that gained less formally. Sometimes this view seems to sit uncomfortably with the picture of the tradition gained elsewhere. At other times the two pictures appear complementary, with various formal approaches providing a conceptual framework and a clear set of moral guidelines which, for young people spanning two cultures, provides the means to give intelligibility to the Hindu tradition.

A global perspective

A third reason for including material from Hinduism in religious education relates to the network of projects and teaching strategies whose work is placed under such headings as 'education for international understanding', 'world studies', 'development studies', and the like. The World Studies Projects, for example, have done much to promote an awareness in schools of the increasing global interdependence between peoples and nations. Further, events in India – such as the troubles in the Panjab and the assassination of Mrs Gandhi – were widely reported in the British media, highlighting the religious dimension to India's political life. Richard Attenborough's film *Gandhi* also created much interest among young people in Britain and an array of teaching materials on the religious and political aspects of Gandhi's life became available as a result. There are exciting opportunities for inter-departmental work on 'world studies' topics, and it need hardly be said that a junior school project on India, a fourth-year secondary school study of an Indian school inspired by Gandhi's thought and writings, or a sixth-form discussion of the Indian political scene can make little sense without due attention to Hinduism.

Fundamental questions

A fourth reason for studying Hinduism in schools is that its themes and concerns raise some of the more fundamental questions of life. Reflection on how a less familiar tradition deals with such questions can stimulate pupils into stating and refining their own views. Simon Weightman actually suggests that their capability to raise and implant fundamental questions is the key criterion for selecting topics for children from the Hindu tradition.

In discussing the complex of phenomena that constitute the Hindu tradition Weightman writes:

> Just as a philosopher, a theologian, a historian can apply his systematics to this structural complexity, so may we as teachers be equally selective in applying our own systematics. That is to say we can, with justice and with no greater distortion than anyone else who has ever attempted to represent South Asian religion, take from the totality those parts that meet our needs. For children in schools, since we are dealing with religious education and not history, anthropology, mythology, art and archaeology or any other subject, we can take material – why not at random and out of any historical sequence – that is the answer to real religious questions. By the answer, I mean an answer, as clearly to every religious question different faiths have provided different answers. What matters for children is that through this material we can implant in them the questions. (Weightman 1978: 41–2)

Weightman's suggested topics include the caste system, related to the ideas of *karma* (action) and *dharma* ('law') and linked with discussion of the individual's rights and responsibilities as a member of society; the *mārgas* or paths of liberation, with particular reference to *bhakti* (devotion) – 'expose children to this, to the mysterious and the holy so that they can know that religion has great power though it may not show our Englishness'; personal mystical experience such as that described by Ramakrishna; *samsāra* (the cycle of birth and rebirth), related to the question 'Who am I?', and so on. It is notable that Weightman's own set of examples show his extensive knowledge of Hinduism and an ability to identify its distinctive features. Those with little knowledge or experience of the tradition, however, are in danger of introducing Hinduism through an idiosyncratic range of topics if they rely exclusively on the 'fundamental questions' criterion. The approach of this book is to take a middle way, covering topics which are central to the tradition and point up its distinctiveness and yet recommending learning activities which are intended to maximise participation and a reflective response by pupils. But first we must introduce the Hindu tradition and some of the issues associated with the term 'Hinduism'.

2

Finding a Way into Hinduism

Attempting an overview

Hinduism has a history of over 5000 years. It has no founder, no essential creeds or doctrines and no single concept of God. The diversity of its practices is compounded by the geographical and linguistic variety of the Indian subcontinent.

Even the word Hinduism is a Western term. The word may lead us to expect a single set of beliefs and practices. However, any attempt to encompass India's religious firework display – whether made from inside or outside the subcontinent – will inevitably result in distortion. To use an old Hindu and Buddhist parable in a different way, those who attempt to describe Hinduism fully are in the same position as blind men trying to perceive an elephant. One blind man, grasping the trunk, believes the elephant to be a snake. Another, who encounters its leg, believes the elephant to be a tree, and so on. We can only grasp parts of Hinduism; we must not mistake them for the whole.

The concept of Hinduism

The word *Hinduism* is derived from a Persian name for India. *Hindu* in Persian was at first the name of the river Indus; the English name of this river is derived from the Persian, through Greek and Latin. The Persians called the country around and beyond the Indus *Hindustan* ('the place of the Indus'), and called its people *Hindu* also; our names *India* and *Indian* come from Latin derivatives of the same Persian name *Hindu*.

When Muslim power was established in India from about 1000 CE onwards, the word *Hindu* was applied especially to those Indians who were not Muslims. Religion was thus part of the meaning of the word, but not the whole of it; in the early nineteenth century it was still possible to speak of a Hindu Christian, meaning a Christian of Indian origin and cultural background. It was in the early nineteenth century that the suffix *-ism* was added to *Hindu* to create the word *Hinduism*.[1] The concept of Hinduism is not part of the Hindu tradition, but is brought in from the outside; so too is the concept of religion, since in Hindu culture, as in many traditional cultures, the modern separation of religion from secular life is not made.

A modern Hindu, Professor T.M.P. Mahadevan (pp. 168–71), finds the key to defining Hinduism in its allegiance to the Vedas, its belief in an all-pervading God, and its stress on non-violence (Mahadevan 1960: 22–7). Others would include belief in karma and rebirth (p. 16; p. 172) as a defining characteristic. A leading Hindu organisation, the UK branch of the Vishwa Hindu Parishad ('universal Hindu council'), defines a Hindu as 'a person believing in and respecting eternal values of life, ethical and spiritual, which have sprung up in India' (Knott 1986: 77). While some non-Hindus may associate the idea of Hinduism with some of its objectionable aspects, Hindus distinguish true Hinduism from false; many would agree with Mahadevan that 'untouchability is the greatest blot on Hinduism' (Mahadevan 1960: 74).

While recognising that the term Hinduism is not traditional, Hindus often point to the Sanskrit term *sanātana dharma* as having the same sense. Literally this means 'the eternal norms of behaviour'; since *dharma* is often used to translate the English 'religion', it can be taken to mean 'the eternal religion'. It refers to norms revealed in the Vedas; sometimes the term *Vedic dharma* or *Vaidika dharma* is also used. The Vedas (pp. 158–60) are texts whose origin modern historians place in the last two millennia BCE; but many Hindus believe that they are far more ancient, or even literally eternal. Though the Vedas have great authority for Hindus, many Hindu beliefs and practices are not found in them.

The inclusion of Hinduism in RE syllabuses in schools, and in Religious Studies syllabuses in higher education, has encouraged teachers in Britain to clarify their ideas of what Hinduism is; it is time for the blind men to pool their impressions of the elephant. At the same time the presence of Hindus in Britain, which we have noted as one of the reasons for studying Hinduism in schools (p. 8), has brought the practical and experiential aspects of Hinduism to the fore instead of the study of ancient texts. Both these developments are welcome, but there are hidden dangers in them also. When a subject is included in the curriculum, there is a tendency to organise it into a syllabus which then takes on a life of its own; school Hinduism may lose touch with living Hinduism to such an extent that Hindu parents may find themselves being corrected by their children who have brought home a view of Hinduism learnt from British books and a non-Hindu teacher. There is also a tendency to talk of 'the Hindu community', as if all Hindus in this country formed a single group (Knott 1986: 53). Because much of the material that has found its way into school teaching on Hinduism is Gujarati, people may get the impression that Gujarati practices or terms are common to all Hindus. Never forget that elephant.

Again, Hinduism appears on the syllabus alongside Islam, Judaism and Sikhism, while the 'Hindu community' may be listed with the Muslim, Jewish and Sikh communities, as if these 'isms' and these 'communities' were all of the same kind. Talking of 'Hindu scriptures', 'Christian scriptures' and so on may also make people think that scriptures play the same part in different traditions. Talking of the origins or history of Hinduism may give the impression that distant historical events have the same value for Hindus as, say, the Babylonian captivity, the life and death of Jesus, or the founding of the Khalsa have for Jews, Christians or Sikhs.[2]

Historical and geographical background

Since in Hinduism's case we are still in the position of blind, or at best partially-sighted people, let us risk comparing Hinduism with a very old tree – perhaps a banyan, the Indian tree whose branches send down roots which become separate trunks, so that it is impossible to tell where the original tree began. We must forget that a real tree originated in one seed, and just think of the tree as it is now, with its many widespread roots. Some roots of the tree are over 5000 years old: they represent the Indus Valley or Harappan civilisation. This civilisation, discovered by archaeologists in the 1920s, may have contributed the goddess cult to Indian religion, perhaps a male divinity resembling Shiva, perhaps the use of water in religious rituals.

Another old cluster of roots represents Vedic religion, brought to India in the second millenium BCE as a result of conquest and settlement by the Āryans, a semi-nomadic people whose name is etymologically linked with the name 'Iran'. One of these roots gives us Hinduism's oldest text, the *Rig-Veda*, a collection of hymns recited by priests who made offerings in fire to the gods or *devas* (p. 158). Another, exemplified by the body of texts called the *Upanishads*, composed in the last millennium BCE, reveals the search for a single cosmic force underlying the devas, sometimes pictured in anthropomorphic terms as Purusha ('Man') or Pra-jāpati ('Lord of Creatures'), and sometimes as the impersonal Absolute, Brahman (p. 159; p. 173). The Upanishads also examine the relationship between the individual self (*ātman*) and the One (*brahman*) – an exploration which gave rise to some of India's great philosophical systems (pp. 168–178). They also introduce the idea of *samsāra*, the endless cycle of birth and rebirth to which each soul is subject until it obtains liberation (*moksha*) (pp. 172–6). The sanctity of the *Brahmins*, the Aryan priestly class, took root in India in this period.

The Aryans also introduced Sanskrit, a language closely related to that of ancient Iran, and more remotely to those of Europe. While Sanskrit is used today mainly for ritual and learned purposes, it has contributed largely to the vocabulary of the vernacular languages spoken in India today.[3] Many of the words we shall use in this book are Sanskrit; others belong to vernacular languages.

Other roots are of more recent growth. The kingdoms and empires which rose and fell in India from before 500 BCE to the establishment of British power in the eighteenth and early nineteenth centuries were responsible for building the great temples, with their elaborate rituals in which the god is a divine counterpart of the king. Of humbler origin are the simple shrines set up by unknown people in every village of India, and wherever Hindus have settled (p. 108; pp. 146–50). Since the seventh century, beginning at first in South India, devotional movements have gathered around the gods Vishnu and Shiva, expressing loving devotion to their chosen god through poetry, song and dance, and challenging the priestly privileges of the brahmins. At the same time the intellectual roots of Hinduism were streng-thened through the development of philosophical schools (pp. 168–78), partly in confrontation with Buddhism, which was planted by the Buddha in North Indian soil around 500 BCE.

The establishment of Muslim powers in India from the eleventh century onwards led to a rich composite culture, in which Islamic and Hindu arts and learning flourished in the courts, while Muslim mystics and Hindu sadhus exchanged ideas and attracted followers. From the mid-eighteenth century British power led to a further intertwining of roots, and made English the commonest means of communication between the different parts of the sub-continent.

The banyan has struck its roots over the centuries in many different soils: the Indus valley and Vedic cultures were rooted in north-west India, while other roots are 1500 miles to the south in Tamil Nādu, 1200 miles to the east in Bengal, and throughout the subcontinent.

Key concepts and social structures

The trunk of the tree represents Hinduism's key concepts, social structures, practices and beliefs. None of these is universal, but together with the Hindu sense of self-identity (which can transcend striking individual differences), they give Hinduism its essential unity. Key concepts include *dharma*, a particularly elusive term which can mean, for example, 'sacred duty' and 'function' (the dharma of fire is to burn). Dharma can represent a whole range of moral and ritual norms that apply to a member of a particular caste. Within the extended family dharma is transmitted especially by example and by myths and stories. The Hindu family ethic is strong, and the various roles and responsibilities in the moral sphere are generally taken very seriously (pp. 59–68). Related to dharma are the doctrines of *karma*, which means that one's actions determine one's future destiny, for good or for ill (p. 172), and *samsāra*, the cycle of birth and rebirth which the soul goes through. A person who is true to his dharma will generate good karma and will be reborn at a higher point on the scale of ritual purity. Dharma, in the sense of the acquisition of religious merit through right living, is one of the traditional aims of life, the others being *artha* (wealth and power), *kāma* (the satisfaction of desire) and *moksha* (liberation from this world) (pp. 172–3).

An important feature of Hindu life is caste. Each person is born into a caste (*jāti*), a hereditary group which is normally endogamous (that is, marriage takes place only within the caste). Castes are ranked hierarchically with Brahmin castes at the top and with groups engaging in the most ritually polluting activities – handling the dead, and tanning, for example – at the bottom. The scale of ritual purity and pollution is the main factor in determining the hierarchy of the numerous castes. Ritual purity (pp. 66–8) should not be confused with moral goodness.

Key practices and beliefs

The principal Hindu religious practices include daily and seasonal rituals (which vary from caste to caste, being particularly elaborate for devout Brahmins), the *samskāras* or life-cycle rites (marking the main transitions of a Hindu's life such as birth, marriage and death (pp. 88–97), and worship (pp. 103–111). Worship may take the form of *pūjā* (pp. 103–5) in the home or in a temple, or *bhajan*, the group-singing of devotional hymns (p. 163; p. 182). Another meritorious religious act is pilgrimage to local, regional or national sites such as Vārānasī (Benares) (pp. 141–8). The most colourful feature of Hindu practice is the annual cycle of festivals (pp. 128–35) which again may be local, regional or all-Indian (for example Diwālī and Navarātri). The festivals bring gaiety and life to Hinduism, being occasions of celebration as well as a yearly reminder of religious values.

If Hindus are highly restricted in the realm of conduct, they are relatively free in the domain of belief. Nevertheless there are certain tendencies which are strong enough to make belief part of the tree-trunk of the religion. One is the notion of *brahman*, the impersonal Absolute or World Soul that pervades the universe (p. 122; p. 173). The fact that brahman is considered to be immanent as well as transcendent gives rise to a pantheistic tendency in Hinduism – a belief that the divine principle is present in everything. At the same time there is a tendency to personalise the divine, perhaps as *bhagavān* or *ishvara* (the Lord) and in this sense Hindu religion has a strongly monotheistic current. Hinduism is certainly not crudely polytheistic, and the *devas*, the gods, are generally regarded as different facets of the same jewel. A peasant may make offerings to several gods and yet still affirm 'bhagvān ek hai' – 'God is one'. Further there is the notion of the *ishta-devatā*, the chosen diety who is worshipped by a person as the Supreme God, although that same individual does not deny either the reality of other gods or that other people will have different chosen deities.

The principal gods

The main branches of our tree represent the three main theistic strands of Hinduism, involving devotion of Vishnu (*Vaishnavism*), to Shiva (*Shaivism*) or to the Goddess (*Shāktism*) (p. 122). Vishnu is regarded as a benevolent god, who in times of moral decline appears in the world in various forms (*avatāras*, literally 'descents') to restore justice (pp. 118–20). Shiva's character is complex. He is loving and full of grace, but he is also the fearsome destroyer; a great ascetic and a god of procreation (p. 120); he is worshipped in the form of the *linga*, an ancient male fertility symbol (p. 109). Female fertility is represented by the Mother Goddess, who is often identified as Shiva's wife – Durgā in her fierce form, Pārvatī in her benevolent aspect. Her followers are called *Shāktas*, since they believe the goddess to be the Shakati – the energy, immanent and active in the world – of the remote and transcendent Shiva. The Goddess is known under many names, and she is often simply called *Devī*, 'the Goddess' (p. 121).

There are many sects devoted to an avatāra of Vishnu (generally *Krishna* or *Rāma*), to Shiva or to the Goddess, typically having a founder whose teachings are followed closely by adherents (pp. 187–9). Many of these sects have had a profound importance in providing a bridge between some of the basic forms of Hinduism and its more sophisticated aspects as well as being a source for many Hindus of religious and moral renewal. It should be noted that, generally speaking, devotion to one of the principal gods does not preclude worship of the others. A temple dedicated to Krishna, for example, may have shrines to Shiva and Durgā.

Village gods and goddesses

The many minor branches and twigs of our tree represent the amazingly diverse beliefs and practices to be found in village Hinduism (about 80 per cent of the Hindu population lives in villages). Although the full range of Hindu religious activity is to be found in the villages, there is a tendency in rural Hinduism for the more practical rather than metaphysical features of the religion to receive most attention. A considerable amount of care is given, for example, to the *grāma-devatās*, village deities or 'godlings' who, while lacking the great power of the principal gods, are less remote and have sufficient power to affect a villager's welfare, granting benefits such as a cure, a birth or a good harvest if they are suitably propitiated, or bringing disaster if they are not. Some are associated with diseases, natural forces or spirits of the dead. Others may be linked with particular caste groups or geographical locations. Many are conceived of in female form; often a particular village goddess is identified with the great Goddess, the wife of Shiva, while retaining her own character, and village gods may be similarly identified with Shiva or Vishnu. Contact with a village deity may be through individual worship, through a ritual specialist such as a non-Brahmin priest, or through a person who becomes possessed by the deity and goes into a trance. A villager who propitiates a local god or goddess may also venerate one or more of the principal gods, and still affirm that God is one.

Adaptation to environment

The tree of Hinduism has adapted to many different environmental conditions, and like any other organism it is in a constant state of change. Now and again its seeds have grown into new plants, some of which have become new trees. Buddhism and Jainism are now solid and venerable specimens, while Sikhism, relatively speaking, is still a thriving sapling. Political, social and technological upheavals in India have led to changes in the relation of traditional practice to daily life, and in ways of passing on the tradition (pp. 114–6; pp. 128–31; pp. 154–7; pp. 168–71). Lastly, the tree has struck root in other lands, adapting remarkably well to the soil and climate of Africa, the Caribbean, Fiji, Malaysia, Britain, or wherever Hindus have migrated in the past hundred years (pp. 43–4; pp. 59–62; pp. 88–92; pp. 182–4).

Is 'Hinduism' a useful term?

If Hindu practices and beliefs are so varied, are we justified in treating Hinduism as one entity at all? Are we dealing with a single tree or a clump of several plants? A radical approach to this question was made by the Canadian Islamicist W. Cantwell Smith. He says Hinduism

> is a Western (and Muslim) concept, which Westerners (and Muslims) have tried to impose upon their understanding of India; but it does not fit. There are Hindus, but there is no Hinduism. (Smith 1978: 65)

Of course, it would be very incovenient if we were to refuse to talk about 'Hinduism' any more: it is on the syllabus, and it is in the title of this book. But we should be clear in our minds what we are talking about when we use the term. We are not talking about a unity, but a diversity linked by many shared traits. 'Hinduism' is an umbrella term for a great number of beliefs and practices, each of which belongs to some of the millions of people who for historical reasons are called Hindus. Some of these beliefs and practices are highly characteristic of Hinduism, in that they are found among most groups of Hindus: karma, rebirth, caste, offerings to an object representing a god. Others are less so: the Pongal festival, in which rice is boiled in milk and offered to the sun at the winter solstice, is a Tamil festival which would seem strange in northern India; the typical British Hindu worship, on Sunday and in a temple in the form of a large hall, would be out of place in most Indian villages. What is unknown to many Hindus is part of Hinduism none the less, if it is familiar to some Hindus. But it is in individual Hindus that the tradition lives; not the whole tradition in each Hindu, but each part of the tradition in many Hindus.

Among our reasons for studying Hinduism we mentioned the need to understand religion (pp. 7–8), and concern with fundamental questions (p. 10). Since 'Hinduism' is an extreme example of how misleading a label can be, it may set us thinking about other labels. When we speak of Christianity or Islam, are we misled by the label into thinking of a single entity to which individuals approximate, or do we remember that each of these labels represents a diversity of tradition, and that it is in the individual Christian or Muslim, faced with the fundamental questions that face all individuals, that the tradition lives[5]?

Selecting from the tradition

We have seen that there have been many different attempts to encompass Hinduism, from inside and outside the tradition, all of them inadequate in one way or another. Our banyan tree metaphor of Hinduism also inevitably has its weaknesses. It gives an incomplete picture – nothing has been said yet about some of the major texts (pp. 157–62), the *āshramas* or stages of life (p. 97), the role of the *guru* (pp. 184–5), and so on. Also a tree is a unity and there is little room for debate as to what is part of it and what is not. Hindu tradition is more complex and there is room for debate as to whether a particular feature is or is not part of it. However, we believe such debate to be unimportant for understanding the faith of Hindus; 'Hinduism' is a convenient label, but by worrying over boundaries we make it inconvenient. Some elements of the tradition date from pre-Vedic times: the worship of a mother goddess may be among them. Others originate with the Vedic peoples: for instance, the Sanskrit verse called the *Gāyatrī* (or *Sāvitrī*) mantra, recited by many Hindus in their daily worship

(p. 96). Some are found first in the nineteenth century, including the search for a true 'Hinduism' – and despite what we have said about the pitfalls of the term 'Hinduism', this search is a genuine part of Hinduism, because it is a concern of Hindus. Others, again, are products of the twentieth century, such as Sunday classes on the *Bhagavad-Gītā*. It is the individual Hindu that we must try to understand; we need not worry if he or she is different from other Hindus.

These points have consequences for the ways in which we select ideas for teaching to children. Firstly, since no attempt to en-capsulate Hinduism can possibly be successful, we can select from the tradition material which relates to children's questions, con-cerns and interests. We should, however, give an eye to the general framework outlined above (so that we do not make eccen-tric choices or repeat earlier mistakes, especially the one of over-emphasising the past). Hindu festivals, for instance, can provide younger children with material through which to explore the experience of celebration; preparing and eating festive sweets and savouries will open children's minds as well as their mouths (pp. 36–7) and will raise many questions which may direct the teacher back to Hinduism for more material. Older children may find, for example, that a consideration of the caste system, related to the concepts of dharma and karma, will enlighten a discussion of the individual's rights and responsibilities as a member of the society (pp. 72–87). The possibilities for creative teaching are endless and the situation in which a topic from Hinduism is chosen merely 'because it is in the syllabus' should never arise.

Secondly, frequent references to the life and faith of individual Hindus makes Hinduism far more accessible for children and young people than a study through topics abstracted from the tradition. This is one of the reasons why we have started our chapters in Part 2 with case studies of real people. Chapter 4, furthermore, encourages teachers to develop contacts with mem-bers of the various Hindu communities in Britain so that, through welcoming Hindu visitors into the school or through visiting temples, children can gain some first-hand experience of Hindu faith and practice.

Notes

1   The earliest occurrence recorded in the *Oxford English Diction-ary* is in 1829 but it was used at least as early as 1808 (Burghart 1987: 226).

2   Some current books on Hinduism concentrate on the past and on the textual tradition. Zaehner's *Hindu Scriptures* (1966) contains Vedic texts and the *Bhagavad-Gītā*, but none of the later texts in Sanskrit or other languages which are far more familiar to most Hindus. His *Hinduism* (1962) is concerned with the traditions contained in texts, and the adaptation of these traditions made by those in contact with the West in the nineteenth and twentieth centuries. M. and J. Stutley's *Dictionary of Hinduism* (1977) deals mainly with the past, and ignores many topics that one might have expected from the title.

3   On Indian languages and words, see Killingley (1984: 105–23); Shackle (1985).

4   For brief surveys of history, see Bahree (1982); Killingley (1984: 82–96).

5   Smith (1978) proposes to abandon not only the term 'Hinduism' but the whole concept of 'a religion', and discusses at length the ideas sketched here.

Teaching about Hinduism

Introduction

In Chapter 1 we argued for a particular philosophy of religious education and for Hinduism's place in the subject. We also considered in Chapter 2 the problems of answering the question 'What is Hinduism?', and argued that, although Hinduism may not have a universally accepted core, it does have a family of distinctive concepts and social structures, and it also has certain tendencies in practice and belief. Turning to the treatment of Hinduism in schools, it will already be evident that we are advocating an approach that combines an accurate and well-balanced presentation of the tradition with teaching methods and ideas that draw on pupils' and teachers' direct or indirect experience of religion and which prompts a reflective response. We are also recommending activities which are potentially interesting, stimulating and challenging to pupils. Part 2 will introduce some of Hinduism's distinctive features together with ideas for selecting material and teaching it in schools. But first, we need to consider a range of learning methods and activities appropriate for introducing Hinduism to beginners.

Appropriate attitudes and methods

For most people, whether children or adults, an attempt to understand an unfamiliar religion or way of life represents a difficult challenge. Inevitably, when trying to grasp someone else's world-view, we tend to reduce it to categories and concepts that are already familiar to us, and in doing so we may make some fundamental mistakes. Further, the introduction of art, customs, rituals, beliefs and languages which may initially seem strange and alien can provoke negative responses from some pupils. These might be relatively innocent and good humoured, but the fear that can be generated by the sudden introduction of new experiences can bring to the surface deep feelings of hostility which may be expressed in racist terms.

An empathy game

This activity has been used extensively with children in junior and secondary schools and with adults and it – or some other activity like it – is recommended as a preliminary to studying Hinduism with a class. Another reason for using the game is that students and teachers have found that it significantly reduces the sort of instant, racist response which may come from a minority of children when Asian or Afro-Caribbean topics are presented for the first time. There can be little more dispiriting for a teacher than to prepare an interesting and well-researched series of lessons, illustrated with pictorial and audio material, and yet to hear a racist remark as soon as the first slide is shown or the first record played. Of course, good teachers adapt their lessons accordingly and deal with racism head-on. But it is better to anticipate prejudice and to place pupils in a situation in which they can work out for themselves the sorts of attitudes and methods required for understanding an unfamiliar way of life.

The class is divided into groups of about four, and each group appoints a secretary. The following instructions are given. They can be adapted according to age and ability of the audience. 'You are Martians. You have exceedingly high intelligence, and X-ray vision. You are travelling as part of an exploratory mission to other parts of the solar system, and your instructions are to land on earth and to report your observations regularly to your base commander. You do not understand Earth languages, and you have no previous knowledge of planet Earth or its inhabitants. Your ship lands some distance from what is actually a human dwelling place. You approach the building and, looking through the wall, you see before you a scene which you observe closely. Using your highly developed intelligence you write a short report (a few sentences) to be transmitted to your base commander. *We* know that the Martian is looking at a living room in a house. In the middle of the room is a Christmas tree, and members of the family are placing parcels at the foot of the tree. The Martian, of course, does not know this.'

Leave a few moments for questions before the exercise begins.

Someone usually asks whether they can write a report in Martian (answer: 'Yes, as long as you provide an English translation!') while older students and teachers may also ask some variant on the question: 'Do the Martians share our concepts?' to which an appropriate answer is 'Give the Martian whatever range of concepts you wish'. Around five minutes is usually enough for discussion and writing, though the teacher needs to keep an eye on the progress of each group and to be available for consultation. The reports are then read to the class in turn by a representative from each group. The reports tend to be rich in imagination and strong on humour, with those of younger children being some-times shorter rather than less imaginative than those of their older schoolfellows.

The ensuing discussion deals with a number of questions. Given that the Martian had very high intelligence, did he (or she or it) interpret the scene correctly? What would the Martian have needed to do in order to have an accurate picture of what was happening? Groups always answer the first question in the nega-tive, though some add that the Martian may have partially understood what was happening. Answers to the second question include 'He should have learned their language or had an inter-preter'; 'the Martian should have *asked* the people what they were doing'; 'the Martian needed to observe the people over a long period' or 'He should have contacted Mars to find whether there were earlier records of explorations of Earth which explained this practice'. The point is taken that, however intelligent a pupil or student is, without the proper attitudes (having an open mind; not jumping to conclusions) and appropriate methods (e.g. interview-ing in order to grasp concepts and the significance of practices; observing over a period and consulting authoritative sources) serious errors of interpretation are likely to be made when describ-ing features of an unfamiliar way of life. One can refer back to the game at later stages in preparation for new work, such as a visit to a Hindu temple, or should anyone be seen to be sliding away from an open-minded approach.

Relevant and associated experiences

The empathy game emphasises the distinctiveness of traditions such as Hinduism and cautions against imposing one's own preconceptions on material to be studied. To call the festival of Diwālī the 'Hindu Christmas' or to say that Hindu and Christian weddings are fundamentally 'the same' is to make a category mistake. There are, however, various similarities between the two festivals, especially in terms of the experience of celebration, which participants in either are likely to share (see pp. 128–39). And, although there are important differences between Hindu and Christian weddings, direct experience of the latter can be of assistance in relating to the former (see pp. 88–101). Thus, in experiential terms, the Hindu tradition is not entirely foreign even to an all-white rural class. Children may have had experiences which, when recalled, may help them and their classmates to empathise with their Hindu counterparts. In addition analogies can be made between familiar and less familiar rituals or beliefs which, without being over-pressed, can be an aid to understanding. The theme of the interplay between the distinctiveness of the Hindu tradition on the one hand and the universality of human experience on the other will recur at various points in this book.

Learning activities

What has been written already about the importance of drawing on the personal experiences of children (p. 7; pp. 8–10; pp. 25–6) and of preparatory work on attitudes (pp. 23–5) indicates the need to engage children actively in the process of religious education. The methods suggested below all aim to promote active learning. All are suitable for children working in small groups from two to six, and some are appropriate for, or can be adapted to, work with individuals or with a full class. This section has been cross-referenced with the teaching ideas that are placed at the end of the chapters in Part 2 dealing with various aspects of the Hindu tradition.

Brainstorming, ranking and classification

'Brainstorming' is making a list, without discussion, prompted by a word or topic supplied by the teacher. If children are working in a group only one person need act as a scribe. With a whole class each pupil can make a list, and with young children brainstorming can be done orally with the teacher making a written list on the blackboard. The value of the activity is that in preparing a list, children are likely to draw upon their own experiences which can be shared, discussed and related to analogous but unfamiliar experiences. In preparing to do work on Hindu festivals, for example, children can be given the instruction 'list everything you can think of connected with Christmas'. After a few minutes (no more than five), lists can be read out and discussed. The activity works for any age group, however, with adults tending to produce longer lists, often including some variant on 'indigestion tablets' as well as the usual mixture of celebratory and more overtly religious words. Children can enjoy reading the lists aloud before proceeding to other activities, such as ranking and classification.

In 'ranking', each child is asked to choose three or four words from the list which are especially important to them. These may be placed in rank order. In 'classification', children are asked to put the words which are associated with one another into groups. The teacher needs to explain that children can devise their own systems of classification and that there are no 'wrong answers'. Both ranking and classification are aids to discussing the relative importance to children of different features of the lists.

Artefacts and print-objects

One way to arouse interest in religious education and to give children a form of direct experience of religion is to allow them to look at and handle religious artefacts. Devotional Hinduism is rich in artefacts of various kinds which are readily available from suppliers in Britain (see pp. 230–1 for a list of artefacts and pp. 236–7 for addresses of suppliers). These include such inexpensive items as *dīvās* (small clay vessels used as lamps) and incense sticks, through medium-priced items – plaster of paris or plastic *mūrtis* (images of gods), a wedding garland or a moderately-priced sari – to more expensive items such as a pūjā set (*āratī* lamp, tray [*thālī*], bell, water vessel and ladle) or metal images of deities. Whatever activity is devised using artefacts, pupils should be told that the objects may be held in reverence by Hindus and should be treated with great care and respect. In addition to artefacts there are a number of 'print-objects' which make very useful resources. These include calendars of the 'block' or tear-off variety, wedding invitations and Diwālī cards.

One way of using artefacts and print-objects (as well as slides, pictures and videos – pp. 28–30), which has been used successfully, is to get children to guess what particular objects are or what they are used for. Each group can be given one or two objects and a card bearing a set of short questions. The group considers the questions and a spokesperson reports back to the whole class. This activity can be done in groups and follows on very well from the empathy game (pp. 24–5). The Martian was probably cautious in his judgements and used his intelligence in guessing what the humans around the Christmas tree were doing. Nevertheless, some of his deductions were wrong, and he had to admit the need to go to other sources to get correct answers. In the same way, children will make some imaginative but wrong guesses as well as some accurate deductions. The wrong answers are not a sign of low intelligence or lack of effort (remember the Martian), but simply an indication that other sources need to be consulted.

Another use of artefacts is to help in the simulation of a religious activity, such as a wedding or domestic worship. Artefacts also enhance displays of work on Hinduism done by pupils. The use of particular artefacts will be described at appropriate points in Part 2.

Pictures, slides, videos

The visual appeal of many features of the Hindu tradition is obvious and a variety of resources is readily available. Brightly coloured pictures of deities, religious leaders and scenes from myths can be obtained from suppliers (listed on pp. 236–7). Similar pictures are available more cheaply as illustrations to calendars. These can often be seen in Hindu homes and may be purchased from Asian stores and from printing firms such as Printrite of Coventry (p. 236).

A fairly good range of commercially produced colour slides is currently available and is reviewed on pp. 219–23. A visit to a Hindu temple or a wedding can give teachers and their pupils an opportunity to do some of their own photography and have a personal record of an experience of Hinduism as well as a resource that others can use and appreciate (p. 49; pp. 52–3). Some publishers still produce filmstrips and a number are available either on Hinduism or including some aspects of Hindu religion and life (see p. 223). It is difficult to be flexible in the use of filmstrips and many teachers prefer to mount each frame as a separate colour slide. The slides can then either be used with the filmstrip notes or tape, or can be rearranged or used selectively to suit teachers' and pupils' needs.

Schools are increasingly using videotape as a resource in religious education. A few videotapes on Hinduism are available commercially and schools also have the opportunity to make their own video recordings of educational broadcasts (pp. 229–30).

All of these visual resources can be used to illustrate teaching or to reinforce points that have already been covered. As with artefacts, a highly effective way of using pictures, slides and photographs is as picture puzzles. A class of third-year secondary school children with no previous knowledge of Hinduism were shown a calendar picture of the goddess Ambājī and managed to make some correct deductions with no further information. Her smile was regarded as evidence of a benevolent side to her character, while the fact that she carried weapons and rode on a tiger whose fangs dripped with blood was taken to signify power and a destructive tendency. Although some would describe Indian calendar art as gaudy, the children found it immediately appealing and there were no negative responses to the exercise. Slides can be used equally or even more effectively as puzzle pictures. Try projecting a slide of a pūjā or a wedding, for example, and get a class to guess what is happening in the picture. Children often notice features that the teacher may have missed incidentally, and there will be occasions when neither teacher nor pupils know the answer. Since no individual can possibly understand the entire Hindu tradition, teachers should feel liberated rather than daunted by such cases of collective ignorance! Fun can be had finding out the right answers – if there *are* 'right' answers.

Slides can also be used as visual puzzles by small groups of children using a daylight viewer. This piece of equipment looks like a small television set. A slide is slotted into the machine and the image is back-projected on to the screen. Most types of daylight viewer are simple to operate and children learn how to use them very quickly. Viewers manufactured by Diastar are robust and relatively inexpensive compared with other electrical equipment. A cheaper way to use photographic material with small groups is to supply them with photographs mounted on card and accompanied by simple questions about what is happening in the picture. Other exercises which could be undertaken by small groups include: looking at a photograph for a minute, turning it over and writing a description of it; writing one or more titles or captions for the picture; listing, within a specified short time, everything that can be seen in the picture. Extracts from the videotape, *Aspects of Hinduism* published by Videotext can also be used for puzzling, since this particular programme has no spoken commentary (see p. 229). The freeze-frame facility can be used to give pupils an opportunity to guess what is happening in shots or indeed what happens next.

Audiotape recording

Given their potential as tools for learning and expression, cassette audio-tape recorders are a good investment for use by small groups of children. An obvious use is to play the whole or part of pre-recorded radio programmes or commercial tapes. BBC Education has broadcast a variety of twenty-minute programmes on Hinduism for all junior and secondary age groups. These are listed on p. 225. Some local teachers' centres and all the major religious education in-service and resources centres (pp. 236–7) stock these and they may be copied for use in school. BBC Education now has a Radio Shop which publishes a selection of broadcasts in cassette form (see Part 3). The most economical way to build up a collection of tapes, however, is to obtain details of forthcoming programmes from BBC Education and to record them off-air. Most programmes can be divided into short sections which can be used as a stimulus for discussion, as a source of information or as a preliminary to some other activity such as drama. Programmes in the 'Quest' series (earlier programmes were for 9–11 year olds; more recent programmes are for the 10–13 range) often include a story which can be used to stimulate the kind of activities described below under the heading of 'story' (pp. 32–6). The 1977 'Quest' programmes on Holī and Navarātri include dramatisations of stories about Prahlāda and Saraswatī respectively, while the 1987 'Quest' programmes use a storyteller to relate tales of Durgā, Lakshmī and Holikā. Programmes on (or including) Hinduism in the sixth form series 'Religion and Life' are still obtainable at resources centres, but the BBC no longer has a sixth-form religious education series. The fourth and fifth form series 'Religious Education' continues to be a good source of audio material.

Children and young people can also use cassette recorders for various dramatic activities. Hindu stories can be improvised or scripted and then recorded or a short news programme can be made, providing information for others, e.g. on work completed or about a visit to a temple (pp. 52–3). Making a news programme requires the development of interviewing skills which can be put to good use during outside visits or if a Hindu guest visits the school (p. 55).

Using printed or written material

There is an increasingly large amount of textbook material on Hinduism available for use by pupils of various ages and abilities. Most of the books available at the time of writing are described in Part 3 (pp. 206–19). Good textbooks are particularly useful as school or class library books. For most schools, however, multiple purchase of expensive texts is out of the question, so it is important to find interesting and productive ways of using a selection of good books with small groups of pupils.

One method is to choose a section or paragraph from a book and to get small groups of pupils to undertake various tasks collectively. The discussion required to undertake the tasks helps pupils to understand the text and helps them to grasp new concepts and terms much more readily than through silent reading. The following paragraph is from Patricia Bahree's book *Hinduism* (1984) and the tasks were completed by a small group of fourth-form secondary pupils. Passages can be selected to suit different ages and abilities and the tasks can be adjusted accordingly.

> Pilgrimage places can be grouped into two main types. Many are natural creations such as rivers and mountains. These may be considered sacred because of their great importance to life or because they are particularly beautiful or inspire awe and wonder. A second type of pilgrimage spot includes man-made structures or places associated with important events. Great temples and places where famous teachers taught make up this group. Sometimes the two overlap. For instance, many great temples have been built along the Ganges river. Pilgrims visit both the river and the nearby temples. (Bahree 1984: 41–2)

Tasks:

1 *Make up a title for the paragraph.*
   Indian pilgrimage.

2 *Choose a phrase in the paragraph itself to be a title for the passage.*
   Pilgrimage places.

3 *Pick out the five most important words in the paragraph. If it is helpful, choose phrases rather than single words.*
   Pilgrimage; natural creations; sacred; man-made structures; temples.

4 *Summarise the paragraph in one sentence of your own.*

Indian pilgrimages are made to sites on rivers or mountains, or to man-made structures, but these two phenomena overlap sometimes in that temples can be built near rivers or on mountains.

5   *Write down one or more questions you would like to ask which are raised by the paragraph but not answered by it.*
Why do people go on pilgrimages?

6   *Draw a flowchart, diagram or picture to summarise the main points.*

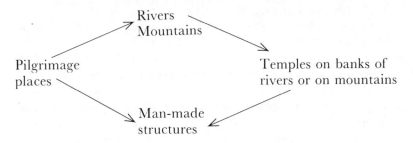

Sequencing and prediction:

Another way to recall a passage – such as a story – and to check comprehension, is by supplying individuals or small groups of children with a copy of the text which has been cut into sections and asking them to sort the pieces into the correct order. Short versions of Hindu stories can be divided into paragraphs which can be duplicated and cut into sections. Children work out the correct order and then stick the pieces on to a piece of paper or card.

Children can be helped to concentrate on story material by being asked at various points to guess what happens next. This can be done informally or in a more structured way by preparing copies of the story in booklet form. Children read or follow the text on the first page, and then guess what happens next before moving on to page two.

Note that these activities are aids to concentration, comprehension and revision. They need to be supplemented by other methods if children are to gain understanding and to make their own contributions. Methods for using story are discussed below.

Story and the expressive arts

Hindu myths provide access to some of the distinctive features and concepts of the tradition. Yet they are also part of the common stock of world mythology handling such universal themes as origins, morality and human destiny. Sita's devotion to Rama, and Arjuna's sense of his identity as a member of the warrior class (the Kshatriya varna), not only raise general questions about duty and moral dilemmas but also show the special nature of the Indian concept of dharma. Children's work on Hindu myth and story can reflect both these aspects. They can learn new vocabulary and new concepts, and thus may be initiated into the uniqueness of the Hindu tradition. But they can also enter the world of myth and explore some of its universals through its relationship to their own experience.

In order to do this, however, children need to be helped to grasp the idea that questions about the historicity of the myths are largely irrelevant to an understanding of their significance. Some discussion of the world of science fiction – Dr. Who or Star Wars, for example – can help young people to appreciate the distinction between historical truth and whether there is any 'truth' in a story. The point is an important one for it is still very common – among adults as well as children – to hear stories dismissed because their mythic elements seem nonsensical in historical terms. Some young Hindus in Britain, whom one might have expected to have retained a capacity to appreciate story, are influenced by a narrow, positivistic view of truth and have become embarrassed by their own heritage. J. H. Taylor reports comments from two Hindu teenage boys in Newcastle upon Tyne:

> 'Some of the things I've heard about the religion, they're ridiculous. Like gods with elephants' heads, and some of these gods flying to the moon – ridiculous really . . .'

> '. . . well how could it be true, you know, all these fantastic stories? Well, there's a man going into the jungle for 14 years without food or anything, coming back as young as he was when he went, and such like. And people having blue skins . . .' (Taylor 1976: 82)

Young people need their imaginations stimulated in order to avoid literalism (pp. 123–6). Drama can be an effective complement to listening and discussion, for it is through performance that individuals give something of their own experience to the story as well as bring it to life.

When considering how children might work with story it is worth reminding ourselves that the medium is not entirely a written one. The writings of Iona and Peter Opie testify to an

evolving oral tradition of stories as part of the lore and language of
children (Opie and Opie 1959). Similarly, in the case of Hindu
stories, the textual versions are not the only ones. Apart from the
epics, the other major textual source of Hindu myths is the
Purānas, including the countless local *Sthalapurānas* – each a
written record, made at a particular time and place, of an ongoing
oral tradition (p. 161). R. K. Narayan emphasises the richness
and life of this continuing oral story tradition in Hinduism:

> Every day one hears of these stories and professional narrators address
> huge gatherings – with song and description and partly adding their
> own ideas and dialogue and relevance . . . In the villages they may
> find some place, in a temple corridor or a blocked-off street. All their
> stories have their origins in the Indian epics, and they will take and
> narrate with proper treatment, so that an episode is made full of juice
> and song. (*The Guardian*, 12 September 1978. See also Narayan 1965).

Such tellers of myths and legends are called *paurānikas*, and there is
a case study of one on pp. 114–6.

Hindu myths are also brought to life in folk song, in India's rich
dance traditions, by troupes of itinerant actors (as in the annual
Rām Līlā in Delhi; see also p. 130; p. 156) by puppeteers and in
popular films. If we allow children to draw on their experience
and imagination in exploring Hindu stories, and if we encourage
them to use the media of the creative and performing arts in
expressing their own versions we can help to bring some of
Narayan's 'juice and song' into the classroom.

BBC 2's 1986 'But Is It True?' (p. 230) programme shows
children and actors manipulating huge home-made puppets in
the cosmic battle between good and evil which marks the climax of
the *Rāmāyana* (p. 130). Colour slides available from Coventry's
Minority Group Support Service charmingly show the same story
acted by infants 'on location' at a stately home (p. 222). The fact
that Sītā is pictured against the background of mock Tudor
buildings with Rāvana peering wickedly at his adversaries across
a moat from the turret of a castle adds to the mythic quality of the
performance. One school has used shadow-theatre in conjunction
with a tape-recorded narration of the Rāma and Sītā story from
the Rāmāyana (p. 161), while another depicted the tale in a
sequence of paintings which were displayed in the classroom and
later photographed and made into a series of colour slides,
accompanied by a tape-recording of the children's retelling of the
story. Stories of Krishna and the tale of Prahlāda's victory over
the demoness Holikā have been danced by children at another

junior school while sixth-formers and university students have learned the basic hand gestures of classical dance from a professional Indian dancer before watching her perform the story of the infant Krishna eating dirt and being punished by his mother (when Krishna opened his mouth to cry, his mother saw the whole universe inside it).

Merlin Price, in discussing the use of story in religious education, emphasises the need to give children sufficient time to explore and respond to story – especially in making an oral response. Oral work can include making links with other stories or with common themes which appear in religious myths. He goes on to identify various activities that can follow the initial telling of the story. The following points summarise Price's suggestions and are relevant to a treatment of Hindu story with primary and lower secondary children (Price 1985).

(a) Retelling the story in the children's own words. Possibly a small group activity to ensure that everyone can participate.

(b) Using a lead sheet or cue cards, small group discussion to promote empathy.
- (i) Eliciting insights into feelings and relationships within the story.
- (ii) To explore insights into characters and situations by extension or change of story-line and characters.
- (iii) Evoking the child's own reaction to the story.

(c) Language development.
- (i) Identification of words and phrases that evoke feelings and emotions.
- (ii) 'Brainstorming' sessions to discover other emotive words.
- (iii) Sequencing – pictorial or textual (p. 32).
- (iv) Extending the story – what happened before and after? (p. 32).

(d) Interpretation.
- (i) Developing the acceptance of more than one interpretation.
- (ii) Evaluation of other interpretations (supplied by teacher or other children).

(e) Start from the child's own experience.
- (i) How does the story relate to the children's own experience?
- (ii) How does the story elicit concerns and questions?
- (iii) How does the story help us to come to terms with such concerns?

(iv) Does the story introduce ways in which beliefs affect actions?

(f) Make links with other stories.
  (i) Discussion of other stories on similar themes.
  (ii) Construction of new stories around children's interpretations.

(g) Creative arts responses. Allow reflection over time and in various different ways.

(i)   Immediate art/drama response. This helps the child to 'live through' the events and can be adapted to the modern world.

  (ii) Use previously identified phrases in the following cycle: Phrase or imagery; 2-D art; oral or written poetry; 3-D art; further language response.

  (iii) Music – produced by children or selected as an appropriate response to the telling of the story or to the above cycle.

  (iv) Puppetry.

Some of these activities can be enhanced by the use of pictures, posters, slides and filmstrips as visual aids in addition to any available artefacts, e.g. statues of different Hindu deities. Food and clothes associated with Hinduism and India may also be used.

Food and cookery

Topics in Hinduism such as caste, festivals, worship, *ahimsā* (non-violence), fasting, the cow and even philosophical speculation about the nature of matter all raise questions about food. At the classroom level, some pupils will have misapprehensions and prejudices about Indian food which may inhibit a serious consideration of the culinary aspects of these topics. It is suggested that teachers start from pupils' own experience of food and their current knowledge of Indian cuisine before moving to more challenging areas of study.

Children enjoy seeing a display of different spices and experiencing their varied aromas. It is not a good idea to encourage children to taste spices in their raw state since a misleading impression of their flavour will be given. It is much better to involve young people in the preparation of Indian dishes, and recipes are given in the cookery books listed in the bibliography (Jaffrey 1978, 1985; Santa Maria 1973, 1979; Singh 1970). Teachers with Hindu or other Asian students may be able to invite parents to lend their knowledge and expertise. Pupils need to grasp that there are wide regional and local variations in cuisine (Jaffrey 1985, has recipes arranged by region) and that most Indian restaurants in Britain present a limited and rather generalised north Indian style of cooking. Most of these restaurants are run by Bangladeshi Muslims, though the number of restaurants staffed by Hindu families and offering regional cooking is growing. Occasionally one might find Brahmin families running restaurants offering regional, e.g. Gujarati, vegetarian food. Since food prepared by Brahmins is ritually pure for all castes, it is not surprising that some families have diversified into the catering industry (p. 77).

Indian cookery requires scrupulous cleanliness and there are a number of conventions that children cooking Indian food can be encouraged to follow. Hands should be thoroughly washed before coming into contact with food, and only the right hand should be used for eating. Food is not tasted during cooking. If it proves necessary to taste in order to check seasonings, the spoon should never be returned to the pan. The person serving food should not eat at the same time as those served, and eaters should not exchange food with one another. Left-over food (*jutha*) should never be eaten (p. 66), though food which has been offered to the gods can be distributed as *prasāda* (p. 107). Hindu cooks usually offer a little of their food to the god Agni or to the birds. For further details of food in relation to worship, see Chapter 8, and in connection with purity and pollution see p. 61, pp. 66–7, pp. 76–8 and the 'Food and philosophy' section below.

Vegetarianism in India

The doctrine of *ahimsā* (non-violence) was emphasised by Gandhi and has a long history in India. It was known in the time of the Upanishads and was elaborated by Buddhism, and Jainism. The reign of Ashoka (c.269–232 BCE) is a landmark, since he became a vegetarian and forbade the slaughter of many animals. Vegetarianism, however, has never been universal. Many castes eat meat, and fish is eaten in some coastal regions, e.g. parts of Bengal, by Hindus who regard themselves as vegetarian but who may not be so regarded by Hindus from other areas. The universal taboo on beef eating is associated with the sanctity of the cow in the Hindu tradition. Eggs are avoided by many Hindus in case they are fertile, and therefore contain the embryo of an animal (pp. 193–4).

Food and philosophy

In the Hindu tradition foods are considered to have a number of characteristics. One is the degree to which they are prone to ritual pollution (pp. 66–7, pp. 76–8). Uncooked food is far less pollution-prone than cooked food, so raw food, e.g. grains, may be received from members of a lower caste, but not most cooked foods. Cooking removes any pollution from the donor or vendor, but in the act of cooking something of the nature of the cook has passed into the food. In eating the food, the eater takes up certain qualities from the cook, and others who have come into contact with the cooked food, as well as those inherent in the food itself. To receive food from another person is to share, to some extent, in that person's nature.

A second characteristic is the capacity for foods to have a 'heating' or 'cooling' effect on the body. The 'heating' effect does not correspond always to the hotness (in the sense of pungency) of foods. Thus, although chilli has a 'heating' effect, ginger is cooling; oranges are 'cooling' but mangoes are 'heating'. The heating and cooling properties of food play an important part in traditional Indian medicine and are significant in some religious rituals. Incidentally, some foods – onions and garlic in particular – are believed to have an aphrodisiac quality and are avoided by many ascetics and members of some religious sects (e.g. members of the International Society for Krishna Consciousness – pp. 188, 191, 194).

A third characteristic of foods is their inherent capacity to convey certain qualities to the eater. Foods with the quality of *tamas* (e.g. meat) promote inertia and dullness while those with the quality of *rajas* (e.g. chilli) stimulate excitement and action (p. 176). The best foods are those which promote *sattva* – harmony, elevation of the spirit, intelligence. Sattvic foods include milk products, sugar, rice, wheat, pulses, fruit and many vegetables. The *Bhagavad-Gītā* (ch. 17, v. 8–10) includes left-over, decomposing, and stale foods in the tamasic category, while foods that lack balance, e.g. too hot, too dry, too salty, it regards as rajasic, causing 'distress, misery and disease'. Sattvic foods, however, are tasty, rich and well balanced, promoting long life, happiness and health.

Activities

(a) Ask pupils to make lists of foods they like best. In discussion pupils can be asked to give reasons for their choices. Issues of nutritional value, advertising, family tradition, regional preferences and so on are likely to come up.

(b) Ask pupils to make a list of dishes or ingredients that commonly appear in western European cookery, starting with foods that most people might be willing to eat and moving into the more exotic. Go through the list with the class, asking children to raise their hands when you get to a food they refuse to eat. Ask for reasons. The activity tends to reveal that the question of food can arouse strong feelings, and that family background is an influence on determining attitudes to different foods. Some foods are ruled out because of moral and religious beliefs. Religious reasons may be given for vegetarianism or, in the case of Jews and Muslims, for refusing pork and shell fish or meat not slaughtered in the appropriate manner. Hindus and Sikhs may specifically mention beef as not to be eaten. There will be a penumbra of disagreement as to whether certain foods are good to eat.

(c) Ask pupils to make a list of seasonings, spices and herbs they know or have tried and give examples of foods in which they might be used. Even the more basic lists tend to include pepper, salt and mint (all used in Indian cookery). The more adventurous or knowledgeable might include cinnamon, cloves and ginger (all used in Indian dishes). Parsley, thyme and sage do not figure in Indian cuisine, although parsley is used sometimes as a substitute for coriander – a herb that was used extensively in English cookery up to the time of Elizabeth I. Small groups can discuss the uses of spices and seasonings they are familiar with and report back to the whole class. A wide range of spices used in Indian cookery is described in Jaffrey (1985), Santa Maria (1973), and Singh (1970). Further teaching ideas on food occur on p. 69 and p. 193.

4

Hindus in Britain and Religious Education

Hinduism in Britain

Hindu communities in Britain represent a small fraction of contemporary Hinduism, and they are subject to the influences of an alien cultural environment. Nevertheless they are an important part of the Hindu tradition, and for many teachers and children they provide the sole means of direct access to the religion (pp. 8–10). Hence, although we will attempt in Part 2 to portray the Hindu tradition through varied examples from the Indian context, there will be regular reference to Hindus in Britain, and three of our case studies are of British Hindus.

Apart from a few Hindu migrants whose families settled in Britain before 1914, the bulk of the Hindu population migrated after the Second World War. The first significant movement was by male Hindus who responded to the labour shortage in Britain's industrial cities in the 1950s with the aim of gaining employment in order to supplement the family income in India. By a process of 'chain migration', early migrants were joined by men of similar caste – relatives or fellow villagers – the established residents providing accommodation and helping to find work for the new arrivals. By the mid to late 1960s the situation had changed, with an increasing number of wives and children migrating to join their husbands, establishing a more permanent form of settlement, while continuing to preserve economic and other ties with families in India. The majority of these migrants were from Gujarat and the Panjab, two Indian states with traditions of population movement.

The second wave of migration began in the late 1960s, not directly from India but from Eastern and Central African states to which Indians had moved – often as indentured labourers but also as traders or professionals – in the nineteenth or early twentieth century. Africanisation policies in countries such as Kenya and Tanzania were an important reason for moving. Ugandan Asians had no choice in the matter and were expelled from the country in 1972. Of those Asians who came to Britain, around 60% were Hindus, mainly Gujarati by ethnicity, that is by language and culture. One of the prominent differences between this and the earlier wave of migration was that, where passports permitted it, whole families entered the United Kingdom together.

It is extremely difficult to assess the size of the British Hindu population. It has been calculated that by 1977 nearly 30% of the British South Asian population was Hindu – almost 307,000 people. Of these some 46% were born either in an African state or to African Asian parents. Hindus of Gujarati cultural origin are the majority group, representing 70% of the total Hindu population, while ethnically Panjabi Hindus are the largest minority (15%). The remaining 15% represents Hindus with various linguistic and cultural backgrounds including Maharashtrians, Rajasthanis, Bengalis and Tamils (Knott 1986a: 9). It should not be forgotten that many Hindus in Britain are children (pp. 8–10).

Religious practice

There are several factors which determine the nature of Hindu religious life in Britain. Because Hinduism is such an amorphous phenomenon, with a wide variety of practice and belief, one would expect some diversity of religious activity among British Hindus. The principal factor in determining this variety is ethnicity. Gujaratis and Panjabis, for example, speak different languages, have notable variations in their religious festivals and life-cycle rituals and have different food preferences. In tracing the pattern of settlement of the two groups, it comes as no surprise to discover that Gujaratis moved to areas of cities already with a Gujarati community, while Panjabis tended to set up homes near other Panjabis, whether Hindus or Sikh by religion. Most temples and religious organisations cater for a single ethnic group, though there are some exceptions.

A second factor which has influenced the development of Hindu practice in Britain is the difference between the first and second waves of migration. The most important aspect of this is that while the first 'Indian' movement consisted initially of men of wage-earning age, the second 'African' group comprised a population of all ages. Among the latter were many respected

elders whose knowledge and influence have done much to preserve the religious life and caste structure of the Gujarati population.

Reference to caste introduces a further factor which plays a part
in determining the variety of religious life among British Hindus.
There are many temples whose worship expressing bhakti (loving
devotion) attracts people from across caste boundaries. Likewise
there are *bhajan mandal* – devotional singing groups – and various
satsangs or religious meetings which attract people from a range of
castes. There are other organisations and activities that are open
only to members of individual castes. In Coventry, for example,
there is a range of caste associations which, in various ways, cater
for certain aspects of the religious and social life of caste members.
Moreover, the details of domestic religious practices and life-cycle
rites tend to vary from caste to caste.

Sectarianism provides another variable in the pattern of Hindu
life. Membership of a sect or *sampradāya* (p. 185) is a long-
established feature of the Hindu tradition. Although the majority
of British Hindus are not sect members, several Hindu sects
flourish in the United Kingdom, some – like the distinctively
Gujarati Pushti Mārga and Swāminārāyan sects – being associated with (though not exclusive to) certain Gujarati castes.
Others transcend caste and regional barriers; the *Ārya Samāj*
opposes caste distinctions as a matter of principle.

The International Society for Krishna Consciousness, more
popularly known as the Hare Krishna Movement, has proved
attractive to a segment of the British Hindu population. This
group is rooted in the medieval bhakti (devotional) sect founded
by Shri Chaitanya, and brought to the West in 1965 by A. C.
Bhaktivedanta Swami Prabhupada. It attracted followers in
North America and the United Kingdom and is now going
through a process of 'Indianisation' as it is joined and influenced
by Indian and migrant Hindus (p. 188; p. 191).

British Hindus find themselves cut off from the implicit and
informal ways of handing on tradition which surround Hindus in
an Indian village. Many of them therefore feel that they do not
know enough about their religion; this may lead them to read
about the theology and philosophy of Hinduism (pp. 168–78) or to
attach themselves to sects.

Hindu life in Britain, then, is highly variegated, with linguistic
and cultural background (ethnicity), the Indian/African distinction, caste and sect being factors which determine its variety. One

should also remember that much religious practice goes on outside temples, caste organisations and sectarian meetings. Much of it is domestic and some of it is individual. Such practice includes fasting, making vows, undertaking pilgrimages to sacred sites in India (pp. 141–48), and, most important, the celebration of samskāras or life-cycle rites (pp. 88–97).

Change and continuity

We have noted that British Hindus have to adapt to an alien cultural environment. Such adaptation results in change, but continuity with the Hindu tradition is not lost. When, for example, visitors enter a Hindu temple in Britain they see something very different from what they would most likely see in an Indian temple (pp. 148–50). The building is a different shape, to begin with. It may be the front room of a terraced house, or a converted church, or a converted cinema; the Newcastle temple is a converted working men's club and the Shree Krishna temple in Coventry is a converted school. Whatever the origin of the building, visitors are likely to see four walls enclosing a space, as they would in many buildings with quite different purposes; take away the pictures of deities, holy men and so on that have been attached to the walls, and remove the shrines and furniture that have been put into the space, and it is simply an empty room. An Indian temple is different: it will have a pillared hall, perhaps approached by a pillared porch, leading to a small, dark shrine; everything is directed towards the shrine, and its centre is marked by a tall spire or peak. Meaning is built into the shape of the temple: it symbolises a mountain on which the god dwells, a chariot on which he rides, the tree at the centre of the world. It is not just a space to hold a lot of people; indeed, it may not have room for many people. Its function is not to bring people together, but to house the god and protect him from the profane world outside.

There are other differences in the Indian temple. People come and go at different times according to their private wish or the needs of their family life: to pray in a crisis, to give thanks for a birth or to fulfil a vow. People also crowd together in the temple and around it at certain times of the year, governed by the phases of the moon (pp. 132–5). In the British temple, although these functions are by no means absent, people often come together at certain times on Sundays, like a church congregation; the British working week grew up round church worship, and Hinduism has to adapt to this pattern.

The British temple is also a community centre, where the local Hindu community asserts or renews its solidarity, holds study classes on texts such as the *Bhagavad-Gītā*, holds classes in Indian languages, meets to sing bhajans (devotional songs) or cooks and eats traditional food. In India the sense of belonging and the assimilation of traditional values and teachings, like language and food, come from the home; there is no need for the temple to perform these functions. Most British temples are funded and maintained by a local Hindu community; Indian temples are often founded by a wealthy person and maintained from endowments in the form of land.

So when we compare British Hinduism with Indian Hinduism, we find change, adaptation to the conditions of British life, following earlier adaptation to East African life in the case of those families who came here from East Africa. As the tradition is transmitted to new generations of British-born Hindus the process of adaptation will continue (pp. 8–10).

But again, change does not necessarily imply a loss of continuity. The British temple is, consciously but genuinely, a place for maintaining traditional ways and values which are hard to maintain in British surroundings. British Hinduism is therefore a valuable resource to teaching about Hinduism as a whole.

Visiting a Hindu temple

Children can gain some experience of Hindu communities in Britain through the increasingly wide variety of audio-visual materials and textbooks which are currently available (see Part 3). But there is no real substitute for meeting Hindus either as visitors to schools or in other contexts, such as Hindu temples. Care should be taken, however, to set British examples of Hinduism in the wider context of the Indian tradition.

For many pupils and students a visit to a place of worship such as a Hindu temple is a highly motivating experience. Some seem to perceive for the first time that religion is not a purely intellectual or book-bound activity but is concerned with persons – with their beliefs and rituals, but also with their emotions. Personal accounts from adherents of what it feels like to engage in worship or to have participated in a life-cycle ritual give insight into the meaning of religion that cannot be grasped solely through a formal understanding of religious concepts. It is in the behaviour and responses of worshippers that pupils begin to grasp the idea of sacred place (pp. 103–13; pp. 141–50).

Further, a Hindu temple provides a feast of visual experience, being full of colourful and vivid images, pictures and artefacts. Most Hindu images and religious pictures might be described as freeze-frames of Hindu myths. The images are a focus for worship – this should soon be grasped by a visitor to a Hindu temple. But they are also educational aids which often prompt or recall key stories from the tradition – Rāma's triumph over Rāvana, the flute-playing Lord Krishna, with his beloved Rādhā, Durgā's defeat of the buffalo demon and so on. During worship the sounds of prayers and songs, the smell of incense and the taste of *prasāda* – food offered to the gods and later shared by the worshippers (p. 107) – complement the temple's visual features and combine to make an impact on both devotees and observers. Learning activities based on visits are not difficult to devise, since most of the data will have been experienced or witnessed by all partici-pants; everyone should have some question, observation or anec-dote to contribute. The activity of sharing and analysing experi-ences and observations from a visit sometimes raises questions about the students' personal beliefs in relation to what has been witnessed, questions that can lead to some introductory theologic-al discussion on inter-faith relations or more philosophical reflec-tion about the relationship between the claims of different faiths and belief systems (pp. 179–81).

The potential of visits for enhancing good community relations should not be ignored, nor should opportunities for informing Hindu communities about the kind of religious education current-ly being taught in schools. But these reasons for making visits, though important, are secondary to pupils gaining first-hand experience of sacred place and worship.

Preparation for visits

Organising a visit to a Hindu temple involves at least four different groups of people and it is important that each group is given proper attention during preparation for the visit. The children and the Hindu community immediately spring to mind, but there are also parents and colleagues to be taken into consideration.

The Hindu community

In our experience Hindu communities are very welcoming and hospitable and they are happy to receive school parties at appropriate times. Community leaders with whom we have talked were unanimous in asserting the educational value of visits, though a few reservations were made about occasional insensitivity or lack of preparation. Their comments have been taken into account in the following points:

(a) Give the temple committee plenty of notice – two weeks at least, but preferably more. Addresses of over thirty temples are available from the National Council of Hindu Temples (p. 236). Local Community Relations Councils should also have addresses of temples and their current officers. If telephone numbers are available, it is suggested that contact is first made by telephone and confirmation of arrangements is made by letter.

(b) Explain to your contact, by telephone or letter, the educational purpose of your visit. Do you need a speaker? If so, what material do you wish to be covered?

(c) Make a preliminary visit to the temple to meet members of the committee and to discuss the details of the visit. As well as breaking the ice, the occasion is likely to prompt further ideas for the kinds of work you can expect children to do during or after their visit. In consultation with your contacts decide whether the visit should be to a communal activity – an ārati ceremony or a festival – or to the building when the congregation is not present. Since ceremonies and festivals are conducted in the evenings a visit during the school day is likely to focus on your host and on the building and its contents rather than on worshippers. However, individual devotees visit the temple at any time, and may do so while a school party is present.

(d) Make sure that the children are well prepared for the visit. Classes showing complete ignorance of the Hindu tradition and of how to behave do not make a good impression.

(e) All visitors should be properly dressed. Everyone should be ready to remove shoes before entering the prayer hall of the temple. Wear clean, smart clothes which will be comfortable and decent when sitting cross-legged on the floor. (All visitors should have legs covered if attending a Swāminārāyan temple.) Head covering is not essential, though Hindu women tend to cover the head during ārati Double-check these details with your contact before the visit takes place.

(f) Traditional views about ritual purity may require that women should not visit a temple during menstruation (p. 149).

(g) Encourage children and young people to be sensitive both to the place they are visiting and to the people who use it. Temples are not museums or leisure centres but are places of prayer and worship. If corporate or individual devotions are taking place, parties should sit quietly and observe the proceedings. Try to sit cross-legged if possible. A good impression is not given by visitors who sit with feet pointing towards the shrine. Usually boys and girls should sit on different sides of the hall.

(h) If a temple congregation is small the presence of a large group of visitors during a festival or an act of worship may be distracting, even if the visitors behave impeccably. Groups of around twelve are relatively easy to organise (with a couple of teachers they can fit into a minibus) and can be unobtrusive. As a rule of thumb, parties of between twenty and thirty should not be taken to the temple when congregational devotions are taking place. Large parties need to have adequate supervision and, if the visit is to be of value to individuals, a good deal of planning of the activities which children will be expected to do at the temple needs to be undertaken.

(i) Photography and tape-recording should only be allowed if permission is given by the host. Flash cameras can be very distracting, so if the visit is taking place while worship is in progress limit the number of people taking photographs to one or two and encourage sensitivity in the selection of subjects to be photographed. If in doubt, consult your host.

(j) Thank-you letters are warmly appreciated by Hindu communities and by the individuals who have helped with the visit. Letters from teachers and from children are often read out to the assembled congregation. Children can send examples of their work – pictures, poems, photographs – to the temple, or your hosts can be invited to the school to see a display of children's work or an assembly based on their visit. Every effort should be made to demonstrate to the community that the exercise has been a valuable learning experience for children and not a casual visit.

The children

It has already been suggested that visits should take place after children have been given a grounding in Hinduism and should not be placed too early in a course. The anticipation of a visit, further, helps to motivate children to study new material in preparation for it. If children help to plan the visit and to design the work to be carried out their motivation will be even stronger.

What follows is an account of the preparation for a visit by a class of eleven-year-olds in an all-white South Warwickshire junior school. The teacher was undertaking her first school visit to a temple, and her experiences are likely to be of value to others contemplating a similar venture. The teacher, in this case, was a third-year student on teaching practice, assisted by the class teacher and the Head Teacher. The work on Hinduism constituted half of a topic on 'places of worship', the rest of the work being on Christianity and involving a visit to the local parish church. Since children had had no previous experience of Hinduism some of the exercises outlined in Chapter 3 were carried out.

In groups of five, children were given various tasks and asked to report back to the whole class. One group used a Diastar daylight viewer to work with slides showing the ārātī ceremony (p. 29). Their task was to try and guess what the slides depicted. Another group did a similar 'puzzling' activity with a collection of artefacts (ārātī lamp, bell, water pot and ladle, image of Ganesha). A third group was given a Gujarati tear-off calendar, bearing both Gregorian and Hindu (Vikram era) dates (p. 133), and a series of questions, e.g. What do you think the object is? Why are many of the pages coloured green? (Answer: they are holy days – new moon, full moon, festivals, fasts, etc.) The activities generated interest and prompted questions. The teacher was able to supplement and to correct answers in the ensuing discussion. Further activities concentrated on arousing interest and making children feel comfortable with new experiences. They listened to Indian music, examined a wedding garland and a sari (modelled by one of the girls) and they smelt incense burning. Pupils were also introduced to the Rāma and Sītā story. It was read to them, they discussed issues arising from the story and the symbolism of the characters, they responded to the story in their work and wrote their own versions. Gradually the children became aware of the range of artefacts and experiences they might encounter at the Hindu temple and they learned a little about the people who regularly used the building; the sequence of migrations that older members of the community had been through; and about the part of India (Gujarat) whose culture and language was maintained by those who used the temple.

The children were also involved in designing activities to be carried out in the temple. Since the visit was for a whole class, it was decided that children should not attend a congregational act of worship and that they should work in groups after an initial welcome and brief talk by the temple's president. Two groups decided to record interviews with members of the temple committee and in preparation they conducted interviews with the school secretary, the Deputy Head, the Head Teacher and the cook. Schedules of appropriate questions were prepared and the techniques of interviewing and of using a cassette recorder were practised. The groups then prepared specific questions about the temple and its use as well as more general questions about Hinduism. Time was also allowed for spontaneous questions, and interviewing duties were shared out among the children in each group. A third group decided to make a photographic record of the visit. The president of the temple gave his approval to this idea and an automatic camera and flash unit were borrowed. A provisional list of shots was discussed with the student teacher who had made the preliminary visit. The activity of guessing and puzzling was chosen by a fourth group. Their idea was to extend the work that had been done in class with slides. They would be accompanied by a person who knew the answers, but they would try to work out for themselves what was depicted in each of the three main shrines at the temple and in some of the pictures on the walls. The last group decided to make drawings of shrines and of gods and goddesses portrayed on the various pictures around the temple. There was unanimous enthusiasm for the project and all the children looked forward to the visit.

Parents

It is, of course, essential that permission from parents is sought for visits away from school. Since some parents are likely to be unfamiliar with recent developments in religious education it is important that an educational justification for the trip is made. The following account continues the story of a visit to a Hindu temple by children from a Warwickshire junior school.

A letter was sent by the Head Teacher to the parents of the children in the class, explaining the reasons for the visit and its place in the work that the children were currently doing. Details about lunch arrangements and cost of transport were also given. All but one parent gave permission for their children to take part, and some expressed as much enthusiasm for the visit as their offspring. A small minority of parents expressed strong reservations: 'They don't want to know about us, so why should we learn about them?' But only one parent refused permission, and this was on theological grounds.

To its credit, the school argued the educational case for the visit with all who expressed reservations and, although it is doubtful that attitudes were changed in a dramatic way, questions of racial, cultural and religious conflict were brought into the open and were approached rationally.

Had the visit been from a multi-faith school the question of theological objection might possibly have arisen in other forms. In our experience most parents, regardless of their religious affiliation, are happy for their children to undertake visits provided that the reasons for the visit are explained and that it is made clear that children are not participating in worship nor being expected to affirm Hindu beliefs. Some parents may object to their children receiving prasāda (p. 107), on the grounds that it is food that has been offered to idols; some pupils may have such objections themselves. This could lead to useful classroom discussion on how people with different views can still respect one another's practices. Pupils can be advised that they do not have to eat prasāda if it is offered to them in the temple.

Teachers

Visits require adequate supervision, and it is unlikely that one teacher could cope adequately with more than a dozen pupils. Also for reasons of safety and security it is better always to have more than one teacher involved in a visit. Colleagues who lack recent experience in religious education may require some informal in-service training by the organiser. The story of our school visit continues.

Since no work on Asian religious traditions had previously been done in the school, the student teacher found that she had to argue a case for the visit with some colleagues. It is interesting that reservations were not expressed openly about classroom-based work on Hinduism, but they were uttered when a visit to a Hindu temple was proposed. The student had the support of the Head Teacher, several colleagues and the County Agreed Syllabus in

Religious Education, so she felt confident enough to encourage discussions about the concerns felt by some teachers. The main gist of what was being said was as follows:

(a) Since we live in a Christian country we should be teaching children to be Christians, not Hindus.

(b) That children would be confused by something that was so complicated and 'different' as Hinduism.

The student teacher and the staff who supported her replied along these lines:

(a) Although we live in a country that has a Christian heritage, only a minority of people today are practising Christians. Religious education must cover Christianity, but it should not be confined to it.

(b) Religious education does not aim to proselytise for individual religions or for a general religious outlook. One of its principal aims, however, is to develop children's understanding of religion.

(c) The presence in the region of substantial numbers practising a faith other than Christianity afforded an excellent opportunity to study it and to meet the people who practised it.

(d) Whether or not children would be confused by Hinduism or mathematics or any other subject depended largely on the teacher's skill in selecting appropriate material and teaching methods. The children's enthusiasm for the topic, it was pointed out, was evidence that they were not finding the work difficult to understand.

Without the support of the Head Teacher and of other teachers it is doubtful whether the student teacher would have had the confidence and status to carry her case. As it happened, there were open and rational discussions, and plans for the visit went ahead. What became clear during the period of preparation for the visit was that the apparent reluctance of some teachers to support the enterprise masked their own anxiety about coping with new and unfamiliar experiences and about their own lack of knowledge of religions other than Christianity. In the case of one teacher it was the removal of these anxieties – through working cooperatively with another person, through the experience of the visit and in realising that the teacher does not have to be an authority or 'expert' – that changed her attitudes, rather than simply being defeated by counter-arguments.

To summarise, one should take care not to underestimate the amount of preparation required for a successful visit to a Hindu temple. Direct contact with the community needs to be established through a preliminary visit, and the reasons for the activity given. Similarly, parents and colleagues need to have the educational rationale of the trip explained to them. Finally, children should be involved in preparing for the visit, and should be given the opportunity to suggest and practise appropriate learning activities.

The visit

Careful and detailed preparation may occasionally seem tedious, but there is little doubt that when the visit takes place, the time spent will be seen to have been worthwhile. In the case of our Warwickshire party, the children were excited, but they were reasonably well informed and they knew how to conduct themselves. They were properly dressed and knew that they would be expected to remove their shoes. The two interviewing groups were ready with their tape recorders and interview schedules, the 'puzzling' group was armed with a short questionnaire prepared by the student-teacher in consultation with the President of the temple, the photographer was equipped with cameras and film and the drawing group had a list of possible subjects. The aroma of incense was recognised by the children as they went into the temple, and some reported later that their initial experience of it in class had 'made us feel less strange' during the visit. After some minutes spent quietly absorbing the surroundings, the President gave the children a five-minute introduction to the temple, and then the class split into groups, each with a teacher or a student, and work began. Many of the questions addressed to Mr Lad, the President, asked for explanations about images, pictures, stories and festivals, but he was also asked about his own personal history and his likes and dislikes. The drawing group settled on Ganesha, Rāma and Krishna as subjects, and the photographers began taking pictures of shrines and of their classmates working. The 'puzzling' group worked their way around the temple, making notes on their questionnaires as they went. At one point a worshipper entered the temple and performed his devotions, sat down and proceeded to read a text while most of the children quietly observed this activity. Having explained why they were at the temple, a group of them asked him if he was willing to be interviewed. This example of flexibility on the part of the second 'interviewing' group resulted in their learning information about the *Bhagavad-Gītā*, seeing pages of the Sanskrit text, recording passages intoned by their new friend and hearing about the importance of prayer. After about an hour the activities were drawn to a close and the Head Teacher thanked the President and other members of the community for their warm welcome and their efforts on behalf of the children. He invited the President to visit the school and to see the children's work arising from the project, and after signing the visitors' book, the children returned to school.

Visits during worship require different ways of working, though thorough preparation is a must. During ārati children or young people might simply sit or stand attentively, listening and looking, gaining an impression rather than checking off the details of the ritual in a notebook. Later, the experience of the rituals can be discussed in relation to information already given, and new material can be introduced as appropriate. Attendance at a festival might not turn out to be so passive. Groups of third-year juniors and fifth-form secondary students attending one of the nine nights of the Navarātri festival in Coventry have found themselves encouraged by their hosts to participate in the *garba* (a clapping dance for the mother goddess) or the *rās dandiān* (a stick dance re-enacting the *gopīs* dancing for Krishna). Such experiences are likely to be remembered.

Follow-up work

To return to our example, both staff and the children found the visit a highly motivating experience. The Head Teacher followed up the occasion with a visit by his own family, and the staff who accompanied the children were all keen to participate in follow-up activities. Although several children admitted to feeling slightly apprehensive on first entering the temple, there was general agreement that their preparation and the welcome they received soon made them feel comfortable.

Of the different activities which the children engaged in, the most successful was that done by the 'puzzling' group. In the student-teacher's words:

> This activity really sparked off an interest which continued long after the visit. Each child wanted to find out more about the shrines and pictures they had seen. None of them was satisfied with just the basic answers needed for the questionnaire – they wanted explanations.

They found the method absorbing and of all the groups they were the best informed.

Also they wanted to discuss issues arising from the work, even questions like 'Who is God?' and 'Why do different people think there are different Gods?' These children were a good source of information for the other children and were keen to explain points from the photographs and pictures. Also they were keen to explain things to children in other classes and I found groups at break and lunchtime showing other children photographs and objects on display – a real question/answer activity in progress!

Interviewing also proved to be a very fruitful method and the tapes provided an excellent source of information which was incorporated by children into their poems and reports. The photographers were able to mount a display of colour prints which illustrated the iconography of the temple, but also showed children doing their various activities. Drawing turned out to be the least successful learning method. Some good pictures of Ganesha, Rāma and Krishna were produced, but the children had learned little about the Hindu tradition, even though they enjoyed the activity. Some of the best artwork produced in class was by children from other groups whose interest had been stimulated by 'puzzling' and interviewing. Follow-up work in class included painting, poetry-writing, news reporting (for a magazine and for a television news bulletin) and a display of photographs.

Assembly

The climax of the children's follow-up work was an assembly drawing on material from their visits to the parish church and the Hindu temple. The President of the temple and the vicar were both guests on this occasion and they witnessed a delightful sequence of sketches, reports and poems including the two quoted above. They were then taken round a display of the children's work in the classroom, and the President of the temple was presented with a book, made by the children and containing examples of their work following the visit. Finally, the guests were treated to coffee and a huge chocolate cake made by the children. The children had remembered that the President of the Hindu temple liked cake, and so had taken the trouble to provide it. (Many, though by no means all, Hindus would avoid cake if it contained eggs (p. 38).) It is hard to calculate the good effects of occasions like this. At the very least a member of a Hindu community was made to feel that a visit by a group of children to his temple had been undertaken seriously and had resulted in a good deal of thoughtful work and learning.

Visitors

Work on Hinduism in school can be enhanced by a visit by one or more members of a Hindu community. Generally, visits contributing to work on Hinduism which is already in progress are more effective than talks given by outsiders introducing the subject for the first time. Teachers in multi-faith schools often have the particular advantage of being able to invite Hindu parents to make a contribution. There are many examples of parental contributions to infant and junior topics such as festivals – introducing dress, food and hand decoration as well as more devotional topics such as worship in the home. If parents are inexperienced at talking to groups, children can prepare a schedule of questions and interview their guest about topics that interest them. In any case children are likely to learn more using active methods rather than sitting passively listening to a talk. Some schools in multi-faith areas have also invited Hindu dance and music groups into school to great effect. Contact has usually been made by way of parents, Asian teachers or local Community Relations Councils.

The National Council of Hindu Temples will assist in finding speakers, as will the International Society for Krishna Conciousness (p. 236), but enquirers should be precise in stating their requirements. Needless to say, enquirers should observe the kind of courtesies mentioned above and should be prepared to cover the expenses of visitors.

Part Two

The Hindu Religious Tradition

5

The Family

It is through the family that most Hindus learn and experience Hinduism. We shall examine this topic through the eyes of a Hindu woman in east London, who told her own story, in her own language, Panjabi, to a British anthropologist. Like most Hindus she was originally a villager, and like many Indian villagers she is a good talker, with a fund of stories and proverbs (Sharma 1971).

Case study: Satya

Satya came to Britain with her three children in the late 1960s to join her husband Rāmpāl, an electrician. Her father was a shopkeeper and small farmer. He was a Sikh, though the rest of the family were Hindu. This may seem strange, but Satya explains that it was due to a vow made by her grandmother, whose previous children had died in infancy. She prayed to Guru Nānak, the sixteenth-century founder of the Sikhs (p. 191), and promised that if she had a son who survived, she would make him a Sikh. Satya was closer to this grandmother than to her own mother, 'My mother used to spank us if we were naughty, but Dadi would always try to stop her.' Dadi means 'paternal grandmother'; Indian kinship terms are often more precise than those in English (p. 64).

Guru Nānak was a holy man in the Hindu tradition, and is still venerated by Hindus. Hindu prayers and vows often override the boundaries which we may be used to making between religions; alongside the Hindu pictures on Rāmpāl and Satya's mantelpiece there are not only Sikh saints but also a Virgin and Child. It is not unusual to find both Hindus and Sikhs in a Panjabi family, as they sometimes intermarry if they are of the same caste.

Satya was eighteen when she married. The marriage had been

arranged three years before, and it was Satya's parents who initiated the negotiations. Until the wedding Rampal did not see Satya; if he had even gone to her village, the engagement would have been broken off. A marriage was arranged at the same time between Baldev, Rāmpāl's younger brother, and Gītā, Satya's younger sister; the double wedding took place on an auspicious day chosen by an astrologer. Marrying both couples together simplified the negotiations, and lessened the expense, both for Rampal, who came back to his home village from his job in Delhi and entertained Satya's family for the wedding itself, and for her family when they entertained his family for three days afterwards. After that he went back to his one-roomed flat in Delhi; Satya stayed with her parents for some time before joining him. Both Rampal and Satya believe firmly in arranged marriages, though they recognise that their children may have their own ideas. They think young people are too impetuous to choose for themselves, and their elders are impartial and experienced enough to decide for them.

Satya had her first baby, a girl, at her parents' house. After the birth she was given strengthening food – almonds, butter, milk, sweets – and stayed in bed for thirteen days. At the end of this time she got up and took a bath, to mark the end of a time of impurity. When her first son was born, the excitement was greater. Satya loves her daughters as much as her sons, and does not believe that you should boast of having boys; it is God who decides which they shall be, she says, not you.

Rampal, like his father, is interested in religion; he would like to meet Christian monks and nuns of the enclosed orders. Satya is more practical and adaptable, with a cheerful outlook on life; but she expresses that outlook in a religious way. When they lived in Delhi, Satya usually went to a temple after her morning bath, before starting the cooking. She and Rampal sometimes went to a Hindu temple or a Sikh gurdwara as a Sunday outing with the children; and just before going to England he took her for a holiday to Vrindāvan, where Krishna lived among the cowherds: 'There are lots of holy places there and you will enjoy yourself.' (p. 146)

In England, Satya had to get used to new ways. Food was an obvious problem; she was first prompted to learn to read English by the need to recognise the word 'beef' on the tins in the supermarket, so that she could avoid it. Not only the food but the ways of eating were different. Hindus are very particular about avoiding contact with food that anyone, even oneself, has started to eat; such left-over food is called jutha, and Rampal was surprised that the English had no such word or concept. He explains that Hindus eat with their hands, and when your hands have been in your mouth they are impure. People who are eating will ask someone who has not yet started eating, or who has already finished and washed their hands, to serve them. Food left over, unless it is untouched, is thrown away.

Even in India there are differences. When Rampal and Satya were on holiday in Agra on the way to Vrindavan, they found the people there not only washed their hands before a meal but took a bath, if they had been out of the house, and would never carry food about to eat away from home, as Rampal and Satya did.

Another thing that struck them about life in England was the weakness of family ties. Children please themselves, not their parents, in choosing whom to go out with and whom to marry. Satya finds that English mothers feel their daughters are off their hands when they marry, and no one minds if they divorce soon afterwards. What she has seen in England convinces her that Indian marriages are very firmly based. She makes sure her children get the best she can provide, so that they will learn to trust her. 'As they get bigger', she says, 'they will come to know that we will get them married and provide everything at their marriages.' Arranged marriages thus seem to her a natural expression of the bond between parents and children.

Satya regrets that in England her children cannot enjoy the love of the aunts, uncles and grandparents who surrounded them in India. By moving to London, the family had become more like an English one. They had no relatives living near; they had thought of bringing Rampal's father over, but decided that he was too old to adapt to a strange country away from his old friends, and they would not have been able to look after him. 'I can get a baby-minder for my baby, but where can I leave my poor old father-in-law?'

When Satya came over with the children she took a part-time job while they were at school, to help towards buying a house. Family life took place mainly in the evening when everyone was tired and the television was on. Satya remembers a very different kind of childhood; she had no schooling, though later she taught herself to read Panjabi when she was in Delhi, and English in London. She played out of doors with her sisters, making mud chapattis and making and dressing rag dolls until, at seven or eight, she was old enough to join in the real housework: folding the bedding, fetching the water, washing the dishes. From time to time the girls and their mother would re-plaster the floors of the house together. This was done by mixing mud and cow-dung with water, and spreading it smoothly. Then there were pots to scour, clothes to wash, and even buffaloes and cattle to look after. Satya describes all these tasks with enthusiasm.

Rampal is very concerned about how his eldest son is getting on at school; education is traditionally the family's responsibility. In return for the money spent on them, sons are expected to remit money to their parents when they start earning, or to bring their parents to live with them. When Rampal and Satya were living in Delhi, his father came to live with them; when she left for England, he went to live with Rampal's younger brother. Satya got on very well with him, although a wife is expected to be subdued in front of her father-in-law, and veil her face with the end of her sari in his presence. It is the custom, Satya explains, for a married woman to veil her face from the older men in her husband's village, or at least from his elder male relatives. She found it difficult, on the rare occasions when she visited Rampal's village, to know who were his relatives, and whether they were his elders.

Satya recognises that the Hindu family system does not always work as it should; people do not always do their duty by their relatives. One example of neglect occurred when Rampal was first in England and she was in Delhi. The daughter of Rampal's sister was seriously ill. Her mother had died and her father had married again, and the girl's husband and his family did nothing for her.

So it was Satya who took the girl to hospital, and eventually arranged her funeral. Normally the pyre is lit by the eldest son or another close male relative, but in this case

> the funeral priest told us that as there was no very close relative present that person who had loved her the most ought to be the one to ignite the funeral pyre. So it was I who had to do this, although my heart rebelled so that I could hardly bring myself to set light to the wood.

The joint family

Not all Hindu families follow the same pattern, and times are changing; but Rampal's and Satya's experiences illustrate many of the tendencies of Hindu families. While the term 'family' can refer to a husband and wife and their children – a 'nuclear family'

– it can also refer to a wider group, including several related couples and their children – a 'joint family'. Among Hindus, these couples are usually related through the husbands, who are brothers, or else father and son; the typical pattern is thus the 'patrilineal joint family'. The sons of one father, with their wives and children, will not necessarily all live with him at the same time, but some of them are likely to do so some of the time. Thus, Rampal and his two brothers lived in their home village at various times; Rampal's father lived with him in Delhi, and with his younger brother when he had left for England. It is common for the elder couple to live in one room and their son and his wife in the next, even if lack of space means that their children have to sleep with them. On the other hand it is not customary for parents to live with a married daughter and her husband.

Even where the whole joint family does not share a house, it shares wealth to some extent. Men who are working away from home remit money to their fathers or, if the father is not alive, to their elder brothers. Conversely, fathers provide capital to set up their sons in business, or get them training. Prestige is also shared; children are brought up in the hope that they will bring credit to the family through their behaviour and style of life. Any failure to carry out obligations to groups outside the family, any lapse from religious norms, any vice or sign of impoverishment, brings disgrace not just on the individual but on the family.

Linked with the solidarity of the family is the sense of attachment to the home village. Even where more than one generation of a family has lived in one of the modern cities of India, or overseas, for the sake of work, people regard themselves as belonging to a village; they may remit part of their earnings to their relatives there, and go there for family occasions such as weddings, so long as any members of the joint family are there. Strangers meeting in cities are apt to ask each other what village they come from, and to exchange village news if they find they are connected.

Marriage

The family tends to make joint decisions under the leadership of its elders, even where the lives of individuals are concerned; the choice of marriage partners is a clear example (p. 89). The birth of a daughter carries with it the obligation to get her suitably married, and when she is approaching marriageable age her family spreads the word among families of the same caste who have eligible sons. For ritual purposes, marriage is regarded as the gift of a girl from one family to another, and although the inclinations of the bride and groom are not necessarily ignored, the question of how the bride will fit into the new family, not just how she will get on with her husband, is important. This matters from the bride's point of view: 'To tell you the truth,' Satya says, 'I thought more about what sort of mother-in-law I should get than about the husband chosen for me.' The head of the bridegroom's family makes his choice, consulting the elder women of the family and the young man himself as he sees fit; typical criteria are the status of the bride's family, her looks, her educational qualifications and her domestic and artisitic skills. A photograph is often a useful aid in making the choice. Traditionally, at least among the higher castes, a substantial dowry went with the girl, and was often in inverse proportion to her other assets; the dowry was abolished by law in 1961, but the law is often circumvented through the gifts which the bridegroom's family expect before and after marriage.

While marriage is normally within the caste, it is often outside the village. Women thus act as links between families of the same caste in different villages, and carry news from one village to another. A wife retains her links with her parents' village, and often goes back there, for instance, to have her first child. Her assimilation into the new family is therefore gradual; in the days of child marriage, which has declined considerably since the early nineteenth century, she spent the early years of marriage in her old home.

Kinship terms

A child thus has a very different set of relationships with relatives on the mother's side from those on the father's side, who are involved in decisions affecting the child's immediate family and may live in the same house. Indian languages have different words for maternal and paternal grandfather, for maternal and paternal uncle and aunt, and for wife's brother and husband's sister. Relations are addressed and referred to by kinship terms, often added after the name. Some kinship terms, such as Hindi or Gujarati *bhāī* ('brother'), can also be used outside the family, and even to strangers.

Cousins are commonly referred to as brothers or sisters, even when speaking English. English-speaking Hindus also use the phrase 'cousin brother' or 'cousin sister', as opposed to 'real brother' or 'real sister'.

Roles of women

Deference is due to elders in the family, and from the women to the men. Wives are expected to eat after their husbands, go to sleep after them, get up before them, and walk behind them. Traditionally, a wife does not speak her husband's name, whether in addressing him or referring to him. She is expected to be deferential to his elder relatives and in some families she covers her face in front of his elder male relatives. However, deference does not invariably mean subordination in terms of real power; men often consult their wives before making decisions.

While modern employment and education patterns bring women into trades and professions, their traditional role is domestic unless poverty forces them into manual labour. A woman's concerns are the rearing of children, especially sons, the comfort of her husband, and thrifty housekeeping; her work is demanding and highly skilled.

A new wife has to be assessed and trained by her mother-in-law; her status rises when she has borne a son, which not only ensures the continuance of the line, but gives her a chance to become a mother-in-law herself in due course. Since a woman traditionally owes her status to being a wife and mother, widows and barren women tend to be neglected, and spinsters are a rare anomaly.

In Indian villages, women's work includes fetching water and grinding grain; in warm, humid weather flour needs to be ground daily because it would go bad if kept for long. Women are also responsible for the striking patterns which are painted on the walls of the house, or sprinkled on the floor in coloured powder, on auspicious occasions such as a wedding or the birth of a son, and for the elaborate adornment of a bride, including the delicate patterns painted on her face, hands and feet. Some women have other artistic skills such as singing and dancing, though until the twentieth century these were considered disreputable. Women also have an important role in the daily worship of the gods at the household shrine (pp. 103–5).

Since young children are part of the women's domestic concerns, while men's activities are often outside the house, it is from their mothers, grandmothers and aunts that children get their first nurturing in the Hindu tradition, and become familiar with its routine of worship, ideas about people and gods, and attitudes to the world. Children are allowed considerable indulgence and licence in their first few years but from the age of two or three, they are gradually taught what they should and should not do. In Britain, women are more often at work, and so less involved in nurturing.

Pollution

Among the things learnt by children from the women of the family are attitudes to the pollution which is inevitably involved in bodily functions: eating, excretion, perspiration, menstruation, birth, death.

The need to keep food and dirt separate, and to avoid eating what is not fit to eat is universal, but takes different forms in different cultures. In Hinduism, it is an example of the general rule that one's actions (karma) affect one's future destiny (p. 16, p. 172), breaches of purity can bring misfortune. We have already seen that beef is not eaten by Hindus (except of very low caste, or very lax observance), because the cow is sacred; many Hindus avoid pork, and some are vegetarians or even vegans. Such practices vary greatly according to caste and region, and partly also according to vows undertaken by individuals. The avoidance of left-over food (*jutha*) can be carried as far as throwing away a meal if one has been interrupted after starting it. The idea that a person who is eating cannot serve others, which Rāmpāl mentioned, makes it convenient that different members of the family should eat in turn. The practice of drinking from a cup by pouring, without touching it with one's lips, is also a way of avoiding contact with one's own jutha; so is the care with which Hindus rinse their hands and mouths after a meal (pp. 36–9).

Because the preparation of food has to be kept free from pollution, the kitchen is a centre of purity. Shoes are removed before entering the kitchen, if they have not already been removed on entering the house as they often are. Some Hindus will take a bath before entering the kitchen. Because it is kept pure, the kitchen often contains the household shrine, with the images of the gods that are habitually worshipped by the family (p. 108).

The opposition between food and excrement is obvious. Bodily functions are more public in traditional India than in modern life, and village Hindus may be seen, especially in the early morning, going to a latrine across the yard or even in the open air some distance from the house, carrying a metal pot (*lota*) of water to clean themselves; this function is for the left hand, the right being reserved for eating.

Anything that comes out of the body is polluting; the laundry-man's occupation is polluting because he handles sweaty clothes, and so is the barber's, because hair and nails that have been cut are considered dead matter. Traditional Hindus do not shave themselves, but are shaved by a barber every few days. Men-struating women do not enter the kitchen; there are often enough women or young girls in the household to keep the meals going, but sometimes men do the cooking.

Birth is a particularly polluting as well as dangerous event, and not only the mother and child but the whole family have to undergo a series of purification rituals after a birth (p. 95). Death is also polluting, and the bereaved family are barred from their normal social and ritual life for a period of ten or twelve days, after which they clean or replace the household utensils, bathe, and change their clothes (p. 97). Even someone who hears of a death in the family while living elsewhere has to undergo purification:

> Someone who hears that a relative has died in a foreign country, if not more than ten days have passed, shall be impure only for the rest of the ten nights. If ten days have passed, he becomes pure merely by bathing (*Manu*, 5, 75–6).

That is to say, pollution by death results not only from proximity in space, but from kinship. This is an example of what is called 'group pollution', which affects all members of a group even where there is no physical contact. In a similar way all members of a caste of barbers or laundrymen are polluted, whether or not they actually do the polluting work (p. 76).

Purification

Since life itself involves pollution, repeated purification is needed. Washing with water is an obvious form of purification. A person washes himself in running water such as a river, or, if this is not available, in a large area of water such as the artificial pools which are called tanks in India. Traditional Hindus do not sit in a bath to wash; they stand and pour water over their heads, since the head is the part which it is most important to keep pure, while the feet are in constant danger of pollution from the ground. Drinking the water of the Ganges is a form of purification for people guilty of offences such as harming a cow.

The sun is another purifier; mild pollution can be removed by looking at the sun. The cow is a source of purification in several ways. A polluted object can be passed under a cow, or a cow led over a polluted piece of ground; a polluted person can be purified by touching a cow. The cow is considered so pure by nature that her five products – milk, curd, *ghī* (clarified butter), dung and urine – are a means of purification, although in non-ritual situations the last two can evoke disgust. Dung is important as fuel and for making plaster for the floor of the house (p. 62; p. 104) and the urine is traditionally used for making ink, and even to make lye for washing clothes. A mixture of these five products can be drunk as a purification ritual, for instance on returning to India from overseas, since sea travel is polluting, or after eating forbidden food. Sometimes, instead of the five products of the cow, a mixture called *panchāmrita* (the five immortal or life-giving things) is drunk as a purification: milk, curd, ghi, honey and sugar.

Detailed prescriptions for avoiding or removing pollution are to be found in the Sanskrit texts on dharma – the norms of behaviour (p. 16; p. 161). The best-known of these texts, compiled in the second century CE, has passages listing types of forbidden food (*Manu*, 5, 5–19), on the impurity resulting from birth, death and menstruation (*Manu*, 5, 58–92), and on ways of purifying utensils, clothes and foodstuffs (*Manu*, 5, 111–26). But it is not from texts that a typical Hindu learns the rules, but from the home, and later from local elders; the people who composed the texts were not so much lawgivers as compilers of traditions already current in their time, and the similarity of the texts to the practices in the villages today testifies to the persistence of these traditions over the centuries.

Besides being the place where such ideas and attitudes are learnt and put into practice, the home is the place where most of the Hindu life-cycle rituals take place (pp. 88–102); the gods are also worshipped in the home, whether they are represented by elaborate images in a special pūjā room, simple clay images on a shelf in the kitchen, or brightly coloured pictures (pp. 103–5; p. 108; p. 117). The home is not just a place to live in but the centre of a Hindu's ritual life and the place where he or she learns and passes on the complex mass of ideas and practices which we refer to as Hinduism.

Teaching ideas

Early years

Material to contribute to topics such as 'families' and 'homes'.

(a) *Family tree*   Brainstorm the word 'family' orally, with the teacher writing words up on the board, OHP or large card. A discussion is then based on the responses. The term family tree can be explained. Children can make family trees as far as grandparents, discussing where grandparents live. Make a display of photographs showing family relationships.

(b) *Hindu families*   Introduce some basic information about Hindu families: married daughters go to live at their husband's family home; grandparents are a close part of the family and in an Indian village the paternal grandparents, their sons and their sons' wives and children would all live together as one family. There is a close relationship between cousins (they call each other 'brother' or 'sister'). What do the children think would be the advantages and disadvantages of these traditions?

(c) *Migration*   Ask if any children have any relatives who have gone to live in another country. Ask if any children have family members who come from another country. Explain that some Hindu families from India have gone to live in other countries, including Britain, and have maintained many of their customs and traditions.

(d) *Food*   Brainstorming of the word 'food' orally, with the teacher writing words up on the board, OHP or large card. Discussion: favourite foods and foods we do not like. Who eats and who does not eat meat and why? Hygiene and cooking – why is it important to keep hands and utensils clean? What cooking implements do we use? Who does the cooking at home? What happens to left-overs at home?

Introduce the following information:

(i)   Many Hindus (not all) are vegetarian.

(ii)   Since the cow is a special, sacred animal, even Hindus who eat meat do not eat beef.

(iii)   Milk, curds (yoghurt) and butter are considered by Hindus to be very good foods from the cow. They are often used to make sweets.

(iv)   Hindus do not eat food that has been in contact with anyone else's lips (therefore food is not tasted during cooking).

(v)   Hindus use the right hand for eating (one table could practise this at school dinner).

(vi) People from India often use spices to flavour foods.

See pp. 36–9 for further information on food. For ideas related to marriage see Chapter 7, for stories see Chapters 9 and 12, and for festivals see Chapter 10.

The Middle Years

(a) Brainstorm the word 'family' in small groups. Written responses are reported to the whole class by group representatives. A discussion is based on the responses. Poetry can be used as a means for children to express their views of family.

(b) Children can invent a number of imaginary families using ideas from the brainstorming exercise, e.g two parents and two children; a family with a grandparent living with them; a single parent family. Alternatively, the empathy game (pp. 24f.) can be adapted so that an alien from another planet observes and reports on incidents during a day in the life of a family. Introduce the idea of the joint or extended family as in the Hindu tradition, using a simplified version of the story of Rāmpāl and Satya and/or Aggarwal, *I am a Hindu*. Discuss relationships within the imaginary families and in the Hindu family (in the latter between cousins or between parents and grandparents, for example). Patterns of child rearing and marriage systems could be discussed. The idea of 'family honour' could be introduced. There is scope here for drama and for tape recordings, e.g. a 'radio feature' on different family systems (p. 30).

(c) *Hindu families in Britain.*   Aggarwal, *I am a Hindu*; Ray, *A Hindu Family in Britain* and Ewan, *Understanding Your Hindu Neighbour* are all useful resources for looking at aspects of Hindu family life in the British context. Audio-visual stimulus could be provided by the BBC 'Quest' Radiovision *Hindus and Sikhs in Britain*.

(d) Hinduism and Food. See pp. 36–9.

Adolescence and post-16

(a) Marriage (this topic can also be dealt with in the context of life-cycle rituals (p. 100)). Brainstorm the word 'marriage' in small groups. Group leaders report back and lists of related words can be made or a diagram can be designed showing features of the marriage systems known to class members. These might include economic and social factors (e.g. inheritance; marrying within a social class) as well as personal matters such as romance and love. Questions such as 'How far is marriage a free choice for those who marry?' and 'How risky in the long term is a marriage based on romantic love?' can be considered. The Indian marriage system can then be introduced, noting:

(i) marriage is, in a sense, between two families rather than two individuals. The marriage introduces a whole range of responsibilities and obligations between the families.

(ii) marriage ceremonies are universal 'rites of passage' (see Chapter 7), having certain features in common. Look for ceremonies which mark the separation of the young people from their peer groups, ceremonies or customs which represent a transitional stage between being unmarried and married, and ceremonies which mark the entry of the couple into the new state of married life.

(iii) though there are common elements in different marriage systems, there are features distinctive of different traditions. In Hindu marriage, for example, the bride and groom are dressed like gods, since marriage marks the highest point of ritual purity in the life-cycle between the pollution of birth and the pollution of death.

Having considered these points, students should be in a position to discuss the strengths and weaknesses of their own and of the Indian marriage system.

(b) *Values* Individuals can list three values they think are important (e.g. honesty, self-reliance, compassion). Small groups discuss from where they think they mainly derived their values (parents, relatives, school, friends, other). Consider how values are passed on in Hindu families. From the discussion do we gain insights as to how values are passed on in our own families? (See also pp. 193f.)

(c) *Child-rearing* List customs and practices concerning the bringing up of children in the Hindu tradition. Compare these with your own memories of growing up.

(d) *Food and Hinduism* For ideas see pp. 36–9.

Further reading

Mandelbaum (1970); Sharma (1971); Srinivas (1976).

6

Society

Since Hinduism includes the social norms followed by Hindus, and is learnt through interaction with other Hindus, a look at Hindu society is necessary. The feature of Hindu society that may come to mind first is caste; but this cannot be understood without relating it to other forms of grouping such as the family, which we have already seen, and the village, and to economic as well as religious life. We will look first at a village in southern India, around 1950, in the state which was then called Mysore but is now Karnātaka; we will concentrate on the person who had most to do with its varied inhabitants (Srinivas, 1976).

Case study: the Headman of Rampura

The Headman of Rāmpura was tall and powerful, with the look of a man with many demands on his attention. He had few words to spare, except with intimate friends, and when he spoke it was often in the rasping voice that he used for giving orders, sometimes reinforced with insults and obscenities. His dress was not the cheap shirt and shorts of the other villagers, but a wide-sleeved shirt, long thick white shorts, and over these a *dhoti* – a long white cloth worn round the legs, with the end drawn between them and tucked in at the back. This style, generally associated in South India with Brahmins, marked him not only as conservative but as a person of high standing. On state occasions he wore a high-collared silk coat, a gold-laced scarf, and a white and gold turban.

Rampura in 1948 had 1523 people, making it one of the larger villages in Mysore, though many villages elsewhere in India have several thousand. Eighteen Hindu castes were represented, and also Muslims. Most of the people lived by agriculture, whether as landowners, tenant cultivators or labourers; even people whose caste had another traditional occupation, such as shepherds, fishermen or oil-pressers, worked the land.

The main crop was rice, but there were also coarser grains – sorghum and millet – as well as sugar cane, vegetables and mangoes. Most villagers ate rice only on special occasions; it was grown as a cash crop, and the time for buying clothes and utensils, and repairing houses, was after the rice harvest, from December to January; from then to June was the time for pilgrimages, visits and weddings.

The Headman's function was to preside over the village council (*panchāyat*) and to be the intermediary between the village and important visitors such as officials of the state government. The position used to be hereditary; in post-Independence times it became elective, but the position still often goes to powerful landowners.

The Headman of Rampura belonged to a caste of peasants, whose members owned most of the land in the region. Besides land he also owned houses and buses, and was quick to find new forms of investment; but land was the traditionally valued form of wealth, and villagers acquired as much of it as they could. Like other wealthy villagers, the Headman lent money, and was patron to a large number of clients who were bound to him in various ways – as debtors, tenants, or as regular or occasional employees. His skill in agriculture affected the whole village, and it was through him that new ideas from visiting agricultural experts were diffused. Since most of the villagers regarded agriculture as the most important form of work, his skill enhanced his prestige. As president of the village council he arbitrated in personal disputes, and reported the village's needs to the state government of Mysore.

Unlike his father, who had kept a carriage and been ostentatiously generous, the Headman adopted an austere style of leadership. Servants and tenants dared not look him in the face, though they spoke disrespectfully behind his back. He often sent villagers on casual errands; they complied, not because they owed him any specific duty but because they knew that at some time they would need his favour. His closest friendships were with men of his own caste; people of different castes would not eat together, and close relationships with women outside one's own family were always assumed to be sexual.

There was some rivalry in the village between two lineages of the peasant caste (a lineage is a group of families descended in the male line from a common ancestor). The second most powerful member of the peasant caste was the head of the other lineage, but he and the Headman were old friends from schooldays, and carefully avoided antagonising each other. The skill and tact of these two men helped to keep the village relatively free from faction. Other members of the caste often ate at the Headman's house, and stayed there if they came from another village.

Relationships with Brahmins were more complex, since they would not take meals cooked by the Headman's family, though they might take milk, fruit or tea. For important Brahmin visitors he would get a Brahmin to supply food (p. 37; p. 76). He was anxious that Brahmins, his superiors in the caste hierarchy, should maintain their proper rules of purity, at least so long as they were in his village. Even if visiting Brahmins from the cities were progressive enough to eat in a non-Brahmin house, the Headman would cater for them in an adjoining building, not in his own house where the household images of the gods were, and where his widowed mother was the guardian of tradition. M. N. Srinivas, the anthropologist who studied Rampura, was a Brahmin from the city of Mysore; the Headman gave him quarters in an outbuilding. Srinivas had some habits which were not those of the village, such as shaving himself instead of being shaved by a member of the barber caste. The Headman tolerated this, but reprimanded his guest when he found him shaving after his bath instead of before it; for shaving, being a polluting operation, should be followed by a bath. While the Headman and his family showed respect to all Brahmins, poorer Brahmins such as the village priest were also deferential to him.

The Headman depended for services on members of lower castes, such as the washermen, the barbers, or the smiths (who are also carpenters). Like other cultivators in the village he paid them not in cash for each job, but in grain and other produce at harvest.

There were about thirty families of an Untouchable caste in a separate quarter on the outskirts of Rampura. Some of the men were hereditary village messengers under the Headman's orders; others worked for other landowners, while the women winnowed and pounded grain, and planted, weeded and harvested rice. Dead cattle were a perquisite of the Untouchables, providing them with hides, horns and meat; the fact that they ate beef was considered by the Headman to be a clear mark of their low status, and a sufficient argument against the new view, promoted by Gandhi, that they should be admitted to temples – the Untouchables had their own temples and priests. Yet the Headman's attitude was not one of total exclusion. He relied on the expertise of one of his Untouchable servants to judge how much water his rice seedlings needed. Another had the task of taking the Headman's little grandson to school; even when the reluctant boy had to be carried kicking and screaming, the villagers who watched from their verandahs were amused, not shocked.

One of the Headman's clients was a Muslim, the son of the previous Headman's coachman. He lived in the group of buildings adjoining the Headman's house, not in the Muslim quarter near the edge of Rampura, and was the Headman's trusted agent in collecting debts, recruiting labourers, and even investigating the status of a prospective bridegroom for the Headman's daughter.

Besides his power and wealth, the Headman had duties. He was expected to protect his clients, to dispense local justice, and to take the lead in providing the hospitality which was due from wealthy villagers to visitors, and to the whole village at festivals. Villagers were quick to assess the generosity or niggardliness of all givers, and in this and other matters public opinion was an effective form of control.

The Indian village

Though some Hindus live in the cities of India or in other countries, four-fifths of them live in India's half a million villages. While Hinduism in an Indian or Western city is no less real than that of a village, the village is the setting in which Hinduism can be observed most clearly. Many city-dwellers have relatives in villages, and still feel that they belong there.

The Indian village has sometimes been seen as a self-sufficient unit, providing for all its needs and unaffected by changes outside it. But this is an exaggeration; villages have always been affected by events elsewhere. Rampura could not have sold its rice or sugar without markets in the towns, nor could it have grown the rice if the rulers of Mysore in the seventeenth and eighteenth centuries had not dug the canals, which brought the waters of the River Kāveri to irrigate the fields. Some villages depend for certain services on neighbouring villages or towns. Moreover, brides usually come from outside the village (p. 64), so that, while a Hindu's relatives in the male line often live in the same village, those in the female line live in another. Nevertheless, villagers are aware of the unity and distinctiveness of their village; they praise it to the detriment of other villages, contribute to its festivals, and support its wrestlers in the inter-village matches which are often a feature of such festivals.

An Indian village brings together people who depend on one another for goods such as food, clothes and utensils, and for various services, including ritual services. The exchange of goods and services is often regulated by custom rather than by contract or by cash transactions. The deep-rooted ideas about purity and pollution which we have already noted (pp. 66–8) make it desirable that some functions in the village should be kept separate from others. While the service of a god in his temple, and the conduct of family rituals, require a high level of purity, the cleaning of latrines or the preparation of hides necessarily involve pollution.

Caste

We have already mentioned group pollution, which affects all members of a group regardless of physical contact (p. 67). This concept helps to explain the complex phenomenon of caste. A caste is a group of people who are considered to be related to each other, usually claiming a legendary common ancestor. They also often share a common traditional occupation; there are castes of oil-pressers (who produce sesame oil for cooking and fuel), washermen, potters, peasants and so on. Certain occupations are polluting: the barber's, the washerman's, the tanner's, and especially the sweeper's and scavenger's. All members of a caste are polluted by its traditional occupation, whether or not they actually practise it. Moreover, some food is polluting, especially meat, and beef most of all; different castes have different traditional diets.

Caste is hereditary; a person belongs to the same caste as his parents, marriage being usually within the caste. Because food is particularly vulnerable to pollution, especially when it is ready to eat, Hindus avoid receiving cooked food from, or eating with, members of a caste they consider more polluted than their own. This causes complications on such occasions as wedding feasts: people of different castes sit in separate rows, and a non-Brahmin host may need the services of a Brahmin cook to prepare food for his Brahmin guests (p. 37). Generally, the more castes will accept drinking water or food from a caste the higher it ranks. A caste is therefore a group of people linked by common ancestry (real or legendary), common occupation (actual or imputed), endogamy (marriage within the group), commensality (eating together), and a common rank in a hierarchy. A caste is also based on a particular region of India, though its members may of course migrate.

At the top of the hierarchy of castes are the Brahmins. The traditional occupation of Brahmin men is the performance of rituals and the study and teaching of sacred texts. Most Brahmins, however, have other occupations, including the running of restaurants, since all can receive cooked food from them. At the bottom are the Untouchables, who traditionally work as sweepers and scavengers, handling such highly polluting things as excrement and dead cattle. Most regions have more than one caste in each of these categories. Between these extremes the ranking order is often disputed. It might seem to be possible to observe who receives food from whom and plot the results in a diagram in which the giver always ranks higher than or equal to the recipient; but the actual facts are more complex. In a village in central India the barber caste accepts food from the gardeners, but not vice versa; the barbers therefore seem to rank below the gardeners. However, another caste, the Rājputs, accept food from barbers but not from gardeners, which would place the barbers above the gardeners (Mayer 1960: 33–40). Different castes have different estimates of their own and others' place in the hierarchy.

A village may contain a dozen to twenty castes, including Brahmins, peasants, potters, oil-pressers, barbers, washermen and sweepers. Some villages have only one or two castes; if a village lacks the castes to provide all the services its people need, they either rely on another village or perform them themselves. Often there is a dominant caste, such as the peasants in Rampura, whose members hold most of the land, wealth and power, though it may not rank highest in terms of purity. Caste is not peculiar to Hinduism, since other groups in India such as Muslims and Christians are similarly divided; but it is peculiar to India, since no other part of the world has such an elaborate pattern of hereditary endogamous groups.

The word 'caste' is not Indian; it comes from Portuguese *casta* meaning 'lineage, breed'. Most Indian words for 'caste' come from the Sanskrit *jāti*, which also means 'birth', or any group linked by birth, such as 'family, breed, race, species', or *kula*, which also means 'family, lineage'. A caste can be thought of as a family on a large scale; its members may in fact all be related by blood or by marriage. Sometimes what is treated by other castes as one caste may itself contain two or more endogamous groups, so that it is hard to decide whether to call it a cluster of castes or a caste divided into subcastes. This makes it impossible to say how many castes there are; three thousand is a rough estimate. Moreover, castes can merge if one group starts accepting food and marriage partners where it hitherto did not; they can also split.

A caste may be regulated by a council (panchāyat) of caste elders who decide on what behaviour is acceptable in the caste; members who refuse to conform may be excommunicated or 'outcasted' by the council, so that other members will no longer accept food from them until they undergo a purification and are readmitted.

Varna

The Sanskrit tradition speaks frequently of a fourfold division of society into Brahmins, *Kshatriyas* (kings and warrior nobles), *Vaishyas* (cultivators and traders) and *Shūdras* (serfs, who serve the other three groups). These groups are called the four *varnas*, a word which usually means 'colour'. The list appears first in the *Rig-Veda* (p. 198), where they are linked to parts of a mythical original man:

> The brahmin was his mouth;
> His arms were made the prince;
> His thighs were the vaishya;
> From his feet the Shūdra was born (*Rig-Veda*, 10, 90, 12)[1].

The myth is referred to constantly in later literature as giving the pattern for the organisation of society; the parts of the body symbolise both the ranking order of the four varnas, from the Brahmin down to the Shūdra, and their functions: speech (since the Brahmins speak the Veda and other texts), fighting, physical work, and support of the whole social body. Sometimes the Untouchables are added as a fifth varna, or a fifth group outside the varnas; otherwise they are thought of as a particularly unclean kind of Shūdra.

Within the four varnas there is an important division between the Shūdras and the other three. The three upper varnas – Brahmin, Kshatriya and Vaishya – are called 'twice-born'; this is because boys of these varnas are entitled to undergo an initiation which marks their entry into full ritual life, and is called a second birth. In this ceremony they put on the sacred thread which is the mark of twice-born status (p. 91; p. 95).

Whether or not this fourfold society existed in ancient India, the dharma texts (such as the Laws of Manu, dating from about 150 CE) show that the situation in their time was more complex. They speak of dozens of castes, which they explain as having their origin in the four varnas: some through mixed marriages between varnas, and some from members of varnas who have lapsed from their dharma and so become separated from the rest. The complexities of caste are thus explained as a falling away from the original perfection of the relatively simple system of varna; but this explanation has little historical value.

Some modern writers translate the word *varna* as 'caste'; but this is very misleading, as the two words refer to quite different concepts. There is an indefinite number of castes, of which only some are known in each part of India, ranked in an uncertain order which changes with time. On the other hand the number of varnas is always four (or five if the Untouchables are counted separately), and the order is fixed and known throughout India. Moreover, the concept of caste results from observation of how Hindu society works; the concept of varna is a theory found in texts dealing with dharma. The theory that the castes originated from the varnas is an attempt on the part of the dharma writers to bridge the gap between the norms of varna and the observable facts of their time.

But though the two concepts are clearly different from each other, there is a complex relation between them. The varna model, known throughout India, provides a common framework through which Hindus see the facts of caste. Since it is found in the Veda, and is mentioned throughout the later literature, it provides religious sanction for a hierarchical view of society, even if the hierarchy it embodies does not match the one which is observed. It also provides norms on which individual castes can model themselves in their attempts to reinforce or raise their place in the ranking order. In the past, men who founded dynasties claimed to belong to the Kshatriya varna, and so claimed high status for their castes. Meat-eating, though generally polluting, is associated with Kshatriyas. In the central Indian village referred to above, the meat-eating Rajputs, who claim to be Kshatriyas, rank next to the Brahmins, although the vegetarian gardeners refuse to take food from them. Castes which are successful in commerce often claim Vaishya status, while craft castes such as smiths and carpenters sometimes claim to be Brahmins. Such claims are usually rejected by rival castes, making it difficult to classify castes in terms of varna. On the whole, the clearest divisions in the caste hierarchy are those between Brahmin and non-Brahmin, and between Untouchables and the rest. Brahmins are under 10% of the Hindu population; Untouchables are about 20%.

When a caste which is thought of as Shudra claims twice-born status, it seeks to justify its claim by changing its behaviour; such changes are sometimes directed by the caste council (p. 78). A caste may give up practices associated with low castes, such as the eating of meat or at least of beef, blood sacrifice, the drinking of alcohol, and the remarriage of widows; it may take up high-caste practices such as the worship of gods who are described in Sanskrit texts, the wearing of the sacred thread, and child marriage (women are less free in the higher castes). They may claim descent from an ancestor drawn from Sanskrit mythology, and give themselves a new name; thus the smiths of South India called themselves Vishvakarma Brahmins, claiming descent from Vishvakarma the builder of the world. They may also engage Brahmins to initiate them with the sacred thread and perform other rituals for them.

Such changes of behaviour are summed up in the term 'sanskritisation' (p. 93). This does not refer only to the use of Sanskrit words and ritual texts. Rather, it is the adoption of a wide range of norms known in Sanskrit as *samskriti*: ritual purity, conformity to the dharma, education and general culture. A long process of sanskritisation, over many centuries, has helped to bring about the unity in the diversity of Hinduism.

Caste as a moral issue

So far we have avoided taking a moral stand about caste. It is easy to condemn it as a system of oppression, exploitation and segregation, without troubling to understand how it works. Without taking too rosy a view of caste, it is possible to see some points in its favour, just as with other social systems. Caste solidarity provides security; it overrides differences of wealth, so that the poor can be helped and respected by their caste-fellows. A caste provides for the handing on of skills and equipment through the generations; so long as the economy and demography are stable, this has some advantages over our system of general education for all. The customary exchange of goods and services between caste-groups in a village helps to distribute the available resources and employment opportunities; caste also helps groups of very different culture to coexist symbiotically in the village. It has been said that 'The caste system should be seen as less "exploitative" than democratic society. If modern man does not see it this way, it is because he no longer conceives justice other than as equality' (Dumont 1970: 147).

Nor is caste as rigid as a brief description may suggest. Friendships are possible between castes, and the degree of separation varies with the situation. People who might be expected not to touch each other do so at wrestling matches, and those who would not eat together at home may do so at work. The verandah of an Indian house provides an area where people may be entertained who would not think of coming inside.

Untouchability

Undoubtedly the most objectionable feature of caste is untouchability. This term refers to the position of those castes who are considered so unclean that even their touch is polluting to those in other castes. (One of the anomalies in the use of the word 'caste' is that those who are not Untouchable are often called 'caste Hindus', which suggests that Untouchables do not belong to castes. In fact, Untouchable castes are castes in every sense, being endogamous hereditary groups with traditional occupations, some of which do not accept food from others.) Whereas elsewhere in the caste hierarchy those who rank below others are not necessarily less wealthy or powerful, most Untouchables are among the poorest and most exploited people in India.

It was Gandhi (pp. 154–7) who gave Untouchables the new name *Harijan*, meaning 'people of God' (Hari is a name of the god Vishnu) in an effort to change the attitudes of other Hindus to them. They are also known as 'Scheduled Castes', because they are listed in a schedule to the Government of India Act 1935, which provides for positive discrimination in their favour. An older official term is 'Depressed Classes'; they are also sometimes called 'outcastes', but this suggests wrongly that they do not belong to castes, and invites confusion with people who have been 'outcasted' (p. 78). Recently they have given themselves a new name, 'Dalit', meaning 'oppressed'; in South India they have for some time called themselves *Ādi Drāvida*, 'original Dravidians'[2]. The constitution of India outlaws all caste discrimination and expressly condemns untouchability; but the law, despite further enactments, has not succeeded in protecting Untouchables from discrimination, exploitation and violence (Minority Rights Group, 1982).

The Brahmins

At the other extreme, the privileges of Brahmins have led to anti-Brahmin movements, especially in twentieth century South India. Not all Brahmins are privileged; some are poor, particularly if they follow their traditional norms of purity, study and abstinence from agriculture. But Brahmins as a whole have a position of power as repositories of tradition and as teachers, and as recipients of pious gifts. Since Vedic times they have been advisers to kings; in modern India, many civil servants and politicians have been Brahmins. Since learning is among their traditional occupations, they are disproportionately represented in the professions – even in medicine, despite the pollution involved in dissection and in medical practice. The whole structure of dharma is codified in books composed and interpreted by Brahmins, and representing their outlook (pp. 161–2); many modern interpreters of tradition – Rāmmohun Roy, Dayānanda Sarasvatī, Rabindranāth Tagore, Rādhākrishnan – have been Brahmins.

Caste, varna and dharma

The view of society found in the Sanskrit texts is that it reflects eternal norms which are to be known from the Veda, (pp. 158–60), or, since in the present fallen age only a fraction of the Veda is known, from the dharma literature (p. 161). But Hindus do not usually refer to the dharma literature to find out how they should behave; rather, they assume that the behaviour they are used to conforms to the eternal norms. In this way they assume that the actual caste system is an elaboration of the varna system. The dharma literature itself is an attempt to reconcile older traditions with the facts as known to its compilers, and commentators on the ancient dharma texts often interpret them in the light of contemporary behaviour. The difference between contemporary facts and Vedic rules is accounted for by the notion that this is the fallen Kali age (p. 136), and that in times of distress certain adjustments are allowable: for instance, a Brahmin may engage in trade like a Vaishya (*Manu* 10, 85).

Modern interpreters of dharma are influenced by egalitarian and humanistic trends, while retaining their hold on the Sanskrit tradition; they see themselves as purging the true Hinduism from the false Hinduism that has grown round it. They accept the idea of four functional groups, defending it as a way of organising people into a stable society. They point out the difference between this ideal four-fold order with its emphasis on function, and the complexities of caste as it now exists with its emphasis on pollution and privilege; they reject untouchability, which is not a part of the Varna system. Though they usually use the term 'caste' when writing in English, it is varna, and not caste in the sense used here, that they defend.

Sannyāsa

Both the traditional concept of dharma and the actual structure of Hindu society contrast sharply with the individualism of modern Western ideology and practice. We could not leave the subject without mentioning another traditional concept, *sannyāsa*. Sannyāsa is the total rejection of social norms and of ritual life. A *sannyāsī* – a man who has taken sannyāsa – has left his home and has no family ties; he owns nothing, and lives on wild plants or by begging. He eats any food, and has no fear of pollution. Described in this way, the sannyāsī presents a complete contrast to the highly structured rigidity of Hindu social life. But this is not all the sannyasi's role. Many act as gurus – religious guides – to particular persons or families (pp. 184–5). They can organise themselves into monasteries. Sannyāsa can thus be an entry into a new social status, rather than a rejection of all social status. But, unlike inherited status, it is voluntary. Another voluntary status open to a Hindu is membership of a sect (in which the leaders are often sannyāsīs); this will be discussed in Chapter 14.

City life

Villages are not the whole of India. In an Indian city, the norms of village life are modified. At work, in the street, in shops and on public transport, it is impossible to maintain the boundaries that separate people in the village. This is not merely a matter of physical proximity; the anonymity of city life also ensures that one cannot distinguish at sight between people of different caste, a money economy replaces the system of customary exchange, employment opportunities are more varied for those who can reach them, and food and water are available regardless of caste. Marriage, however, remains an area in which caste is important. While it is quite possible to meet someone in a city without knowing their caste, it is difficult to marry someone without first meeting their family, so that traditional attitudes prevail, especially if part of the family lives in a village.

Life in Britain

Life in a Western city makes traditional ways even harder to maintain; food rules are often more lax, and endogamy extended to wider groups. However, many British Hindus have links with relatives in villages, and particular cities or districts in Britain have communities from particular parts of India. Many castes have formed associations which organise cultural, religious, social and sporting events. Caste associations can have a liberalising effect – for example, by arbitrating between traditionally minded parents and their less orthodox offspring over marriage arrangements.

Teaching ideas

Early years

(a) Young children can be introduced simply to Indian village life through the use of story. Peter Bonnici's *The First Rains* and *Festival* convey the atmosphere of village life through the eyes of a young boy. Children need to understand, however, that not all Hindus live in villages or even in India. Many Hindu children live, for example, in Britain.

(b) The topic of caste is too complex for younger children to cope with. The Vedic myth of the creation of four classes (varna) in society from a primeval human figure (purusha) is, however, a story that can stimulate the children's imagination. Young children have produced clay work, paintings and much discussion through the stimulus of the story (an adaptation from O'Flaherty 1975: 27–28).

Middle years

(a) *Indian village life*. Teachers can supplement information from the chapter with material from other sources on Hindu village life, e.g. Srinivas (1976) on which our case study is based or R. Durrans and R. Knox, 1982. A plan of a typical village can be made (houses, fields, well, temple/shrine, school) and profiles of key inhabitants can be written, e.g. headman; a family from a particular caste (three generations); craftsmen; barber; a Muslim family etc. Some classes might wish to make a model village, or a wall display. Various aspects of religious, economic and social life can be explored through discussion or role play. A village study can be expanded by reference to teaching ideas offered in other chapters, e.g. the family (Chapter 5); a visit of an itinerant story-teller (paurānika) (see pp. 114–6); domestic worship or worship at a shrine or temple (Chapter 8); the performance of life-cycle rituals (Chapter 7) and the celebration of festivals (Chapter 10). A children's book which deals with village life in Maharashtra is Aruna Hardy, *Ravi of India* (p. 210). Note that children need to understand that not all Hindus live in villages – many live in cities and in other countries and their ways of life will be different in a number of ways. S. Harrison, *Daksa and Arun*, tells the story of two British Hindu children visiting relations in a Gujarati village.

(b) *A note on caste*. Caste is one of the few topics in which starting from the child's own experience may cause misunderstandings rather than help to remove them. Drawing analogies between western and the Indian social systems tends to lead to a confusion of caste with social class. Furthermore, asking children to rank jobs in terms of their 'cleanliness' may reinforce the common confusion between physical cleanness and ritual purity (pp. 66–7), as well as possibly causing offense to some pupils. The caste system is best described in the context of a study of Indian village life and the notion of the interdependence of castes can be emphasised. Study of the technicalities of the caste system is best left for older children.

Adolescence and Post-16

(a) *Caste as a moral issue*. GCSE boards offering syllabuses in personal and social ethics in a religious context may require candidates to be able to discuss caste as a moral issue. Of primary importance is the avoidance of superficial comparisons between caste in the Indian tradition and social class in the west. Caste must be understood in the context of Indian society, especially Indian village society. Thus the concepts of purity and pollution need to be grasped and the relationship between varna (pp. 78–80) and caste should be understood. In the chapter above we note at least six positive features of the system. We also note that the system's most objectionable feature is untouchability. Pupils need to know of reforms and criticisms of untouchability from within the Hindu tradition, and should note adaptations that have taken place as a result of urbanisation in India and of migration to countries outside India.

(b) *The individual and society*   (see also p. 179). A study of the relationship between the individual and wider social groups in India (e.g. family, caste, village) is valuable as a means to understanding the Hindu tradition, but also raises questions for the student in connection with his or her own place in society. Through being a member of a family and a society has the individual certain obligations as well as rights? Students can distinguish between moral obligations and legal obligations. They can further consider the impact of religious beliefs, especially about the nature of the individual person, on the ways in which religious people approach life within society. In the context of Hinduism an individual's place within the social system can be considered in relation to the concepts of karma (action), dharma (duty, law) and samsāra (the process of acting and experiencing perpetuated by rebirth) (p. 172).

(c) *Caste in cities and outside India.*   One way to avoid stereotyping Hinduism as a 'village phenomenon' is to examine the effects on caste of urbanisation and of migration by Hindus to countries outside India, such as the United Kingdom. In what ways is the system adapting and being simplified? What are future developments likely to be? See texts cited in the bibliography, e.g. Bowen (1981) and Burghart (1987).

Further reading

Mandelbaum (1970); Srinivas (1976); Minority Rights Group (1982); Singer (1972).

Notes

1   See O'Flaherty 1981: 30f; Zaehner 1966: 8–10 (full hymn).

2 Dravidian is the name of the family of languages to which the main languages of South India belong, and which existed in India before the coming of the Aryans (p. 11).

7

Life-Cycle Rituals

No one's life consists merely of birth, reproduction and death. In all societies these necessary physical events are organised into patterns, in which each person's life is a repetition of what others have done before and will do afterwards, and its climaxes are marked by rituals which emphasise this. These life-cycle rituals, also called rites of passage, show the entry of a person from one status to another, and his or her relationship to other persons; they also mark the boundaries between unborn and born, single and married, living and dead, and so on. Hindus have a very elaborate series of rituals, which begin even before birth and continue after death (Pandey 1969; Stevenson 1920). They are described in the literature on dharma, in elaborate forms which are followed by Brahmins and other twice-born castes; many accounts of them in English are based on these forms. But practices vary with different castes, families and circumstances, and also, as we shall see, with people's inclinations. We begin with the experience of a Hindu woman in Britain.[1]

Case study: Madhu Lodhia

Mrs Lodhia lives in Coventry with her husband and their two children. His name is Rāmniklāl, but she does not address or refer to him by his name herself (p. 65). She was born in Uganda, but her parents are from Gujarat. They belong to the goldsmith (Soni) caste, and Madhu's father worked as a jeweller in Uganda. Madhu is the tenth of a family of eleven; her eldest sister's son is about the same age as herself. She came to England in 1965, to join her elder brothers.

Her marriage was arranged when she was eighteen, when her father went to India for her younger brother's wedding. Her parents' first consideration in choosing her husband was his caste; it was also important to have a good family. There was no question of a dowry. Madhu herself was consulted; Ramniklal sent her a small black and white photograph of himself, and she agreed to accept her family's choice. She just hoped he would not mind her wanting to wear new clothes, listen to songs, watch films and enjoy the radio.

Her mother Nanduben (whose own marriage had been arranged provisionally before she was born) had begun preparing for her daughters' weddings when they all lived in Uganda, by collecting saris for them. Madhu received sixty, including the one to be worn at the ceremony. Nanduben embroidered it herself, using red, green and gold sequins. Nowadays many people buy them ready-made.

Betrothal

A year and a half before the wedding, when they had not yet met, their engagement was celebrated in England and in India. The lucky days (p. 135) for this are Sunday and Tuesday; Madhu's was on a Sunday. Ramniklal's family sent her clothes and jewellery, and also a coconut and sweets. A cousin of his, who also lives in Coventry, draped the end of a sari over Madhu's head; this would have been done by his mother if she had been able to come. From then on Madhu and her fiancé wrote to each other, but they did not meet until he arrived at the airport for the wedding.

Marriage

There was a civil marriage at Coventry Register Office, after which a few friends came to dinner, but the religious marriage was the main event. The Brahmin priest fixed a date and time (*muhūrta* or *murat*) after consulting the couple's horoscopes and his almanac (p. 132). It had to be on a Sunday as it is convenient as well as auspicious, and it had to be in the wedding season, in the months Jyeshtha to Shrāvana – roughly May to August (pp. 132–5). Madhu's family booked a school hall that would hold two or three hundred guests, and sent out pink invitation cards with a picture of Lord Ganesha (p. 121).

For the week before the wedding there were singing parties in Madhu's house and at Ramniklal's cousin's, and the day before the wedding the priest came to perform puja to Ganesha, who has the privilege of being worshipped before other gods. That evening Madhu's brother's wife and Madhu's mother put turmeric paste on her face and hands to make them fair; when she had washed this off, her eldest sister decorated her hands with little dots of henna. On the wedding morning the same sister made up her face, with an arch of red and white flowers and dots above her eyebrows and curving down to her cheekbones. These preparations should always be made by women whose husbands and children are all living, as such women are considered lucky.

In the wedding hall, the priest had prepared a fire in a portable hearth. Ramniklal and his party arrived by car, with much hooting. The first stage was the giving of the bride by her father, after which Madhu's 'cousin brother' – though her brother would also have been able to do this – poured sesame and barley into the couple's hands which funnelled the grain into the flames. Then Ramniklal took her right hand, making his marriage vows in Sanskrit with the help of the priest. Then he led her three times round the fire, walking in front of her, and a fourth time Madhu walked in front. A stone had been placed to the north of the fire, and at each round they touched the stone with their right toe, as a symbol of firmness. Next Ramniklal led her seven steps northward, at each of which the priest spoke a couple of words in Sanskrit indicating future prosperity, and explained them in Gujarati. Next, Madhu's parents gave her a mixture of sugar and ghi to put into her new husband's mouth, and then he fed her in the same way. This symbolised the mutual support and happiness of their married life.

From the hall, the couple went to Madhu's mother's house, whose lintel was hung with leaves for good luck. Before they left for Ramniklal's cousin's, Madhu made handprints in red powder on a piece of paper fastened to the outside wall, which her mother took down and kept. In India the prints would have been made straight on the wall and left there. Her parents cried, and this made Madhu cry too. As Ramniklal's car was about to go, Madhu's sister-in-law or her mother put a coconut under the right front wheel, so that it shattered as the car moved off, making an auspicious start to the journey.

Birth, naming and first haircut

Madhu's first child, a daughter, was born three years later. On the sixth day after the birth, Madhu prayed to Vidhātā the goddess of destiny, and left paper and a red ball-point pen on a table overnight for the goddess to write the baby's destiny.

Later, she chose her name. Usually it is the husband's sister, or someone of his family, who does this, but Ramniklal has no sister and so it was left to Madhu. The priest, after consulting his almanac against the date and time of birth, told her that the name should begin with S. The family all wrote down names beginning with S, and in the end Madhu chose Sejal. She does not know what it means, but she likes the sound.

Two years later, her son Deepesh was born. When he was thirteen months old, he had his first haircut (*mundana* or *chudākarana*). Some castes, though not Madhu's, have this ritual for girls too. The priest found the auspicious time, and an Indian barber clipped Deepesh bald. Sejal, as his sister, had to catch the hair, and Madhu's mother on her next visit to India placed it in a river. Sejal put some *gur* (raw sugar) in Deepesh's mouth, and Madhu marked his head with a swastika, an ancient Indian symbol of good luck.

Initiation with the sacred thread

Boys of Madhu's caste do no receive the sacred thread which is the mark of twice-born status (p. 78), though she has heard that her great-great-grandfather wore it. She has seen it given to a seven-year-old Brahmin boy. After offerings in the fire, the boy put the triple loop of cotton string over his left shoulder and under the right, hanging down to his right hip. Then the priest whispered a mantra in his ear while their heads were covered in a cloth. This initiation rite is called *upanayana*.

Death

Madhu's mother Nanduben came from Ayodhyā, where Lord Vishnu lived long ago in the form of King Rāma (p. 120); she was devoted to Rāma, and loved to hear his story, the *Rām Charit Mānas* (p. 163). Her brother lives in Ayodhyā; many years ago he gave up his photography business and was initiated as a sannyāsī (p. 83). His wife continues to cook for him; he has no children.

Before she died, Nanduben prepared a bag of things for her laying-out: coral beads and pearls to place on her eyes, leaves of basil (*tulsī*) to put on her tongue, and a white sari (since she was a widow) which had been soaked in the river Yamunā. At the time she died a neighbour saw her soul go past in the form of a lamp flame. For seven months Madhu used to feed a pigeon which sat on her fence and watched her, since she knew it was her mother.

The funeral was at the crematorium, and had to be some days after death; in India it would have been the same day, or soon after. The priest went to the crematorium and recited a prayer for peace, and part of the *Bhagavad-Gītā*. The funeral director was instructed to send the ashes to Ayodhyā, to be thrown in the river there.

Two days before her death, Nanduben had told the family not to mourn, and to eat *khīr* (rice cooked in milk and sugar). This they did, and people commented on the break with tradition; usually sweet food is avoided after a death, but Nanduben characteristically wanted her family to accept her death as cheerfully as she herself did.

Twelve days after the death there was a ceremony called *barmu*, and relatives came for dinner. For six months the family was excluded from normal ritual life; marriages, for instance, could not take place.

Rites for the dead

The dead are remembered annually in the dark half-month preceding Navarātri (p. 130). The rite is called *shrāddha*; in it, a visiting Brahmin is given food and coins. Since Madhu's family are not Brahmins, they give him grain, not cooked food (p. 38; p. 77). Ramniklal's father died on the eleventh day of a half-month, so his shrāddha is performed on the eleventh day of the half-month before Navarātri. His mothers shrāddha is on the ninth, as this is the day for all wives who have predeceased their husbands.

Madhu is involved in the shrāddhas of her husband's relatives, not her own; at marriage, her ritual concerns were transferred from her parents' family to his. But she commemorates her mother informally on the eighth day, by giving khīr and chapattis to the birds.

Samskāra

The Sanskrit term for a life-cycle ritual is *samskāra*. This word, which is also used in other contexts, can be conveniently translated as 'process'; one of the texts on the theory of ritual defines it as 'something after which a thing is suitable for some purpose'.[2] It can refer to cooking, which makes food fit to eat, or the baking of a clay pot which makes it fit to use. In ritual contexts it is sometimes translated as 'sacrament', on the analogy of the Christian sacraments. It is also sometimes translated as 'purification'; this is an important part of the ritual process, but it is not the whole, since the ritual also establishes boundaries between one status and another, provides for a person's needs in his or her new status, and protects him or her from the dangers attending crises such as birth and death. In the case of the funeral it also protects the living. These purposes often require a whole series of processes extending over several days.

A thing or a person that has been through the proper processes is called *samskrita*; the opposite is *asamskrita*, 'unprocessed'. For example, the name of the Sanskrit language is, in Sanskrit, *samskrita*; it is so called because it is the refined, cultivated language, made fit for use in rituals for the gods or in the courts of kings. For a person to be *asamskrita* is to be ignorant, uncultured, lacking proper ritual status, and generally uncouth; such a person lacks samskriti (p. 80). The term *samskāra*, in its ritual sense, refers to that which makes a person fit for the stage of life he has reached, and changes the raw facts of our biological existence into a coherent system acceptable to society.

Despite the variety of regional and caste customs, there is considerable uniformity in the general outline of the samskāras, as a result of the tendency of different communities to adapt their behaviour to that of the twice-born. The samskāras are a sphere in which sanskritisation (p. 80) can be seen at work; a caste which introduces the act of walking round the fire in its marriage ritual, for instance, is in process of sanskritising its rituals (whether or not the Sanskrit language is used). If a caste can persuade Brahmins to act as priests in its samskāras, it is on the way to being recognised as twice-born.

A crucial difference between castes is the presence or absence of Brahmin priests. Another, related to it, is the recitation of Sanskrit texts in the ritual, particularly those from the Veda; such texts are known as *mantras*. Generally, mantras are reserved for the twice-born castes (p. 78), and even in those castes they are often omitted in the case of women, so that the samskāras reinforce the difference between the sexes as well as those between the castes.

The rules for the samskāras are laid down in texts (*grihya-sūtras* 'household rules') dating from the last few centuries BCE; but traces of them may be found in the Vedic hymns (around 1000

BCE) and even in other Indo-European cultures. They continue to the present day, combined with other elements which vary from place to place and from caste to caste, on which women are the authorities. The priests do not necessarily read the ancient rules; they follow modern manuals (*paddhati*) which embody modifications in the ancient rituals, or they follow their own memory of seeing the rituals performed.

Priests

The person we have referred to as a priest may be a Brahmin, as in Madhu's case, or not. This is a point that varies from caste to caste, but generally it is the lower castes that have non-Brahmin priests. We should avoid being influenced by whatever associations the word 'priest' has for us. The priest who conducts the Hindu rituals is essentially a ritual functionary among other such functionaries, including the barber who takes part in the hair-cutting ritual, and the low-caste drummer who plays for weddings, each of whom receives his perquisites in the form of cash, food or clothing in the course of the ritual. The priest contributes to the ritual through the mantras he recites, the acts of worship, purification and so on he performs, and the instructions he gives to the other participants. Some families have a regular arrangement with a priest to conduct their household rituals; he is called their *purohita*.

A priest does not have to be particularly learned so long as he knows his role in the ritual, nor particularly pious so long as he is ritually pure when he performs it. He has no pastoral duties, though the families he serves may sometimes turn to him, among others, for advice. Nor does he necessarily enjoy high prestige; Brahmins who earn their living as priests are looked down on by other Brahmins, particularly if they serve relatively low castes, and even more if they officiate at funerals. Among Hindus in Britain, however, the priest, who is often brought over from India and given quarters in the temple, is acquiring a new role as an authority on traditional ideas and values.

From conception to marriage

The Sanskrit texts which prescribe the ritual life of the twice-born give various lists of samskāras, often numbering ten or sixteen. Even among the twice-born, not everyone will go through all those described below, but they represent a view of life inherited from early times, and to which people try to conform.

A person's ritual life begins before birth (and continues after death), so the first samskāra is conception. Actually no specific rite is performed for this, though ancient texts do lay down procedures and mantras for intercourse.[3] During pregnancy there may be two further rituals, one to ensure the birth of a son, and one to protect the foetus against attack by demons, in which the mother bathes and puts on a new sari, and her hair is combed and parted.

Birth, being a process full of danger, has to be attended by ritual devices to protect the mother and child and facilitate delivery. It is also a polluting process, and the whole family, especially the mother, goes through a period of impurity which has to be removed by ritual bathing and changing of clothes. A horoscope based on the exact moment of birth is an important document which will be used in choosing a marriage partner. Materials for writing the child's destiny, with red ink because it is an auspicious colour, may be placed near it on the sixth day (p. 91). The name may be given on this day or on the twelfth day, and is traditionally chosen by the father's sister. It is often a name associated with a deity, or suggesting some desirable quality (pp. 98–9); children are not named after relatives. Then comes the first outing, the first feeding with rice, the first cutting of the hair, and sometimes the piercing of the ears; each of these is a family occasion.

We have already mentioned the distinction between twice-born and other castes (p. 78). The term 'twice-born' is based on the idea that the learning and recitation of the Veda is a new form of life into which one enters by a second birth, the guru who teaches the Veda being a second father (pp. 184–5). An old verse says:

Of the father who gives natural birth and the one who gives the Veda, the one who gives the Veda is the more important father; for birth into the Veda yields eternal fruit in this world and after death (*Manu*, 2, 146).

At birth, a boy of a twice-born caste is only potentially twice-born; he becomes actually so, at an age ranging from seven to twenty-four, through the initiation called *upanayana* ('bringing near', because he is brought near his teacher), in which he puts on the sacred thread (p. 91). Theoretically this marks the beginning of a twelve-year period of study, in which he lives an ascetic life under his guru, ending with a ritual of return involving a bath and a change of clothes. Usually, however, the period is reduced to a token in which the boy learns the all-important *Gāyatrī* mantra:

> Let us meditate on the excellent splendour of the sun-god Savitri; may
> he rouse our insights. (*Rig-Veda* 3, 62, 10)

This is a literal translation, and does not take account of the layers
of meaning which the verse has acquired through centuries of use
in daily prayer.

It is generally only boys who are initiated. For women, initiation is represented by marriage, the guru by the husband, and the
daily rituals by housework (*Manu* 2, 67). Similarly, in many
cultures, a boy reaches adult status at or after puberty, but a girl at
marriage; this is reflected in the way Western custom distributes
the titles 'Mr' and 'Mrs'. The Hindu tradition, always flexible,
may be able to adjust to new ideas about the status of women, and
Sanskrit literature does contain accounts of women learning the
Veda and wearing the thread. In practice, the boundaries of
twice-born status are not very clear or rigid, since many people of
castes which traditionally are not twice-born are initiated by
Brahmin or non-Brahmin gurus, and printing has made it possible for anyone to learn Vedic mantras who wishes to.

The return from studentship is followed, usually after several
years, by the complex of rituals surrounding marriage. The main
features of this samskāra are common to most castes, though more
elaborate in the higher ones. It includes elements of worship, both
of the gods and of the bride and groom, protection against
demons, and provision for the new life.

Both bride and groom purify themselves by bathing at their
own homes (p. 67). The main ceremonies are at the bride's house,
or at some place arranged by her parents; in Britain this is often a
hired hall or a temple. The bridegroom arrives in procession,
usually with music and wearing elaborate clothes and head-dress,
preferably on horseback. The bride is given away by her father,
while the groom promises to protect her; the groom takes her by
the right hand, and leads her to step on a stone, symbolising the
firmness of the union. The central rite is the leading of the bride
round the fire; either this is done seven times, or it is followed by
seven steps northward. In the evening he shows her the pole star,
another symbol of firmness.

Since marriage is a bond between families, it is the pivot of the
Hindu social system. It is also the most festive and public of the
samskāras. Some texts list it first, emphasising the continuity of
the lineage; others list the samskāras as beginning with concep-

tion and ending with cremation (or with marriage, if cremation is not mentioned), emphasising the life of the individual.

Death rituals

Many of the traditional lists of life-cycle rituals avoid mentioning those associated with death; this reflects a desire to maintain a boundary between the dead and the living. The funeral rites provide for the needs of the dead, and at the same time protect the living from the dangers of contact with them; offerings of food are made to provide the dead with a new body. A dead person who is asamskrita (whose funeral samskāras have not been performed) is often believed to haunt the family as a malevolent ghost.

Among higher castes there is a series of shrāddhas (p. 92) during the year after death. There is also an annual shrāddha on the anniversary of death, and another during the waning moon at the end of the rainy season (pp. 134–5), which is the fortnight of the ancestors. Besides providing for the dead, these occasions mark the solidarity of the family with its deceased ancestors. It is the duty of the male descendants to provide for the ancestors, which helps to explain the importance of sons.

The four stages of life

According to tradition, a man's life, apart from childhood, passes through four stages, called *āshramas* (the same word also means a place where ascetics live). First he becomes a *brahmachārī*, an ascetic student studying the Veda under a guru. Next comes the stage of the householder, *grihastha*, into which he is initiated by marriage; here he provides for his family materially, conducts rituals, and raises children. The third stage, which he can only enter when his line of descent has been secured by his son begetting a son, is that of the forest hermit, *vānaprastha*. Finally comes the *sannyāsī*, who has renounced all ties and no longer performs any ritual (p. 83). The stage of vānaprastha is generally obsolete, and quite early texts claim that one can become a sannyāsī at any time without going through the other stages, and this is frequently done. Nevertheless the pattern of preparation for adult life, followed by active and prosperous married life, and finally by withdrawal from the world, is a powerful ideal for Hindus.

Teaching ideas

Early years

Names.   Help children to find the meaning of their forenames. Why are many forenames known as Christian names? Get children to ask their parents how their (the children's) names were chosen (e.g. after a relative, a famous person etc.) and when their names were formally given (e.g. at a christening). Children can note that in English/Western custom boys' names and girls' names are usually different (with exceptions that sound the same, though they might be spelt differently (e.g. Lesley, Leslie; Frances, Francis)). Children can then learn that the names of Hindu children are often chosen by a sister of the child's father. Hindu children are not named after parents or family members. Give a simplified account of the naming ceremony of Sejal (p. 91) and discuss the details with the children.

Many Hindu names are of characters in myths, gods and goddesses, qualities of character, flowers or different words for light (Killingley 1984: 28). Many are interchangeable between boys and girls (e.g. Krishna can be a girl's name). It is important to pronounce names correctly, or as near correctly as possible, especially since some Hindus believe that a mispronounced name loses its meaning. The same name may be spelt differently in the Roman script (e.g. Puja or Pooja, meaning 'worship'). Many Gujarati names end with the suffix 'ben' (sister) for females and 'bhai' (brother) for males (e.g. Nanduben, Govindbhai) (p. 64; pp. 141–2). Here are some examples of names.

Kamal ⎫
Pankaj ⎬ lotus
Rajiv ⎪
Kam(a)la ⎭

Ushā – dawn
Suraj – sun
Kiran – sunbeam
Tāra – star

Pushpa ⎫ flower
Kusum ⎭
Bhāvna (pron. Bhauna) – feeling
Kalp(a)nā – imagination
Madhu – sweet
Sushīlā – well-behaved
Āshā – hope
Punita – pure, holy

Prakāsh – brightness
Jyoti – light

Gopāl ⎫
Mohan ⎬ names for
Krishna ⎰ Krishna
Govind ⎭

Vinītā – modest	Ār(a)tī – ritual in which lamp is rotated in front of the focus of worship
Prem – love	Sādh(a)nā – devotion
Shānti – peace	Pūjā, Poojā – worship involving offerings

Santosh – contentment
Vivek – discernment
Vinod – wit
Vijay – victory

Middle years

(a) *Initiation ceremonies.* Ask the class to think of times when they have taken part in or been at a ceremony which shows that a person is starting a new phase of their life. Baptisms/christenings, ceremonies marking enrolment into Brownies or Cub Scouts might be mentioned, as might barmitzvah or the Sikh amrit ceremony. A great deal of information can be assembled by sharing the memories of such experiences – details of the ceremony, what it felt like to be involved, what the ceremony stood for – and children can be asked to bring in material for further study, e.g. photographs, baptism certificates. The term 'initiation ceremony' can be introduced as a general label for 'joining' ceremonies. Thus children can learn that baptism and amrit are both initiation ceremonies; amrit is not Sikh baptism just as baptism is not Christian amrit.

(i)   Hindu initiation ceremonies can be introduced. Children need to know that the number of ceremonies and the details of the ceremonies vary from caste to caste and from region to region. In particular they should know that the sacred thread ceremony is not as common as many school books would have us believe. The story of Deepesh's mundana (first haircut) can be told (p. 91). The first haircut is illustrated in the 1987 BBC Quest Radiovision programme 'Hindus and Sikhs in Britain'. Do pupils think that the ceremony marks a new stage in Deepesh's life?

(ii)   Give an account of the sacred thread ceremony described above. Explain how this ceremony fits into the traditional ideal of four āshramas (stages of life), marking entry into the first stage (p. 97). Note that the ceremony is for boys only, and that traditionally it is open to all members of castes corresponding to the top three varnas (p. 78). In practice, however, its performance is far from universal. Pupils can copy the Gāyatrī mantra and discuss its meaning. This prayer has been passed on orally during the thread ceremony for many centuries.

(b) *Weddings*.   Pupils can explore some of the similarities and differences between the wedding ceremonies of different religious traditions. Pupils can follow the different stages in Madhu's wedding – arrangement, engagement, the civil wedding, premarriage rituals and the wedding ceremony – picking out some for discussion (e.g. what differences are there between a civil and religious wedding) and some for practical work (e.g. decorating the bride's hands with henna (*mehndi*) before the wedding; the bride making handprints with red powder (*kanku*) before leaving to join her husband's family).

(c) *Priests/ritual specialists*(p. 82; p. 94; p. 105).   An exploration of the various jobs and functions of ritual specialists in two or three religions. Pupils could start with the variety that exists within Christianity – clergy who are ordained and those who are not ordained; clergy with and without a priestly function (performing rituals that no one else can perform); male and female clergy; the pastoral features of Christian ministry. A study of priesthood in Hinduism could cover some of the following: Brahmin and non-Brahmin priests; that only some Brahmin men work as priests; that Brahmin priesthood (like that in ancient Israel) is hereditary; that the function of the priest is to perform rituals correctly; the absence of a pastoral dimension to a Hindu priest's job, this being provided by other bodies such as the family and the caste; the changing nature of priesthood in Hindu communities in Britain.

Adolescence and post-16

(a) *Marriage*.   See p. 70.

(b) *Death*.   Obviously death can be a very emotive subject to discuss in class, but nevertheless is one which should be covered. It is important that teachers check to find out whether any class member has experienced a recent bereavement before embarking on the topic. Work can focus on two areas, both of which tend to have rituals and ceremonies associated with them.

(i)   Death as a rite of passage.The belief, expressed in many religions, that death is not the end of life, but marks the end of one type of life and the beginning of another.

(ii) Coping with death. Here the focus is on the mourners, not on the deceased. There are likely to be rituals to help relatives to cope with their grief, or to protect mourners from dangers associated with death.

Both of these focuses will raise questions of personal concern to students, which can be explored in discussion, through art work and prose and poetry writing.

A useful resource as a starter is the BBC Education audio-tape on death, broadcast in the series 'Rites of Passage'. This is available from the BBC Radio Shop (p. 236). Although this programme does not deal with Hinduism, it does cover the key issues about death – in the context of a faith likely to be reasonably familiar to some pupils (Anglican Christianity) and one likely to be unfamiliar to them (traditional Chinese religion). Material from the Hindu tradition can be used to supplement the programme. Items to be covered could include the following: how religious faith can sometimes (as in the case of Madhu's mother) give strength and comfort to the dying or to the bereaved and that sometimes, too, people lose religious faith because of the experience of bereavement; ceremonies showing death as a rite of passage (e.g. the cremation; the placing of ashes in a sacred river); rituals to help the bereaved (e.g. a period of communal mourning including weeping, prayer, reading sacred texts); rituals to avoid pollution or danger (bathing; not shaving); personal religious experiences surrounding death and bereavement (e.g. Madhu's experience of her mother's death); actions carried out to perpetuate the memory of the deceased person.

For material and teaching ideas on reincarnation see p. 172; pp. 179–81.

Further reading

Holm (1984); Killingley (1984: 27–30); Pandey (1969); Stevenson (1920); McDonald in Burghart (1987: 50–66).

Notes

1 Material from an unpublished account by Eleanor Nesbitt based on interviews with Madhu Lodhia.

2   Shabarasvāmī's commentary on *Pūrva-Mīmāmsā-Sūtra*, 3, 1, 3.
3   Example in *Brihadāranyaka Upanishad*, 6, 4 (Hume 1921: 168–74).

8
Worship

We have already seen examples of Hindu attitudes to the gods and the ways they are expressed: the pictures on Satya's London mantelpiece, and her love of holy places in India (p. 59); Nanduben's devotion to Rāma (p. 91). Some acts of worship are simple and spontaneous expressions of bhakti – devotion to a god; the following example is elaborate and formal, but none the less prompted by deep personal feeling. It is one of the many forms of pūjā – ritual worship, usually involving offerings to an object representing a deity. It exhibits many of the features of pūjā, which may look tedious or even absurd until one sees their meaning (Babb 1975: 39–46).

Case study: A pūjā to the Goddess

We do not know his name, but we can call him Mr Dutt. He is a Bengali, but he lives in Raipur, the largest city in the Chattisgarh region of Madhya Pradesh in central India. Raipur is the industrial and marketing centre of the region, and Mr Dutt is a prominent figure there, being a well-educated businessman. His family have been there for generations, and he is a fluent speaker of the Chattisgarhi dialect of Hindi. Like many Bengalis he is a devotee of the mother-goddess, Durgā.

Mr Dutt's family faced difficulties; he does not say of what kind. So he made a vow to honour the Goddess in a nine-day ceremony, the main part of which is the daily recitation of a long Sanskrit hymn to the Goddess, known as the *Devī-Māhātmya* ('greatness of the Goddess') or the *Saptashatī* ('seven hundred verses'). This can be an annual event, at Navarātri (p. 130), but it can also be done when the Goddess' favour is particularly sought. The recitation and the accompanying ritual are specialised work, so Mr Dutt called in a Brahmin priest, whom he usually refers to as the Pandit, a title indicating a learned man and also a man with a disciplined way of life. Indians often call each other by honorific titles rather than by their names.

In preparation for the Pandit, the women of the house purified the household pūjā room. They washed the floor with cow dung mixed with water, and made patterns on it with rice paste (p. 65). Framed pictures of Durgā were set on a platform against a wall.

After bathing and putting on a clean dhoti, the Pandit arrived and sat on the floor in the pūjā room; he would not take food until the day's ritual was complete. He then purified himself by sipping water from his right hand, and made a declaration in Sanskrit of his intention to perform the pūjā. He sprinkled perfumed water on the utensils and offerings in front of him, and cleared the room of evil spirits by scattering mustard seeds and rice. Then he set up a brass jar topped with a coconut, to represent the Goddess: 'the infinite in the finite', as the Pandit explained afterwards. While performing these acts, he recited Sanskrit mantras.

The Pandit himself was a devotee of Vishnu. This did not prevent his doing pūjā to other deities, but as a preliminary he worshipped Vishnu, in the form of a *shālgrām*, the spiral fossil shell which is sacred to him.

He then directed his worship to the Goddess herself, treating her as an honoured guest. He placed a small plate of silver near the jar as a seat for her, and welcomed her with the gesture called *anjali*, placing his hands together, slightly cupped and with the fingers pointing upwards, and raising them to his bowed face. A little dish of water represented the washing of her feet. By similar token acts, the Pandit gave the goddess a bath, dressed her by wrapping a cloth round the jar, and decorated her with garlands and loose flowers. He then began the recitation of the hymn.

After the recitation he presented food to her in the form of fruits and sweets; at the end of the day he distributed these to the family and their friends who were in the house.

The same routine was followed for nine days, during which the brass jar remained in its place, covered by a growing pile of flowers, and surrounded by offerings of coconuts, sweets and cloth. On the ninth day, a full dinner was offered, and left on the platform. Then the Pandit waved a number of objects, one after the other, in a circular motion in front of the jar: a five-fold lamp, a conch, clothes, leaves of the bel tree (sacred to Shiva), incense and burning camphor.

For the final stage of the ritual the women brought a basket of sand and a supply of sticks and bel leaves. The Pandit piled the sand into a square, built a fire over it, and lit it with a piece of wood dipped in ghī (clarified butter). He then put on the fire a hundred and eight bel leaves dipped in ghī saying at each offering the old Vedic cry '*Svāhā*', which has been used for over three thousand years when making offerings in fire. The Pandit smeared ashes from this fire on Mr Dutt's forehead, chest and shoulders, and then on the rest of the family. Everyone placed coins in a dish for the Pandit, and bowed to the Goddess. The Pandit sprinkled the family with water from the jar, and finally the food was distributed to the bystanders.

The personnel of worship

The whole nine-day ceremony was initiated by Mr Dutt, and was for his benefit and for general welfare; he provided the bulk of the expenses. He was the *yajamāna*: the one who is having a ritual performed. He also participated in the worship by being the first to receive the sacred ash, as well as by receiving a share of the offered food, and being sprinkled with water; he was not present throughout the ceremony, however, as he had his business to attend to. The rest of the family, and the friends who came to visit during the pūjā, also received the ash and food, and were sprinkled with water; they too were participants in the worship. Some of them played a more active part, such as the women who prepared the room, brought the materials for the fire, and helped the priest select unblemished bel leaves, or the people who distributed the food. But the person who played the most demanding role, and on whose knowledge the success of the ceremony depended, is clearly the Pandit. He was the principal ritual functionary or priest (p. 94). The priest receives money, and sometimes also gifts of food and clothing; these are given to him as part of the ritual, not separately like a clergyman's or solicitor's fee (p. 116).

Not all rituals involve the same personnel. A person may perform a simple act of worship with no priest and no other participants, and one who has sufficient knowledge may perform a full pūjā without calling in a specialist.

The language of worship

Forms of worship vary between regions and groups, and with different occasions. The language used in the verbal part of worship may be Sanskrit or one of the vernaculars, or even English, but the non-verbal part consists of gestures and actions drawn from a common stock which we may call the language of Hindu worship. We need to understand this language if we are not to be like baffled Martians (pp. 24–5).

To start with the body-language of worship, the most common postures are standing and, more frequently, sitting cross-legged on the floor; kneeling is not typical of Hindu worship, and chairs are not generally used. To sit on a couch is appropriate for the one being worshipped, but not for the worshipper; gods are often shown sitting in this way. One of the basic gestures of worship is bowing (*pranāma*), which may range from a slight nod of the head to complete prostration on the ground. Bowing is often accompanied by the anjali (p. 104), not only in religious contexts. Two people may bow and make the anjali to each other, saying '*namas te*' ('homage to you'). When greeting a superior or highly respected person, a further elaboration is to touch his or her feet, or take dust from the feet, before touching one's forehead with the anjali. If we remember the association of the head with purity and the feet with pollution (p. 67), we can translate this gesture into words: 'You are so superior to me that your feet, which are impure to you, are pure to me; my head is less pure than your feet and accepts pollution from them.' To place someone's foot on your head is an extreme form of submission; it is also a way of appealing to their mercy. Devotional poetry often speaks of taking refuge at a god's feet, and if an image has a hand pointing to its foot, as in the dancing images of Shiva, this means: 'Take refuge at my feet.' The body-language of worship is continuous with that of everyday life, and expresses both awe and love.

Another way of worshipping is by circumambulation – walking round an image, a temple, a sacred tree or a fire. This is done clockwise, in the direction of the sun, so that the right hand, which is purer than the left, is towards the deity. An exception is the circumambulation of the funeral pyre, which is anti-clockwise; this reversal is one of the ways of separating rituals for the dead from other rituals (p. 97).

The sight (*darshana*) of an image is in itself a favour from the deity to the worshipper. In some temples a curtain is opened at certain times, or an image is taken out in procession; a notice outside the temple may announce the times when 'the Lord will give darshana'. Religious leaders also give darshana to their devotees, and some people receive darshana of gods in visions or dreams.

Worship often takes the form of personal services such as one would perform for a king in his palace, or for an honoured guest: people bring water for washing and drinking, clothes, and food, or please the deity with flowers, perfumes and music. Images are often swathed in cloth, and sacred trees can be recognised by the little strips of cloth which passing worshippers have hung on them (p. 143). Red powder (*kanku*), yellow turmeric powder, or sandalwood paste are used for making a mark (*tilak* or *chāndlo*) between the eyes of the image. The same mark is made on the participants. Bells, gongs or conches are sounded, to wake the deity or gain attention, and also to drown any inauspicious sounds such as a sneeze or the bark of a dog.

Animals, especially goats, are sometimes sacrificed, but mainly to village deities, not to the ones described in Sanskrit texts and worshipped by Brahmins with formal rituals; with deities as with people, meat-eating generally marks a low place in the hierarchy. When food is distributed to devotees, it is known as *prasāda*. This word means 'favour, grace'; the deity has shown favour to the worshippers by allowing them to eat his food. Usually, left-over food is polluting (p. 66) and would only be given to animals or to low-caste beggars. Sometimes, however, one may accept left-over food from a superior as a mark of respect; a son, for instance, may accept it from his father. This has been called 'respect pollution'; like placing a person's feet, or dust from their feet, on one's head, it is a way of abasing oneself and exalting the other person, which is at the same time a privilege. On the same principle, worshippers may drink the water in which an image has been bathed. Further, it is typically those lower in the caste hierarchy who receive food from the higher; in these terms, prasāda is a natural expression of subservience, since it is the deity who gives to the worshipper. The worshippers are also sharing the god's blessing, and expressing their solidarity with one another by all receiving the same food.

When the Pandit waved a lamp in a circle in front of the jar, he was performing *āratī*, which is a very frequent act of worship. The lamp may afterwards be brought round for worshippers to share in the worship by passing their finger tips over the flame and then bringing them to their foreheads.

Purification is an essential preliminary to a pūjā. Although Mr Dutt's pūjā room is kept scrupulously clean and fit for gods at all times, for this occasion it was specially purified by washing with the purifying agent cow dung (p. 68); in this country it would merely be cleaned in the usual way. The room was further purified by the Pandit's mantras. The Pandit prepared himself with a bath and change of clothes, and also by sipping water.

The Pandit concluded the ninth day of the pūjā with a different method of offering, in fire. This is called *havan* or *homa*; it was the central act of the ancient Vedic ritual. Since it is performed without reference to images, it is acceptable to groups who reject the worship of images, such as the *Ārya Samāj* (p. 190). The fire is said to be the tongue of the gods, by means of which they consume the offerings; in the Veda, fire is called a god, Agni. Since the offerings are destroyed in the fire, there is no prasāda; but the bystanders still participate in the ritual, by receiving the ash.

The main part of the ceremony, however, was the daily recitation of the hymn to the Goddess. There is always a large verbal element in the rituals conducted by Brahmins, and the Pandit accompanied most of his actions with appropriate mantras – Sanskrit verses, often taken from the Veda. We have already mentioned the Gāyatrī mantra (p. 96), which is used by the twice-born as a daily prayer at sunrise and sunset. Some mantras are songs chanted by groups of devotees, like the well-known Hare Krishna mantra. Some are simple phrases such as *namah shivāya* 'homage to Shiva'. Even simpler is the repetition of the name of a deity: in a moment of crisis, or on hearing or seeing something inauspicious, one may say 'Shiva Shiva', or (as Gandhi did when he died) 'Rām Rām'. As a more formal act of worship, a mantra may be repeated 108 times, counting on a necklace (*mālā*) of 108 beads. Some people recite lists of 108 or even 1008 names of a single deity. Each name is a description of the deity, referring to one of his attributes or exploits (see p. 118). To a true devotee, such a recitation is an intense and satisfying emotional experience.

Places of worship

The Dutt family, being well off as well as religious, have a pūjā room. Other families keep their images of the gods in the kitchen or store room, since these are places which need to be kept pure (p. 66). They may also worship outside the home, whether at simple open-air shrines, where anyone may make a small offering, or at temples where priests have the privilege of performing pūjā on behalf of devotees. Some temples have several shrines, and a staff of Brahmin priests supported by cooks, gardeners, musicians and others who provide for daily worship; others are simply a shrine containing an image, on the eastern end of a small shelter, with a single Brahmin or non-Brahmin priest. British Hindu communities often meet for worship in a private house; but in many cities they have raised subsctiptions to acquire and adapt a building, or even to found a purpose-built temple (p. 43; pp. 149–50).

Objects of worship

Pūjā is made to some object representing the deity; it may be a three-dimensional image (*mūrti*), a picture, or it may be aniconic (non-figurative). There were pictures of the Goddess in Mr Dutt's pūjā room, but the pūjā was directed to the brass jar with the coconut on top; this jar (*kalasha*) is a common aniconic representation of the Goddess in rituals. Vishnu is represented by an image or by a shālgrām stone (p. 104). Shiva is often represented by a linga – a column of stone rounded at the top, rising out of a round dish (*yoni*) with a spout at the side, rather like a lemon squeezer. The linga is sometimes carved to represent the sex organ of Shiva, the yoni being that of the Goddess, and the Purānas contain myths identifying the linga in this way.

However, the linga means much more than this. It is the source of energy of the universe, and the pillar upholding it; in worship it marks the ritual centre of the temple or pūjā room, and the form in which the god receives the water for bathing and the offerings of milk, curds, ghī, honey and sugar which are poured onto it. One of the myths about the linga describes it as a fiery column; the god Brahmā tried to find the top of it and Vishnu the bottom of it, but were unable to, and therefore worshipped it. The symbolism of the linga is indeed endless, and to say that Hindus worship a phallus would be no more helpful than to say that Christians worship an ancient Roman gibbet.

Besides gods and their representations, worship may be offered to trees, particularly the *pīpal* and banyan (two species of fig tree), and to animals, especially cows, monkeys and snakes. Pūjā is also performed to the tools of one's trade: ploughs, vehicles, desks and account books can be decorated with flowers and red powder, and until the early nineteenth century the East India Company followed the tradition of Hindu kings by having Brahmins do pūjā to its guns. This does not mean that tools are treated as gods, but it does mean that their efficacy depends on man's relationship with something beyond his control.

Understanding worship

The worship of images raises problems of understanding for the outsider, especially in the Western tradition. Idolatry has a bad name, and the word leads people to assume that the worshipper sees no difference between the image and the deity. Although the word 'idol' originally meant only 'image', it has acquired such associations that it is best avoided. Many English-speaking Hindus, however, refer to their images as 'deities'; they evidently regard them as more than visual aids.

'The "idolator" worships not the stone that I see, but the stone that he sees' (Smith 1978: 141). To understand the place of images in Hinduism, we must try to understand how individual Hindus see them. This, like everything else, will vary (pp. 122–3). Some, perhaps in the face of Muslim or Christian criticism, have denied that images are ever worshipped. Some Hindus say that God is in all things, but they find it easier to contemplate him in an image; others say that God enters into the image to enable his devotees to worship him.

A much-quoted Sanskrit verse says:

Men have gods in water; wise men have gods in the sky;
Fools have gods in wood and stone; the disciplined man's god is in himself.

This implies a hierarchy of ways of worship: the lowest way is in images, the next at places of pilgrimage on rivers, the second-best way is to think of the gods as above our world, but the best way is to know God within ourselves. These are all ways of worshipping 'the infinite in the finite', as Mr Dutt's pandit put it. So is the worship of various gods while affirming that God is one (p. 17).

When an image is installed, a ritual is performed called *prāna-pratishthā*, 'establishment of breath', in which the owner of the image, or the leader of the group which is setting it up, places his hand on its breast and invites the deity to dwell in it. But before he does this, the owner himself is consecrated; the ritual establishes a bond between him and the image, placing on him the duty of maintaining it in daily worship. The ritual transforms the image into a dwelling of the deity – not into the deity itself – but it is also an undertaking by the owner. However, from that time on, the image is sacred not only for the owner but for anyone. A broken image is not just thrown away, but thrown into the sea. Temporary images, such as those used at Durgā Pūjā or Krishna's birthday (Brown 1986: 129–33; Killingley 1984: 37f) are ritually placed in rivers at the end of the festival. Less formally established images can be treated more casually.

Though the image is sacred and may be referred to as a deity, it is not identified with the deity in a way which would limit the deity's power. If food is not placed in front of it, or if a person touches it without having bathed and changed their clothes, the god or goddess will not go hungry or suffer pollution. When food is placed in front of an image, it need not be supposed that the deity eats the food (though some claim that it actually diminishes in quantity (Babb 1975: 56)); the offering is an expression of devotion to the god or goddess, using the image as a means.

Hindus often explain their attitude to images by reference to portraits. They may say: 'If I cannot pay my respects to my father or teacher in person, I do so by putting up his photograph and decorating it with flowers; I do the same for God, since I cannot see him face to face.' Even if we do not treat a photograph in quite this way, we can understand a person's respect for it, at least to the extent of being reluctant to treat it as rubbish. This explanation reminds us of the continuity between Hindu worship of deities and what we might consider secular (p. 106). It also shows how image worship can take its place within a hierarchy: the Hindu who explains his attitude to images in this way may acknowledge that there are people who can know God without the aid of images.

Teaching ideas

These ideas should be considered in conjunction with those listed under Chapter 9. Artefacts which are useful in reconstructing pūjā are listed on pp. 230–1. Other utensils can be substituted if necessary. Other items, e.g. flower petals, fruit, water, cooking oil, cotton wool, are easily available. Multi-faith schools have marvellous opportunities for involving Hindu parents in activities.

Early years

A Hindu domestic shrine can be reconstructed in the classroom or for assembly and pupils can act out a simple pūjā ceremony. This activity could be done as part of a topic on festivals or homes. In all cases when acts of worship are dramatised it should be made clear to children, parents and colleagues that the activity is a reconstruction and not an act of worship.

Middle years

(a) Small groups can brainstorm the word 'worship'. As well as revealing a good deal about the pupils' own knowledge and experience of worship, the word lists can be used as a basis for further discussion. (See p. 124).

(b) A domestic shrine, or a temple shrine (with paintings, cut-outs or collages of deities to represent images) can be reconstructed in class. Pupils can write their own version of the stages in a pūjā ceremony, including explanations of some of the ritual actions. The dramatised pūjā, with narration, could be performed in class or in assembly.

(c) A visit to a Hindu temple. Further ideas for teaching about Hindu worship and a detailed guide to visiting a Hindu temple are included on pp. 44–55.

Adolescence and post-16

These ideas should be considered in conjunction with 'The gods and God' (p. 122–3) and with the related teaching ideas.

(a) The one and the many: small groups can suggest their own ways of reconciling the apparent conflict between polytheism and monotheism in Hinduism. These can be checked against the reasons given on pp. 122–3. Each group can be provided with 'clues', e.g. a picture showing 'plurality in oneness' – the trimūrti of Vishnu, Shiva, Brahmā; a figure showing half Vishnu and half Shiva; a slide showing the six-sided portable shrine which many Gujaratis use at the Navarātri festival (each face bears a picture of a different goddess) (see also p. 180)

(b) The use of images in worship: small groups can pool their knowledge and experience of worship. For an activity to be worship, does there have to be an object of worship? Why do some religious people use images/icons in worship? Why do some religious people reject the use of images? Discussions can lead into consideration of the symbolism of pūjā (pp. 105–11). Possible resources include *A Hindu Puja* (Educational Productions film-strip); *Aspects of Hinduism* (Videotext Video); *Hinduism through the Eyes of Children* (CEM Video).

(c) A visit to a Hindu temple and/or a visit to the school by a member of a Hindu community (pp. 44–55).

Further reading

Babb (1975); Pocock (1973); Weightman (1978b).

9

Mythology and the Gods

Worship is usually offered to a god whose character is known through mythology. Myths are embodied in numerous texts, but it is not by reading texts that most Hindus learn them. They are familiar with them through pictures, images, and countless references in everyday speech, and they hear them told informally as well as recited by storytellers. R. K. Narayan, who is well known through his English novels of South Indian life, has given a description of such a storyteller in the introduction to a book in which he himself retells some Hindu myths and tales (Narayan, 1965). He shows us a man learned in Sanskrit literature, with a warm sense of humour, who goes from village to village, attracting an eager crowd whenever he sits under a tree to tell his stories. He is perhaps a little too good to be true; he is, after all, a storyteller's storyteller. Perhaps he is what Narayan himself would have liked to be, if he had not been a headmaster's son with a voracious appetite for English literature. Here we shall look at a real-life storyteller, more modern than Narayan's, but none the less rooted in tradition (Singer 1972: 150–55).

Case study: the storyteller

He is a paurānika in Tamil Nadu, in South India. A paurānika is a teller of myths and legends, especially those found in the Purānas, which are collections of mythology, legendary history and prescriptions for the worship of the gods (p. 34; p. 161). This particular paurānika is a slim, sharp-eyed, elderly man. The sacred thread across his bare chest shows he is a Brahmin; on ritual occasions men often wear only a dhoti or lower garment.

He is sitting on a platform in a packed school hall in Madras, with an audience of five hundred in front of him sitting on the floor and crowding the balconies outside the windows, and behind him a smaller platform with garlands and a coloured picture of the hero Rāma and his wife Sītā. On either side of him is an oil lamp on a stand. He is giving the last of a series of fifteen recitations of the story of Rāma, and has reached Rāma's coronation after his return from exile.

There are many versions of the story of Rāma, in Sanskrit and in the vernacular languages. The paurānika is reciting from the oldest of them, the *Rāmāyana* by Vālmīki, composed in Sanskrit verse, perhaps in the last few centuries BCE (p. 161). Between the verses he adds explanations in Tamil. This type of recitation is different from the more formal recitation of a text such as the *Rāmāyana*, the *Mahābhārata*, the *Bhagavad-Gītā* or one of the *Purānas*, as part of household or temple worship; such an event, which may last several days, is a ritual act in which the entire text is recited without comment (p. 103–5). Here, the reciter is free to skip parts of the text and to insert his own explanations; part of the purpose of the recitation is to satisfy an audience who are familiar with the traditional story but are also eager for closer contact with its details and its sound. But there are ritual and devotional elements as well: at the end of the story āratī is performed by waving a lamp in front of the picture of Rāma, a bell is rung as in a temple, and the audience call out the name of Rāma, as they have done from time to time throughout.

The storyteller had listened to many paurānikas in his home village as a child, and studied under a village pandit from the age of nine to thirteen. When he was about twenty he decided to give up his agricultural work and become a paurānika himself. At first he recited from a printed text, improvising his explanations of each verse as he went along. But after fifteen years' experience he found that the portions he needed were already imprinted in his mind, and since then he has recited entirely from memory. His repertoire includes the *Bhāgavata Purāna* as well as the *Rāmāyana* (p. 161). His explanations are designed to bring out the moral teaching rather than the excitement of the story; among the moral values he mentions are respect for parents, chastity and family harmony. He keeps the text in the foreground, and avoids jokes, unlike some other paurānikas. He prefers this kind of recitation to the more popular performance in which the story is told in Tamil and embellished with songs and acting.

Nowadays he recites more in towns than in villages; as well as travelling in Tamil Nadu he visits cities to the north where southerners have settled – Bombay, Calcutta and Delhi. For the present series of recitations he came by train to Madras, and is staying with the principal organiser of the series, who works in a bank; another of the organisers, who has a motor spares shop, drives him to the hall for each session. During the series 1000 rupees (about £70) and various other gifts have been donated to the paurānika. Unlike fees, which might be paid before or after a performance, these are given as part of the ritual (p. 105). They are made in the presence of the deity, Rāma, who is represented by his picture on the platform; the paurānika would not accept a gift for his work except in a ritual context.

He finds that his recitations help town dwellers to keep in touch with their religious traditions. The Brahmins who form a large part of his audience have moved from the villages to towns, and have lost touch with Sanskrit learning, besides being exposed to anti-religious ideas. He says that stories give them a link with tradition and an opportunity to think about God, and the experience of hearing them is beneficial in three ways: they teach moral lessons; faith in them destroys bad karma (p. 16; p. 172) accumulated in the past; and the very sound of them cures evil tendencies. This third effect is one which the paurānika's recitations share with the purely ritual recitations mentioned above.

He also explains the popularity of his kind of recitation among town dwellers in terms of the theory of three ways (*mārga*): works, knowledge and devotion (p. 178). Those in towns find it harder than villagers to follow the way of works by performing rituals, or the way of knowledge through study, so they turn to the less demanding way of bhakti – devotion, a personal relationship with a god. He mentions that the *Bhāgavata Purāna*, which is pre-eminently a bhakti text, is becoming as popular as the *Rāmāyana*. The organiser of the Madras recitations adds that for Brahmins like himself, who have little knowledge of Sanskrit and can spare little energy for disciplines such as yoga, the recitations are refreshing, relaxing and inspiring.

The presence of the gods

Rāma, whose story the paurānika told, is an exemplary man, and also a god; to many he is God. Listening to stories is not only an entertainment and an education; it is a way of becoming aware of the presence of God. The man who organised the paurānika's recitation says: 'It charges the air with the divine presence'.

Story-telling is not the only way in which the gods present themselves to the Hindu. Images of gods and goddesses are a common sight in India – in temples, in homes, at work, and in the open air. Some are rough stone images in the open air, or clay or plaster images in the home. The more enduring images are in stone or bronze, usually in temples (p. 109). These are made by skilled craftsmen trained in the rules of iconography (the rules which govern the appearance and posture of each god or other mythological figure, their clothes, and what they hold in their hands). Iconography also governs the scenes in which they take part: each image expresses an aspect of a deity's personality and encapsulates part of their mythology. A deity can be shown in the act of slaying a demon, for instance, or performing some exploit to save the world. The attributes carried by deities may be weapons by which they achieved their exploits, trophies won in them, or gifts bestowed on the worshipper. The portrayal of deities with four or more arms shows their superhuman power, and also enables the image maker to show four or more attributes or gestures.

The most popular form of image today is the printed picture, framed or used as a poster, or distributed on trade calendars; Hindus do not feel that pictures of the gods, or their names are too sacred to appear in secular contexts. These pictures carry on the same conventions as the traditional craftsmen, but modified to suit modern popular taste. Pictures of the gods may be seen in homes, in shops, and in vehicles, often with flowers scattered in front of them or garlands hung over them, showing that puja has been performed to them. The picture of Rāma behind the paurā-nika, for instance, would be instantly recognisable by his crown, his bow and the colour of his skin – traditionally blue, but often toned down in modern prints to a light mauve.

The gods are also seen in dramas presented at festivals, in songs and dances, and in films on mythological themes. The Indian output of feature films is greater than that of the USA and exceeded only by Japan. The first Indian film, made in 1913, is what the trade now calls 'a mythological', on King Harishchan-dra, whose righteousness led him to give away all he had, and in the end to find it restored to him. Indian film actors who have turned to politics owe part of their success to the fact that the public are used to seeing them on the screen not as cowboys, but as gods and mythical heroes.

Everyday conversation contains allusions to mythology. A long tale of misfortune can be called 'a story of Rāma'; if you are being kept in suspense about your future you can say 'I am like Trishanku' – an ancestor of Rāma who was raised to heaven by the powerful sage Vishvāmitra, but thrown down by the gods, so that he remained suspended half way. Little boys are indulged by their mothers as Krishna was by his foster mother Yashodā; girls are thought of as Lakshmī, goddess of wealth and good luck. Hindus dream of mythological figures, seeing them as they appear in popular pictures.

Each god or goddess has many epithets: Vishnu is Chakra-dhara 'bearer of the discus', or Jagan-nātha 'lord of the world'; Shiva is Gangā-dhara 'bearer of the Ganges'; the Goddess is Mahisha-mardinī 'slayer of the buffalo demon'. These epithets, which form a kind of verbal iconography, are given to children as names (p. 98) – yet another way of making mythology present to Hindus.

The mythology of the gods

The mythology of the gods and goddesses is, in its broad outlines, known throughout India, since it is contained in Sanskrit texts such as the epics (*Mahābhārata* and *Rāmāyana*) and the Purānas p. 161. The myths are told in great variety, reflecting successive reworkings.

The two gods around whom most myths are clustered are Vishnu and Shiva. Both occur in the Vedic hymns (Shiva under his older name, Rudra), where their distinctive characters can already be seen, although they are less frequently mentioned in the hymns than other gods who are now little known. Vishnu appears there as the god who has made three steps, in earth, air and heaven. By this exploit, Vishnu created space for the gods, pervaded the universe, and set the three worlds in their places; the third step in heaven is the source of life in air and earth. Rudra-Shiva appears in the hymns as a wild and terrible god, who inflicts disease on people and cattle, and yet is prayed to for healing.

Vishnu and his avataras

Vishnu as the all-pervading source of life is often shown in iconography lying or sitting on a couch formed by a seven-headed snake (called Shesha, meaning 'remainder', because he remains when all the world is destroyed), floating on the ocean. This represents Vishnu before he begins the creation of the world. He wears a distinctive head-dress in the form of a truncated cone, and in his four hands he holds a conch shell (used as a bugle in ancient warfare, and also in temple worship), a club, a lotus and a discus (a weapon, represented in sculpture with flames issuing from it, and in modern pictures as a glowing ring). His skin is blue – the colour of the sky, which, like Vishnu, extends everywhere. He is sometimes attended by the divine bird, Garuda, on which he rides. His wife, Lakshmī is goddess of wealth and cattle; she brings prosperity when she is worshipped at Diwālī (p. 130).

It is the form of his avatāras that Vishnu appears most often as the central figure of a myth. An avatāra or avatār (literally 'descent') is a form in which a god, especially Vishnu, appears in order to undertake some saving exploit. A classic text on this idea says:

> Whenever righteousness (dharma) decays and unrighteousness rises up, I put myself forth; I come into being in every age in order to rescue the good, destroy the evil-doers and establish righteousness. (*Bhagavad-Gītā* 4, 7–8).

The rescuing of the good and the destruction of evil-doers are seen in terms of an eternal struggle between the gods and the demons: Vishnu's avatāras vanquish the demons and rescue the gods and their worshippers from them.

There is a standard list of ten avatāras, but additional ones are often mentioned. The first five of the ten are forms which Vishnu takes for a single exploit. As the Fish avatāra, Vishnu rescued Manu, the ancestor of man, from a flood, or in some versions rescued the Vedas. As the Tortoise, he went under the ocean to support the mountain which the gods and the demons were using to churn the ocean in order to obtain *amrita*, the drink of immortality. As the Boar, he lifted up the earth on his tusks when it was plunged into the ocean by a demon. As the Man-Lion, he killed the demon king Hiranyakashipu, whose son Prahlāda was a steadfast devotee of Vishnu but was persecuted by his father. As the Dwarf, he performed the three strides in order to regain the world from a demon: Vishnu appeared to him in the form of a dwarf and begged for as much space as he could cover in three strides. The demon allowed him this, whereupon the dwarf strode through earth, air and heaven.

The next four avatāras are not simply changes of shape but heroes with complete biographies, born of human parents. Parashurāma is a Brahmin hero who massacred the Kshatriyas in pursuit of a feud. This myth has significance for the theory of varna (p. 78–80). On the one hand it is used to show that kings and others who claim to be Kshatriyas cannot be true Kshatriyas because the latter were all killed; on the other hand some castes, whom others rank as Shūdras, claim to be Kshatriyas whose ancestors escaped from Parashurāma by pretending to be potters, oil pressers or the like.

Rāma or Rāmachandra is the ideal prince whose story is told in the *Rāmāyana* and in many later versions (p. 161). He is worshipped as a god, especially in north India; so is his friend, the monkey Hanuman, who is a powerful protector of his worshippers as well as the ideal devotee of Rāma. Krishna, the eighth avatāra, is also a prince; but whereas Rāma strictly follows the roles of son, husband, warrior and king, Krishna is capricious and unpredictable, though always benevolent. His story is told many times from the Mahābhārata onwards; the most popular versions are based on the *Bhāgavata Purāna* (around the tenth century CE), which dwells on his early life as mischievous child, and then as lover of numerous cowherd girls (p. 161; Archer 1958). In both roles he is loved in spite of his outrageous behaviour, symbolising the worshipper's unconditional love of God. Krishna, like Rāma, is worshipped as a god, and even as God himself (p. 142, p. 188), and is the centre of many forms of bhakti.

The ninth avatāra is the historical figure of the Buddha, who lived in the north of India around 500 BCE, and has been incorporated into Hindu mythology. The last avatāra, Kalkī, is yet to come; when the present evil age is over he will punish evil-doers and inaugurate a new perfect age (p. 137).

Shiva

Shiva – also known as Rudra, Shankara, or Mahādeva – is a terrible and yet merciful god; he is also the source of creation and the destroyer; associated with snakes and poison and a healer; the lord of ascetics and a god of great sexual power and activity. He is shown in iconography with the piled-up hair of an ascetic, with a snake around his neck, wearing a tiger skin, and with a third eye showing superhuman knowledge. In his hands he may hold a drum, a fire, a leaping deer, a trident or an axe. He rides on a bull. The river Ganges or Gangā flows through his hair because he caught it in his hair when it first came down from heaven to save the earth from its impact. He also wears the crescent moon in his hair. His throat is blue from swallowing the poison which appeared when the ocean was churned; only Shiva could withstand it, and thereby save the world. The churning of the ocean, which we have already mentioned in connection with the tortoise avatāra, is an incident around which a great complex of mythology has been built.

Another complex of mythology concerns the marriage of Shiva and Pārvatī the daughter of the Himalaya, and the birth of their son Skanda, Subrahmanya or Murugan. This myth illustrates the paradox of Shiva's sexuality and asceticism: the world can only be saved if a son is born to him, and he is absorbed in yoga. The events leading to the birth of Skanda involve anger, violence and destruction, and yet save the world from evil (O'Flaherty 1975: 154–68).

Devī, Ganesha and Skanda

Besides Shiva himself, his wife Pārvatī and his sons Ganesha and Skanda are worshipped. She is known by many other names: Durgā, Kālī, Umā, Bhavānī, Ambā, Chandikā, or simply Devī 'the Goddess'. She combines destruction with fertility, for she is the shakti ('power') of the gods, without whom they are powerless against the demons and are unable to procreate; for many Hindus she is more important than Shiva or any other god. Ganesha is the elephant-headed god worshipped all over India as the lord of obstacles who must be propitiated before any enterprise; Skanda is worshipped especially in Tamil Nadu, under his Tamil name Murugan.

Brahmā

Brahmā is a god of less fully developed character. He is known as the Grandfather, and incorporates some characteristics of the older Prajāpati, father of gods and demons. In myths, the gods often appeal to Brahmā to save them, but his only resource is to call on Vishnu or Shiva. Brahmā is associated with Vedic ritual: he is shown carrying four books representing the Vedas, or with a book, a ladle and jar – ritual implements – and a string of beads. He has four faces, to face in all directions. His wife Saraswatī is goddess of learning and the arts; she is worshipped on the last three days of Navarātri (p. 130), or on her own day in spring, when she blesses books and school equipment.

The gods and God

The gods and goddesses we have described are the Sanskritic deities known throughout India, though not all are worshipped in every region. But there are innumerable local deities (*grāma-devatā*), having shrines which may be frequented only by the people of one village, or even part of a village (p. 18).

A local god or goddess may be identified with one of the Sanskritic deities. Thus the smallpox goddess, who has shrines all over India where she is known as Shītalā, Mātā ('mother'), Māriyamman or by other names, is considered a form of Shiva's wife. Offerings are made to her to avert smallpox and other diseases and in thanksgiving for release from them, and those who catch the disease are thought to be possessed by her, and therefore able to speak in her name. There are also many heroes and saints whose pictures or monuments are worshipped, and who can work miracles either when living or after death (pp. 141–5; pp. 182–4). The term 'god' does not belong to a clear-cut class, whether we define it as an object of worship or as a being having superhuman powers. Such powers can also belong to demons, enemies of the gods.

Hindus often say that there are 330 million gods. This is an elaboration of the Vedic traditional number of thirty-three gods. Neither is an exact number; the point is that there are many gods. But this does not mean that each Hindu worships them all. One person may regard a particular god as supreme, worshipping other gods on occasions such as their festivals. Such a god is called one's *ishta-devatā*, 'chosen deity'; ultimately it is a matter of choice, though loyalty to particular gods tends to run in families. Thus some are followers of Vishnu (Vaishnavas), others of Shiva (Shaivas), others of the Goddess, regarding her as superior to her husband Shiva; these are called Shāktas, people of the Shakti (p. 121). This does not mean that the whole Hindu population can be divided into Vaishnavas, Shaivas and Shāktas; many take a pragmatic interest in various deities in turn, while some worship no deities.

Most Hindus say that above all the deities there is God, called Nārāyana (a name of Vishnu), Bhagwān or Bhagavat (a title of Vishnu), or Īshwara ('lord'). They may identify this God with their chosen deity, or consider him beyond identification with any particular god (Chapter 13). A popular view is that Bhagwān – God – is like a ruler who delegates particular powers to his ministers and officers of various grades – the gods – and that we can only bring our concerns to the notice of these underlings, not of God himself.

Another view of the relation between gods is represented iconographically as the Trimūrti or triple form, sometimes called the 'Hindu Trinity', consisting of a single body with the faces of Brahmā, Vishnu and Shiva. These have the roles of creator, preserver and destroyer of the world. As we shall see (p. 136), the world is periodically created, maintained and destroyed in an endless series of cycles, besides the fact that each being in it passes through these three phases in the course of its existence. These three phases are all treated in an Upanishadic passage as resulting from the one cause of all, called Brahman (distinct from the god Brahmā, though his name is a form of this word):

> That from which these beings are born, in which when born they live, into which they enter when they perish – seek to know that; that is Brahman. (*Taittirīya Upanishad* 3, 1)

The Trimūrti implies that Brahmā, Vishnu and Shiva – and, by extension, other gods – represent different ways in which Brahman is related to the world.

Brahman, of which we shall say more (p. 168; 173) is beyond the gods. As the infinite ground of being, Brahman can be called God. The term does not necessarily imply a personal being, as Bhagwān or Īshwara does: it is an abstract, learned term, whereas the latter are popular terms. Belief in Brahman, Bhagwān or Īshwara means that Hindus are monotheists, not polytheists, though they may believe in many gods (p. 17; p. 180).

Teaching Ideas

Early Years

The gods are best introduced through stories, preferably illustrated with large calendar pictures, posters or slides. Simple information can be given to younger children in answer to inevitable questions about the colour of gods, their several arms and their displays of superhuman power. In association with story work, young children can take part in the cycle of activities listed on pp. 32–6. Art work could include collage (e.g. collectively making a collage of Lakshmī at Diwālī time) or simple puppetry.

Middle Years

(a) In small groups older middle-years children can discuss what each of them understands by the word 'God'. They can write down a few key phrases from their discussions ('a great power', 'the greatest being', 'like a father' etc.) Discussion can follow on the adequacy of the phrases and on how the characteristics listed could be described pictorially; some art work can follow. (Muslim pupils may be offended by this activity because of the Muslim prohibition on representing God in visual terms.) For others the activity can stimulate an imaginative use of symbols. The exercise of using art to convey ideas such as 'power' and 'caring' can motivate and help children to interpret Hindu pictures.

(b) Puzzle pictures. Using calendar pictures, commercially-produced posters or slides of deities, encourage children to attempt to work out the symbolism of the pictures. Remind children first of the empathy game (pp. 24–5). Information can be fed in by the teacher as appropriate. The activity can be done in small groups or as a 'question/answer' exercise with the whole class. Small images of deities can also be used in this way (pp. 230–1).

(c) Puppet-making. Puppet theatre is especially appropriate for dramatising stories of Hindu gods, since puppet theatre in India is believed to be even older than human theatre, with string, glove and rod puppets as well as various kinds of shadow puppets being represented. Most themes for puppet theatre are based on purānic myths and the epics, and puppets from different parts of India reflect regional styles of painting and sculpture. Discussion on the nature of myth and the symbolism associated with the characters can be incorporated into the project.

(d) Dramatise incidents from the story of Rāma and Sītā linked together by a paurānika, who acts as narrator and draws attention to some of the religious and moral teachings in the story (see p. 130). This work could be performed in assembly.

Adolescence and Post-16

Read pp. 28–30 (pictures, slides and videos) and pp. 32–6 (story and the expressive arts).

(a) Linking deities with their mythology. Small groups can look at pictures or slides (with daylight viewer) of a particular major Hindu deity and make guesses concerning the attributes and character of the god or goddess. These can be checked against the information given above. The imagery can then be related to myths about the deity. The references to versions of the myths written for children can be used (see below) or books such as O'Flaherty, *Hindu Myths* (1975) or Ions, *Indian Mythology* (1967). The statement 'each image expresses an aspect of a deity's personality and encapsulates part of their mythology' (p. 117) can be discussed (see p. 180).

(b) The nature and functions of myth. A number of points can be discussed by groups. Individuals can draw on their own knowledge and commitments as well as using material from the chapter.

(i)   The relationship between myth or story and history within religious traditions. Groups could consider one of the Biblical creation stories. Do Christians and Jews regard these stories as historically true? Do the stories embody a teaching which is clear, regardless of their historical worth? What are the personal views of individuals within the group? Groups are likely to conclude that within Christianity or Judaism there are different yet deeply held views about the historical status of myths, but that all Christians and Jews would regard their religious myths as embodying important teaching.

(ii)   Groups can be given a copy of the quotations reproduced on p. 33. What reasons can you think of for the young men arriving at their views about Hindu myths? Could they have adopted different views and still remained comfortable within the Hindu tradition?

(iii)   Read pp. 32–6. In our chapter the paurānika recited a version of the story of Rāma and Sītā. The class should be given or told a version of the story. Groups can discuss the different functions that they think the story has for those who listen to it or see it performed. Answers might pick out entertainment value; moral teaching (e.g. about duty and loyalty); spiritual teaching (that good ultimately triumphs over evil). Groups can then be introduced to some of the distinctively Hindu functions of the story as told by the paurānika. Note that the paurānika himself wishes to emphasise the following moral teachings: respect for parents; family honour; chastity. Some of his hearers value the links that the story gives them with their tradition, and the opportunity they are given to think of God. The moral lessons are important, but faith in the stories also destroys bad karma accumulated in the past and the very sound of the recited text cures evil tendencies. The recitation is refreshing, relaxing and inspiring and 'charges the air with the divine presence'.

Children's Versions of Hindu Myths

This selection is from items listed in Part 3 pp. 204–16.

Vishnu
Tales of Vishnu (Amar Chitra Katha (ACK) No. 160); *Prahlad* (ACK No. 38); 'How Naradh was Taught a Lesson' in Singh, R., *The Indian Storybook* (1984); Singh, G. 'The Story of Prahlad'; *Parashurama* (ACK No. 42); *Dasha Avatar* (ACK, special issue No. 1); 'Prahlada' in Killingley (1984).

Krishna
Krishna (ACK No. 11); *Mahabharata* (ACK No. 20); *The Gita* (ACK No. 127); *Krishna, Master of All Mystics, Krishna's Birth, Krishna, Krishna and the Demons* (all Bala Books); *Krishna and the Pandavas* (Echo Books); 'The Birth of Lord Krishna' in Gavin, *Stories from the Hindu World*; 'Krishna's Escape' and 'Krishna tames Kaliya' in Kanitkar (1986); 'The Birth of Krishna' in Lefever (1973); Rao, *The Mahabharata* (1986); Singh, R., *The Indian Story Book* (1984); *Krishna and Rukmini* (ACK, 112); various Krishna Stories in Jaffrey (1985) and in Singh, G. (n.d.).

Rāma
Rama (ACK No. 15); *Hanuman* (ACK No. 19); *Hanuman to the Rescue* (ACK No. 254); *Tales the Ramayana Tells* (Echo Books); 'Rama and Sita' in Jaffrey (1985); 'Prince Rama' in Kanitkar (1986); Khanna, G. S., *The Story of Diwali* (1983); 'Rama and Sita' in Lefever (1973); *The Story of Diwali* (MGSS), (1983); *The Prince of Ayodhya* (Nehru Library for Children No. 30); Thompson, B., *The Story of Prince Rama* (1980); Thompson, R., *My Class at Diwali* (1986); Troughton, *The Story of Rama and Sita* (1975).

Shiva
'The Descent of the Ganga', in Dayal, R., *Legends from the Puranas* (Echo Books); *Shiva Parvati* (ACK No. 29); *Sati and Shiva* (ACK No. 111); *Tales of Shiva* (ACK No. 164); 'The Marriage of Shiva' in

Legends from the Puranas, op. cit.; 'The Story of Shiva, the Great God', in Sr. Nivedita (1968); 'The Churning of the Ocean' (Killingley 1984: 55f); 'The Descent of the Ganges' (Killingley 1984: 63f).

Ganesha
Ganesha (ACK No. 89), gives the *Shiva Purāna* version of Ganesha's birth. See also 'The Birth of Ganesha' (Killingly 1984: 58); 'Ganesh', Kanitkar (1986); 'How Ganesh got his Elephant Head' (Jaffrey 1985); Ganesha's birth story is linked to the festival of Ganesha Chaturthi in Jackson, R., 'Hindu Festivals' (Brown 1986: 128). Boothalingam, Sushama, *The Legends of Lord Ganesha* (Echo Books) contains eight stories of Ganesha.

Goddesses
Tales of Durgā (ACK No. 176); 'Lakshmī and the Clever Washerwoman' (Jaffrey 1985); 'Sati, the Perfect Wife' and 'The Tale of Uma Haimavati (Nivedita 1968); *Ganga* (ACK No. 88); stories of Durgā and Lakshmī are read in the 1987 BBC Quest radio programmes *The Festival of Navratri* and *The Festival of Diwali*.

Further reading

Singer (1972); Wilson (1961); Stutley (1977); O'Flaherty (1975); Narayan (1965).

10

Festivals and Sacred Time

Hindus see their lives as part of a cosmic rhythm. Just as our bodily life has its cycles in the heartbeat and the breath, and alternates between sleeping and waking, birth and death, so the world around us alternates between day and night, full moon and new moon, summer and winter, and passes through yet longer cycles in which it is periodically created and destroyed. There are right and wrong times for worshipping particular gods, and for performing various tasks. The changes wrought by historical events are often seen as part of the cosmic rhythm. To exemplify some Hindu views of time, we shall draw on a book which looks back on three generations of a Panjabi family, from before the British annexation of the Panjab in 1849 to the partition of the Panjab between India and Pakistan in 1947 (Tandon 1961). The author is a Khatri, but has a very different background from Satya.

Case study: Prakāsh Tandon

Prakāsh Tandon's grandfather was a minor revenue official in the early days of British rule in the Panjab, and his great-uncle became a successful lawyer. His father was a civil engineer, working on the irrigation canals which transformed the Panjab in the nineteenth century, and he himself became a business executive in Bombay. The family were not formally religious, though the women were more so than the men; the lawyer's wife did a morning pūjā with flowers from a small private garden, and Prakash's mother made offerings to the Goddess when he recovered from chicken-pox. His father was attracted for a time by the Ārya Samāj (p. 190), which combines a modern outlook with belief in God and respect for the Sanskrit tradition. There were few temples, and Brahmins had little influence, except the astrologers who found the auspicious moments for betrothals, marriages, business ventures and journeys, using almanacs produced in Hardwār or Vārānasī. Most Brahmins knew only what they needed for performing a few rituals, and lived on handouts of cooked food from the wealthier families, and gifts of money and cloth at rituals.

Festivals, however, had an important place in the rhythm of life; they marked the seasonal and agricultural cycle. The seasons in the Panjab are winter, spring, summer, rains and autumn. Winter is freezing at night and often wet by day; summer is scorching and dry, with temperatures over 50°C in the sun. Prakash Tandon remembers the effect of the seasons on work and social life. Wheat and other crops were harvested in spring, after which came a time of relative leisure, which was used for making improvements on the land, and also for marriages. As the summer approached, people slept on the roof terraces, and then on verandahs as it grew hotter. Summer brought dust storms and cracked earth, and ended in swirling clouds, thunder and rain, bringing terror and then relief from the heat. After three or four days of rain the land was ready for the plough. Autumn brought shorter and cooler days, and the sugarcane harvest. Winter was the pleasantest time, being cold but bright. It was also busy, with the men working in the fields and the women spinning and embroidering.

Spring festivals

The first festival Prakāsh Tandon describes is *Lohri* (also called *Makara Sankrānti*), in January, when there were bonfires and firecrackers, and sweets. Then came *Basant*, a spring festival when men wore yellow turbans and women wore yellow scarves, to match the ripening corn. *Holī*, around March, was a rowdy festival, when people sprayed each other with coloured water and powder; it was advisable to wear old clothes. In some streets people stood on the roof to throw rubbish on passers-by; all kinds of indignities had to be taken with good humour on Holī and all kinds of pranks were played. Prakash's great-great-uncle, who had fought against the British in 1849, used to dress up as a lion for Holī and carry a goat between his teeth.

Besākhi (Vaishākhi) is a spring festival held on April 13, and common to Hindus, Muslims and Sikhs. Farmers who had harvested their grain brought their families to a river bank on foot, on horseback or in carts, all dressed in their best. Little Prakash had a brightly striped shirt and white trousers, red shoes and a gold-embroidered red pill-box cap. Men got drunk, or at least 'wet their whiskers' as they put it, and danced. There were booths by the river with cosmetics and bangles for the women, wooden toys for the children, roundabouts, animal tamers, ballad singers, medicine sellers, wrestling and horse racing.

Rakshā-bandhana

Summer was bare of festivals, until the *Rakshā-bandhana* ('protection-tie') in August, when sisters tied silk bracelets, often decorated with pompoms and glass beads, on the wrists of their brothers. Prakash had no sister, so he and his two brothers adopted sisters to perform this ceremony for them. The three brothers were given silver rupees to give to their adopted sisters in return; they resented this part, since they thought they had better uses for the money.

Navarātri and Dasahrā

Prakāsh's favourite festival season was in the autumn, with *Dasahrā* and *Diwālī*. Dasahrā, also called *Vijaya Dashamī* ('victory tenth') is the culmination of the festive season of *Navarātri* ('nine nights'). In Prakash's home town, Gujrat, a committee was set up annually to raise money and recruit actors for Rām Līlā, a serial enactment of the story of Rāma (pp. 114–6; p. 161). Prakash and his friends were eager to be chosen to dress up in masks and tails to form the monkey army who assisted Rāma; sometimes they stuck pins in their arrows to prick the boys who played the army of Rāvana. The climax of the show was on Dasahrā day itself, when the defeat of the demon Rāvana was performed. The chief demons were effigies of bamboo and paper, filled with fireworks; when Rāma shot his final arrow, they burst into flames, with crackers and rockets flying out of them, making it clear to everyone that good had triumphed over evil.

Diwālī

Three weeks later came Diwālī. Prakash, who later lived in Sweden for a time, compares it to the Scandinavian Christmas. Diwālī too, was associated with Rāma; it celebrated his home-coming from fourteen years of exile, as well as being the time for

Lakshmī, goddess of prosperity (p. 119), to visit the house. Families gathered at home if they could, and the women spent days decorating the house with red swastikas (p. 91), rolling cotton wicks for the earthenware lamps, and making sweets. Father had the house painted, and bought candles and more sweets. On Diwālī day the family put rows of lamps outside the house, and in the evening they bathed and put on clean clothes. When darkness came at last, the children rushed out to light the lamps, vying with the children in the neighbouring houses. Then pūjā was performed to Lakshmī; it was only after pūjā that the children were allowed to have the sweets as prasāda. Then there were fireworks, and a visit to the bazaar to see the lamps, candles and gaslight illuminating the shops – especially the sweet shops.

Changes

Festivals mark the annual renewal of a recurrent order; but Prakash Tandon, looking back over a century in his family's memories, found that the order was not always the same. Festivals sometimes became occasions for Hindu-Muslim conflict. Hindus then became afraid of celebrating Holī, Dasahrā and Diwālī, because disputes over noise could lead to bloodshed. On the other hand, he says, Christmas celebrations, including children's parties, have become more common in independent India than in the British period, and India also celebrates Republic Day (January 26) as a national secular festival.

But even historical changes were seen as part of a pattern. When political orators came to the Panjab in the 1920s, they spoke of the evils of the present *Kali Yuga*, the fallen age, when food was scarce and falsehood flourished. This was familiar enough, since it was the common talk of grumbling elders. But the new orators claimed that the British were to blame for the evils of the Kali Yuga, and that once they were overthrown the *Satya Yuga* or *Krita Yuga* – the age of truth or perfect age – would be restored. For Hindus in West Panjab, which became part of West Pakistan in 1947, history did not work out in this way. After the riots and massacres which attended independence and partition, Prakash Tandon and his family never returned.

Times and seasons

The intertwining of Hinduism with everyday life is nowhere more clearly seen than in the cycle of festivals. Vaishākhi celebrates the harvest in the Panjab, and provides an occasion for spending some of what has been gained by it. Diwālī is a time for renewal, when new clothes are worn and new utensils are put into use; business people pay off debts and start new account books. The bonfires at Lohri, marking the winter solstice when the days are about to lengthen, symbolise the coming return of warmth and light, as well as being an exhilarating pastime.

There are traditionally six seasons: spring, summer, rains, autumn, winter and cool season (Prakāsh Tandon counts the last two as one). The actual pattern varies geographically; in parts of the south, where no season is cold, the rains come twice a year. The relation of festivals to the agricultural year varies according-ly: in the South the Makara Sankrānti festival (called *Pongal* in Tamil), which takes place at the same time as the Panjabi Lohri, marks the end of the main harvest time, when rice is ceremonially boiled and offered to the sun and part of it is given in thanks to the cattle.

The religious meaning of festivals also varies regionally. In the Panjab, where Rāma is a popular deity, Navarātri is associated with him. But in Bengal, Navarātri is called Durgā Pujā, and the event celebrated is Durgā's killing of the buffalo demon. Some festivals known in one region are unknown in another. The Tamils have *Panguni Uttiram*, which often coincides with Holī but is quite a different festival. It celebrates the marriage of Shiva's son, Skanda, who is rarely worshipped in the north (p. 121).

Not all annual occasions are times of feasting. An all-night vigil and fast in honour of Shiva is held on *Mahāshivarātri* ('the great night of Shiva') around February, and a fortnight around Septem-ber is devoted to rites for the dead (p. 97).

Believing that all life is part of a cosmic rhythm, Hindus are careful in timing their actions. For important events such as weddings and journeys, they consult the experts on time, the astrologers, who use precise data on the apparent movements of the sun, moon, stars and planets. These are printed in almanacs (*panchānga*) compiled by leading astrologers.

The year

A few of the annual festivals are timed by the sun, and therefore always fall on or near the same date each year according to the familiar, internationally used Gregorian calendar. One of these is Vaishākhi or Besakhi, which Prakash Tandon describes; it falls on April 13, and is now a national holiday. It has a special significance for Sikhs, as it commemorates the founding of the Sikh community (Khālsā) by Guru Gobind Singh in 1699. Another is Makara Sankrānti (Lohri, Pongal), on January 14. Modern festivals, like the birthdays of Ramakrishna (p. 190) on March 20, and Gandhi (pp. 154–7) on October 2, are timed by the Gregorian calendar.

The year is divided into two halves: in one, from midwinter to midsummer, the sun moves northward, and in the other it moves southward. The turning points are Makara Sankrānti ('entry into Capricorn') and Karka Sankrānti ('entry into Cancer').[1]

The Gregorian calendar is a solar one: it ignores the phases of the moon, but keeps pace with the sun by means of leap-years, so that each of the four natural reference points of the solar year – the equinoxes and solstices – falls on nearly the same date each calendar year. The timing of most Hindu festivals, however, is based on the lunar month – the period in which the moon completes its cycle of phases – which lasts $29\frac{1}{2}$ days. There are twelve named months, as shown in the diagram; they are grouped in six seasons of two months each. The relation of these lunar months to our Gregorian months varies; the full moon of Chaitra, for instance, can appear on any date from March 14 to April 14. Twelve lunar months make only 354 days; for this reason the Muslim calendar, for instance, which is entirely lunar, places the New Year about eleven days earlier in each solar year. To avoid this, the Hindu calendar inserts an extra month every two and a half to three years, so that each month always comes at roughly the same season of the solar year. The Hindu calendar is thus a luni-solar one, combining a precisely lunar month with an approximately solar year. Its main outlines are shown in the diagram on page 134.

There are various ways of reckoning the beginning of the year. Often it follows the new moon of Chaitra, but in Gujarat it follows the new moon of Kārttika, immediately after Diwālī; in Tamil Nadu it is not fixed by the moon, but falls on Vaisākhi. Various eras are used for numbering years; the commonest are the Vikrama era, counting from 57 BCE, and the Shaka era, counting from 78 CE. 1990 CE is 2047 in the Vikrama era, or 1912 in the Shaka. In rituals the priest may announce the date according to the Kali Yuga (p. 136), so 1990 is 5092.

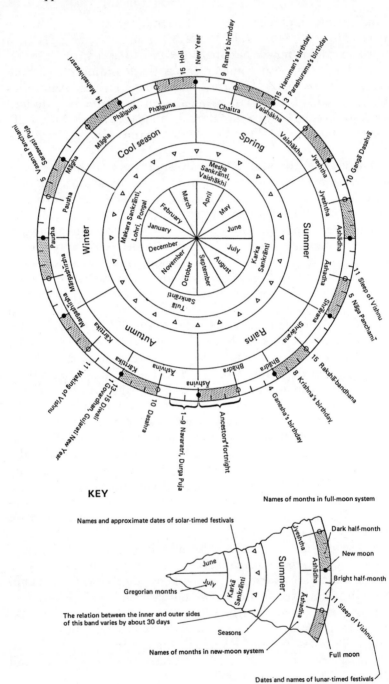

KEY

Names and approximate dates of solar-timed festivals

Names of months in full-moon system

Dark half-month

New moon

Bright half-month

11 Sleep of Vishnu

June

July

Karkā Sankrānti

Summer

Jyeshtha

Āshādha

Āshādha

Gregorian months

The relation between the inner and outer sides of this band varies by about 30 days

Seasons

Names of months in new-moon system

Full moon

Dates and names of lunar-timed festivals

The month

The month, like the year, is divided into two halves, sometimes called fortnights (though they are a little longer than fourteen days): the bright half, when the moon is waxing, and the dark half, when it is waning. The month can be reckoned as beginning either after the new moon or after the full moon, and both systems are used in different parts of India. Roughly, the system of starting the month after the new moon (*amānta*) prevails in South India, and the full-moon system (*pūrnimānta*) in North India. For the names of the bright half-months, both systems agree. But in the dark half-months, where the new-moon system uses the name of the preceding bright half-month, the full-moon system uses the name of the following bright half-month. Thus the first fortnight of the year is the bright half of Chaitra; the next fortnight is called the dark half of Chaitra in the new-moon system, but the dark half of Vaishākha in the full-moon system. In the full-moon system, therefore, the year begins in the middle of a month. This does not affect the timing of festivals. Everyone celebrates Krishna's birthday on the same day, but in the north it is called the 8th of the dark half of Bhādra and in the south it is the 8th of the dark half of Shrāvana.

Each half-month is divided into fifteen 'lunar days', which may begin and end at any time of the solar day. Only astrologers concern themselves with when a lunar day begins and ends; for most purposes it is the solar day that counts, and it begins and ends at sunrise. The day following the full moon is the first of the dark half-month, and the day of the new moon is the fifteenth; the next day is the first of the bright half-month, and the full-moon day is the fifteenth. We can only give the general principles of the system; Hindus usually rely on calendars to find the dates of festivals, and do not concern themselves with the astronomical observations and calculations on which they are based.

Certain days of the month are significant, particularly the new and full moon days, which may be marked by fasting. The fourth lunar day of each half-month belongs to Ganesha, especially the bright fourth of Bhādra. Durgā is worshipped in the bright eighths, and Shītalā, the smallpox goddess (who may be identified with her), on the dark eighths. Elevenths are sacred to Vishnu.

Most Hindu festivals fall on a particular lunar day of a particular half-month, so that it is not possible to date them exactly by the Gregorian calendar; Holī, for instance, can fall in February or

March. The number of the day is often used in the festival's name: Rāma's birthday is called *Rāma Navamī*, 'Rāma's ninth'; Krishna's birthday is *Krishna Janmāshtamī* (janma-ashtamī) 'Krishna's birth eighth' or *Gokulāshtamī* 'Gokula eighth', from Krishna's birthplace.

The week

The week, with its seven days named after the sun, moon and planets, has been used in India from early times. Sunday and Monday are auspicious, and Monday belongs to Shiva; it may be observed as a fast. Tuesday and Saturday are inauspicious, though Saturday is associated with the monkey-god Hanuman. Some people take vows to abstain from particular foods on particular days of the week. In Britain, rituals are often performed on Sunday because it is convenient as well as auspicious.

The day

In each day, sunrise and sunset are critical times. Some people are particular that their first sights and thoughts on waking should be auspicious, since the beginning of the day, like the beginning of the year, determines the character of the whole. Many Brahmins recite the Gāyatrī mantra (p. 96) at sunrise and sunset; some also do so at midday. Within the day, auspicious times for events such as marriages may be determined astrologically (p. 89).

Cycles of years

Some units of time larger than the year are significant. The *Kumbha Melā*, a bathing festival held at Hardwar and Allahabad on the Ganges, and at Ujjain and Nasik in central India, occurs once in the twelve-year cycle of the planet Jupiter. A sixty-year cycle, in which each year has a name, is used in South India.

Years of the gods

Still longer units of time are used when dealing with mythology. Our year is only a day to the gods; the gods' year is 360 of ours. 12,000 years of the gods make up a cycle of four ages or yugas, as follows:

Krita or *Satya Yuga*:	4,800 years of the gods	=	1,728,000 years
Tretā Yuga:	3,600 years of the gods	=	1,296,000 years
Dwāpara Yuga:	2,400 years of the gods	=	864,000 years
Kali Yuga:	1,200 years of the gods	=	432,000 years
Total:	12,000 years of the gods	=	4,320,000 years

The names of the ages are taken from the four sides of the ancient Indian dice. The name Kali has nothing to do with the goddess Kālī; it is the name of the lowest score in the game. In the first age the world is perfect, but in each succeeding age it declines: lives are shorter, food is scarcer and morality lower. We are now in the worst age, and every instance of oppression, dishonesty or misery is evidence of the fact. This fallen age began with the great battle described in the *Mahābhārata*, in 3102 BCE; and it will end when Kalki, the tenth avatāra of Vishnu, comes to begin a new perfect age (p. 120). According to the above scheme, this will not happen for over four thousand centuries, but people still talk like the orators Prakāsh Tandon heard, of the possibility of bringing this evil age to an end.

Like the year, the cycle of four ages repeats itself endlessly. Beyond it are still larger units of time, since in the Hindu view time is infinite and cyclic. After a thousand cycles of four ages, the world will come to an end, and after an equal time, it will be created again, in a series of cosmic days and nights. Nothing, not even the beginning or end of the world, happens only once; if something can happen at all, it will happen again and again when its due time comes.

Teaching Ideas

More books and audio-visual resources exist for teaching about festivals than for any other topic and a substantial selection is listed in Part 3. Not all of this material takes care to point out the diversity of ways in which festivals are celebrated in different parts of India and abroad, or makes it clear that some festivals are regional and local. Therefore it is important for teachers to point out that the class is going to explore a festival as celebrated by a particular group of Hindus rather than by all Hindus. Multi-faith schools will have the opportunity of involving Hindu parents in activities.

Early Years

(a) Celebration. Begin with brainstorming of the word 'Christmas' (see p. 25 and p. 27) in order to explore the various dimensions of a festival which will be familiar to most children. A Hindu festival can then be introduced using slides, pictures or artefacts. Children can suggest similarities (happy times, stories, special meals, visiting relatives and so on) and differences. J. Solomon, *Sweet-tooth Sunil* and C. Deshpande, *Diwali* are appropriate books for introducing Diwālī to infants.

(b) Story. Many festivals have one or more myths associated with them (according to region). Often text books identify the story of Rāma and Sītā as *the* story of Diwālī. As our case study confirms the Rāma and Sītā tale is *one* Diwālī story in some parts of India. Note its association with Navarātri/Dasahrā in some parts of India, and the importance of Lakshmī at Diwālī. M. Jaffrey, *Seasons of Splendour* includes a good Lakshmī story which is read on the 1987 BBC *Quest* programme on Diwālī. Sources for stories associated with particular gods and goddesses are listed on pp. 126–7 and a selection of appropriate activities which relate stories to the experience of children and explore the stories' distinctive features is to be found on pp. 35–6, e.g. art, drama, poetry.

Middle Years

The activities listed under 'Early Years' can be adapted for use with older children.

(a) Cookery. Sweets are offered to the deities and then shared as prasāda in several festivals. See pp. 36–9 for an introduction to Indian food and some teaching ideas. Cookery books containing recipes are listed in the bibliography. Santa Maria (1979) has many recipes for festive sweets.

(b) Calendars. Buy an Indian tear-off calendar from an Asian grocery or one of the suppliers listed (pp. 236–7). These usually print both the Gregorian dates and the dates according to one of the Indian calendars. Thus Gujarati calendars begin with a new year which follows Diwālī in October/November; the new year comes at different times in different parts of India (p. 133). Calendars generally print holy days (festivals, fasts, new and full moon days etc.) in a different colour from the rest. Without telling the children that the object is a calendar, allow them to examine it, to guess what it is, why the pages are different colours, why the first date is in October (or November) and so on. This can lead to work on different calendars and to reflection on how and why people in different cultures and religions divide time up and organise dating systems as they do.

(c) Story. In addition to the ideas given under 'Early Years', children can be introduced to some of the ideas on p. 30 for using audio-tape versions of stories which appear in BBC radio programmes on festivals (see pp. 225–7). For example, incidents from stories can be illustrated with paintings. These can then be photographed and the broadcast and pictures used together as a slide/tape programme. This can be used as a basis for discussion of the story's religious and moral themes or as a presentation for others (parents; assembly). See also ideas for using story on p. 32 (sequencing, prediction), p. 124 and pp. 126–7.

(d) Hindu children in Britain. Hindu children recount some of their own experiences of festivals in R. Jackson, *Religions through Festivals: Hinduism.*

Adolescence and Post-16

(a) Time. Get the pupils to copy the first four sentences of this chapter and ask them to do the tasks listed on pp. 31–2. Discuss questions which are raised, introducing further information (on the seasons, the calendar, the yugas and on samsāra and karma (p. 16; p. 172). The work can lead to a consideration of time in relation to an individual Hindu's needs and goals. Much of day-to-day religious life is likely to be concerned with coping with practical problems of life (making a living, raising a family, avoiding illness, asking for blessing) and with fulfilling family and caste obligations (dharma). The beginning of the day or year determines the character of the whole (p. 136); this idea helps us to understand British New Year customs such as first-footing, as well as the elements of prosperity and renewal in Hindu new year and spring festivals (p. 132). Displays of prosperity at weddings are based on the same idea. The time cycle also includes the individual's death and rebirth, which in turn must be seen in relation to the mythical time cycle of the gods (pp. 136–7). All this gives a perspective on the way in which an individual is perceived within the Hindu tradition. The discussion may raise wider questions about personhood and religious belief (p. 179).

(b) Visit to a Hindu Festival. Most Hindu temples in Britain will welcome parties of visitors during celebrations of festivals such as Navarātri (especially important for Gujaratis), Holī and Diwālī. Details for arranging visits are to be found on pp. 44–55. In addition, students should be familiarised with key features of the festival (many of these are listed in R. Jackson, 'Hindu Festivals' in A. Brown (ed.) (1986)). Note that temple functions are only part of the celebrations. Most temple ceremonies are held in the evening, so this is likely to be an activity for volunteers rather than a whole class. See pp. 47–9 for activities which can be adapted for older students, e.g. photography, interviewing.

Further reading

Tandon (1961); Stevenson (1920); Jackson (1986); Killingley (1984); Shap Calendar.

Note

1   These occur about three weeks later than the winter and summer solstices, because the Indian system is sidereal, not tropical. For the same reason Vaishākhi is later than our spring equinox. The discrepancy is due to the precession of the equinoxes.

11
Pilgrimage and Sacred Places

Many religious traditions hold particular places as sacred; even if the divine is everywhere, it can be experienced more readily in some places than in others. For Hindus there are great sacred places known all over India, such as Vārānasī (Benares), and others attracting pilgrims only from a small region. Just as there is no single authority but many authorities, so there are also many sacred places. Every temple or open-air shrine is a sacred place for some group of Hindus.

It is important not to identify Hinduism exclusively with those features that are most widely known or laid down in Sanskrit texts. The place we are going to look at first will not be found on most maps, or even in most books on Hindu pilgrimage, but it is sacred to thousands of Hindus. The people travelling to it are not interested in ritual precision like Mr Dutt and his pandit (pp. 103–5), but in the spontaneous expression of their love of God as they know him (Binford 1976)[1].

Case study: A pilgrimage to Ramdevra

They were thirteen women, three men and three children, travelling from Bombay to an arid spot over 9000 kilometres to the north, in the Thar desert in Rājasthān. Most of them were poor people from artisan castes; they belonged to a group that met monthly to sing devotional songs to an incarnation of God, Rāmdev. They spent twenty-four hours on the train to Jodhpur, and another ten hours in a special bus which took them and other pilgrims to their destination, all with their bedding, clothing, supplies of food, and offerings. The Bombay group brought a small silver statue of a man on a horse.

One of the women, Sonāben, had been ten times before.

Nānīmā, aged ninety, had also been several times. The others were making their first visit. Dhanjībhāī who had organised the visit, was there with his wife; he kept a flower stall. (The suffix *-ben* means 'sister', *-mā* 'mother', and *-bhaī* 'brother' (p. 64).

Their destination was the village of Rāmdevrā, where there is a temple on a hill above a small lake, surrounded by lesser shrines, with resthouses run by the temple managers. The village had been transformed into a camp for 100,000 pilgrims, for it was the time of the annual *melā* (assembly, especially of pilgrims), in the bright half of the month of Bhādra. This month is in the rainy season; but in Ramdevra it never rains.

In the temple are fourteen graves, marked by ridge-shaped stones in the Muslim manner, one of which is the focus of worship. This is the grave of Rāmdev, the local hero and saint. Little is known about him, except that he was a Rājput – a member of a group of castes, especially in Rājasthān, who claim Kshatriya status (p. 78). He was a king's son, and lived in the fifteenth century; some say he was killed in battle at Rāmdevrā. He is represented in pictures as a bearded man on horseback, carrying a lance from which flies a flag marked with a pair of footprints; his left hand is raised, palm forward, in the gesture which means 'Do not fear'. The horse and lance suggest a military hero, but Rāmdev is remembered as a miracle worker. He is said to have defeated robbers and demons, cured the sick, made a cart move without bullocks, and brought the dead to life, gathering disciples and convincing unbelievers by means of his miracles. While other Rajput heroes are remembered for their fights against Muslims, Rāmdev is supposed to have won over many Muslims, including a king, by means of his miraculous powers.

He is thought of as an avatāra of Krishna – Krishna, not Vishnu, since Krishna himself is often regarded as a god in his own right. He is shown in pictures with the fork-shaped Vaishnava mark on his forehead (p. 185). In this way, a local figure has been integrated into the wider network of Hindu mythology and worship.

Hindu sannyāsīs – men who have renounced the world (p. 83) are not cremated when they die, but buried; for ritual purposes they are already dead on taking sannyāsa. A sannyāsī is not thought of as having died, but as having entered *samādhi*, meaning a state of concentration or heightened consciousness. A sannyāsī's burial-place is also called his samādhi, and such places often become places of pilgrimage. Rāmdev's grave is called his samādhi, and the pilgrimage period culminates in the anniversary of his entry into samādhi. To his devotees, his burial is not a sign of Muslim cultural influence but of sainthood, and miracles have continued to take place there. The other graves in and near the temple are those of his relatives and disciples, and the temple and its surroundings belong to his descendants.

Some of the people from Bombay had special reasons for coming. Triveniben had a vow to fulfil: she had prayed to Rāmdev for a son, and promised that if her prayer was granted she would bring the boy to Rāmdevrā and that until then she would not wear her marriage necklace. Nānīmā was coming to ask Rāmdev's blessing on her grandson's jewellery business. Sonaben was coming for the eleventh time, to give thanks for Rāmdev's help in the past. Everyone was eager to have darshana of Rāmdev by seeing his samādhi and the other signs of his presence, such as the nearly life-size cloth horse in the temple, the tree outside, hung with scraps of cloth offered by devotees (p. 107), and the miraculous well.

The party arrived to find the assembly area full of people who had come by train and bus like themselves, on foot, by camel, by bullock cart, and even by chauffeur-driven car. Pilgrims of all castes could stay in the resthouses; Rāmdev is especially the friend of Untouchables. At the resthouse, they had a small room where they could leave their belongings; they slept on the verandah and roof, and cooked on the verandah. Mixing with fellow-devotees from other places was part of the experience of the pilgrimage. Then there were craftsmen and pedlars from hundreds of miles away, selling figures of Rāmdev, wooden and cloth horses, and stone reliefs of Rāmdev on horseback with his lance and flag, or simply of his footprints. There were also sellers of blankets, bangles, sweets, and other goods which had nothing in particular to do with Rāmdev, but which can be expected at any large gathering. There were preachers and plays, and even a film show from the family planning organisation, spreading its message to people who had come, perhaps, to pray for a son. This is not so inconsistent as it might seem; Triveniben, who had come to give thanks for her first son, had seven daughters, and had undergone sterilization before making her pilgrimage.

On the day they arrived, the pilgrims from Bombay changed into their best clothes and formed their own procession, with a band of hired musicians. The men went ahead carrying flags to be flown from the top of the temple, and Sonaben, as an experienced pilgrim, carried the other offerings on a brass tray on her head: the silver figure of Rāmdev on his horse, some cloth horses, flowers from Dhanjibhai's stall, incense, a clay lamp, and a large silver horse borrowed from the temple. Before starting, they performed a simple pūjā, and scattered red powder over the horses and each other. At last, as the queue moved on, they plunged from the glare of daylight into the dark of the temple, jostled by other pilgrims, and experienced darshana of Rāmdev. A crowned silver mask had been attached to the end of the ridge of the grave, a cloth spread over the ridge, and a garland hung over the mask. Offerings of coconuts, sweets and flowers were placed in front of it, with a box for offerings of money. Two Brahmin priests received the Bombay pilgrims' offerings, and gave them prasāda and water from Rāmdev's well. Then a policeman hurried them on to make room for more pilgrims, while one of the priests picked up the borrowed horse unceremoniously by the ear, and took it back to the store-room.

The ritual was brief, informal, hurried, and in parts even casual, but the place was clearly sacred for the pilgrims, and most of them returned to the temple two or three times a day to experience darshana again. On leaving the temple, the women joined some others singing hymns to Rāmdev, dancing and clapping in a circle as a spontaneous expression of joy. It was Mīrāben, a middle-aged woman in poor health, who had the most intense experience: during the singing she went into a trance, which became deeper when she was brought to the samādhi of Rāmdev's woman disciple Dālībāī. Triveniben, having brought her son to Rāmdev, had his head shaved in a purificatory ritual (p. 91) and put on her wedding necklace again.

At night, some of the women sat by the lake singing, hoping that if they did so for three nights in succession they would have a vision of Rāmdev – another form of darshana. All day and night there was singing, except for a break in the afternoon.

On the second day, the Bombay pilgrims visited Ramdev's family castle, and the samādhi of his guru. On the fourth day some went home, but the rest, led by Sonaben, set out to find the place marked by five trees, where Rāmdev had performed miracles which convinced five sceptical Muslims from Mecca. After an afternoon's ride in two bullock carts, holding blankets over their heads to keep off the sun, they were lost. However, this year's events were being filmed by the University of Wisconsin, and the film crew's jeep, found them and brought them to the oasis with the five trees.

Most of the pilgrims, including the remainder of the Bombay group, left Rāmdevrā before the principal day, the anniversary of Rāmdev's samādhi. Many pilgrims preferred to come at some other time, to avoid the heat and the crowds. Sacred time was less important for them than sacred place. Ritual was minimal, and their main aim was to experience the presence of Rāmdev and of their fellow devotees. Women played a prominent part, and many of the pilgrims were of low caste; low-caste disciples and the woman disciple Dālibāī are a feature of the Rāmdev tradition, though high-caste people also turn to him in times of need.

Making gifts was another part of the pilgrims' experience. In addition to the money in the collection box, fees were payable for the pūjā in the temple and for borrowing the temple's silver horse. Part of the money went to the saint's kin, and part was used to maintain the resthouses and other facilities, and to run the village school, and to care for the sick and poor. Preachers at the assembly reminded pilgrims that almsgiving is one of the ways of gaining merit on a pilgrimage.

Places of pilgrimage

The temple at Ramdevra is sacred not merely because it is a temple, but because of its location. Most Hindu places of pilgrimage are on rivers, and one of the words for a place of pilgrimage, *tīrtha*, originally meant 'ford'. The most famous of all, Vārānasī or Benares, is on the greatest of Indian rivers, the Ganges or Ganga. Another, Prayāga or Allāhābād, is at the confluence of the Ganges and Jumnā. In the upper reaches of the Ganges are Gangotrī, Bādrināth, Rishikesh and Hardwār, whose sanctity attracts determined pilgrims and hardy hermits into the chilly heights of the Himālayas. Other rivers are also sacred, being regarded as manifestations of the heavenly Ganges. Water, being a natural cleansing agent and essential to life, is a symbol of sanctity, and for Hindus especially it represents the washing away of sins and entry into new life. Even parched Rāmdevrā has its sacred well whose water is drunk by pilgrims.

Some holy places are on the sea, such as Dwārkā, where Krishna died, Cape Comorin on the southern tip of India, or Rāmeshwaram between India and Sri Lanka. Others are on mountains, such as Kailāsha, Shiva's home in the Himālaya, Mount Abū in Rajasthan, and Palni in Tamil Nadu, sacred to Murugan (p. 121). Even anthills and trees can be local sacred spots.

The areas from which pilgrims come to a particular place vary greatly. While Vārānasī is the best known, and attracts pilgrims from all over India, it is by no means the place that every Hindu aspires to visit. It is primarily a Shaiva city, and a Bengali Vaishnava, for instance, would be far more interested in going to Vrindāvan, where Krishna played on the banks of the Jumna (p. 60). Holy places belong to particular deities, and Hindus are more attracted to those belonging to their own *ishta-devatā* (p. 17; p. 122). Attachment to sacred places varies according to region also: Vrindavan, though far to the west in Uttar Pradesh, is mainly a resort of Bengalis; Palni, the holy place of Murugan, is frequented mostly by Tamils. Rāmdevrā, originally a local shrine, has increased its catchment area, partly because of migration from Rajasthan to cities in other regions, but also because its reputation for cures and other boons has grown.

Hindus traditionally consider India to be a sacred land, and travel outside it to be polluting; purification rituals are prescribed for those who return from abroad. Nevertheless, places of pilgrimage have been established outside India, among emigrants and their descendants. For instance, the Tamil community of West Malaysia, whose presence there dates mainly from the early part of this century, have a shrine of Murugan (p. 121) at Batu Caves, near Kuala Lumpur, which has become the Malaysian equivalent of Murugan's hill-top shrine at Palni. A park at Bowness in Windermere has become sacred for a section of the Swāminār-āyan sect (p. 188), whose guru Muktajīvandas Swāmī was there on the day of his death in 1979. The growth of such sacred places is evidence of the vigour and adaptability of Hinduism.

Why places are sacred

The holiness of some places goes back beyond the reach of history; others can be traced back to some known historical event. The founder of Bengali Vaishnavism, Chaitanya (p. 188) was born at or near Navadvīpa in Bengal, and spent the last eighteen years of his life in Purī in Orissa; both these places are sacred to his followers. The samādhi (burial place) of a revered person often becomes a pilgrimage centre, as in the case of Rāmdev.

The sacredness of a place is often expressed mythologically. The Ganges, the most sacred of rivers, has a divine origin in the feet of Vishnu; its heavenly form can be seen in the Milky Way. It was brought to earth and led along its course by the sage

Bhagīratha, whose ascetic power enabled him to do this. His purpose was to perform the funeral rites for the sons of his ancestor King Sagara; they had been burnt to ashes by the anger of the sage Kapila. As the impact of the heavenly river threatened to destroy the earth, Shiva broke its fall with his head, so that it now flows through his hair. The sacred mountain Tiruvannamalai in Tamil Nādu is believed to have been formed from the linga of fire which was worshipped by Brahmā and Vishnu (p. 109). The same mountain has acquired additional sanctity as the abode of the saint Ramana Maharshi (p. 170). Many other Shaiva sites are said to contain lingas that have appeared miraculously. Some sites are remembered as places in which avatāras of Vishnu lived especially Rāma's city Ayodhyā (p. 9), Krishna's birthplace Mathurā, or Vrindavan where he lived as a cowherd. Places sacred to the Goddess are often associated with a myth in which her body was dismembered, different parts of it falling in different parts of India.

Not only well-known pilgrimage sites but many local shrines have myths about their origin. In one village in Gujarat, the story goes that a herdsman used to tie his cows at night to a certain tree, but found that they yielded no milk. One night he watched them, and saw them discharging their milk into the ground. He dug, and found a linga, which the cows had been worshipping in their own way; he undertook to worship it, and it was round this miraculous linga that the local Shaiva temple was built (Pocock, 1973: 83f.). Some people have been instructed by a god in a dream to found a temple in a certain place, and some terrace houses in British cities have become holy for devotees of Sathya Sai Baba (b.1926) because his miracle of materialising sacred ash has occurred in them (p. 183).

The motives of pilgrims

The travellers to Rāmdevrā had various motives, and this is true of many places. Some pilgrims come to ask for a cure, for the birth of a son, or some other boon. Some come in fulfilment of a vow; a mother, for instance, may have promised the deity of the place that if her sick child recovered she would perform a pilgrimage and make an offering. Another purpose is purification from sins, removing the effects of past evil deeds, either from the pilgrim himself or from his ancestors. The pilgrim may seek freedom from past deeds in general, or believe that some misfortune is a result of

an unknown sin committed in a previous life, and can be remedied
by washing away the sin. Or the pilgrim may seek to expiate a
specific evil deed of his present life; in this case the pilgrimage may
take a particularly arduous form, such as following a prescribed
route round the sacred place, touching the ground with one's body
all the way.

Sacred places are especially appropriate for certain life-cycle
rituals. Initiation with the sacred thread may be performed there,
and so may the ritual shaving of the head (p. 91; p. 95; p. 144).
Rites for the dead are performed at Vārānasī and other places on
the Ganges; according to the myth, the river was brought to earth
for this very purpose (p. 147). Many people go to the banks of the
Ganges to die, and even ask to be lowered into the water so that
they may die in contact with it; they are then cremated on its
banks. The ashes of those who die elsewhere may be sent to be
thrown into the Ganges or some other river. Places sacred to Shiva
and the Goddess, such as Vārānasī, are often connected with
death, and with salvation from the round of rebirth; people also
resort to them for cures, and to obtain sons.

However, it is not only for specific needs or occasions that
people go on pilgrimage. They may look on it as a way of gaining
merit or prosperity in general, or as an expression of devotion;
they may wish to have darshana of a deity (p. 106), or to enjoy for
a time the bliss of the deity's presence which they long to enjoy
eternally.

The temple as a sacred place

Sacred places exist not only at centres of pilgrimage but in every
village, in the form of temples and shrines. Even a home shrine,
which may only be a shelf in the kitchen, is a sacred place on a
small scale, to be kept pure as a place where a deity manifests
himself and receives worship. A temple is a sacred place on a
larger scale; the same word *mandir* may refer to either.

The central part of a temple for ritual purposes is the shrine,
called the *garbha-griha* (literally 'womb-house'), containing the
image or linga (p. 109). This is typically a small, windowless
chamber with a doorway on the western side. Inside, the walls are
plain; but the outside and doorway may be eleborately carved,
and it is surmounted by a spire or peak (*shikhara*), so that the
central point of the temple is visible from a distance. It is
approached through a hall (*mandapa*), in which the worshippers

stand; they can have darshana of the deity, and receive prasāda (p. 107) but only the priest enters the shrine. The shrine is at the eastern end of the hall, which may be extended round it so that worshippers can walk clockwise round the deity without entering the shrine.

Symbolically, the temple can be seen as a complete world, in which the peak which marks its ritual centre represents the mythical mountain Meru at the centre of the world. It can also be seen as a living person; what we see first of a person, as of a temple, is the outside, but within, in the darkness of the shrine, 'hidden in the cave of the heart' as the ancient texts say, is the deity which animates it and gives it purpose.

From a functional point of view, the temple houses the image and provides for its worship. Besides the shrine and hall, there may be lesser shrines of Ganesha and other deities who are worshipped before the main deity. Large temples, founded by wealthy kings, may have halls for dancing or for the recitation of texts, gardens, tanks, sheds for processional chariots, (which are like mobile temples in which the deity gives darshana to the neighbourhood at festivals), stables for elephants, schoolrooms, libraries and offices. In the great temples of South India, these are surrounded by defensive walls, with gateways surmounted by massive towers (*gopuram*) overtopping the peak which marks the shrine.

Such a temple may show a set of spaces whose sacredness diminishes with their distance from the centre. The shrine is entered only by Brahmin priests, and even they must be free from pollution by birth or death, and have bathed and put on clean clothes (pp. 66–8). Formerly, only Brahmins could enter the hall in front of the shrine, and Untouchables could not enter the temple precincts at all. These restrictions were removed by law in 1939, but even now non-Hindus are barred from the inner areas of some temples, and Hindus do not enter some temples if they are polluted by a birth or death in the family, or by menstruation (p. 47).

Such a hierarchy of spaces is not usual in British temples, where people move freely around a large hall, except perhaps for a curtained shrine which is only entered by the priest and his assistants (Knott 1986: 64–71) (p. 43). There may also be an open fireplace, with a canopy leading to a flue, for havan or homa (p. 108). For some occasions a sacred space may be formed temporarily in a hall or in the open air, by setting up a portable shrine or fireplace. Non-Hindus are generally welcome if they show interest and respect, and adhere to one basic rule of purity which applies to all temples: remove one's shoes before entering. A British temple may be part of a larger building which includes a kitchen, meeting rooms, priest's quarters, toilets, or other facilities; shoes may be worn inside the building, but are left outside the temple itself.

Sacred places and the omnipresence of God

If God is everywhere, or if God is to be found in the heart, why go to sacred places to find him (p. 180). This is not just a question raised by non-Hindus; it has been asked many times from within the tradition. The fifteenth-century devotional poet Kabīr (p. 186) said:

> Kabīr, they all go to the temple
>   and there they bow their heads –
> But God dwells within the heart,
>   so fasten yourself there! (Vaudeville 1974: I, 286)

In the eighteenth century Rāmprasād Sen, a Bengali devotee of the goddess Kālī (p. 121), said he needed no other refuge than her feet (p. 107):

> What have I to do with Vārānasī? Kālī's feet are places of pilgrimage enough for me. Meditating on them deep in the lotus of my heart, I float on an ocean of bliss.

Within Hinduism there are many views on sacred places, and those for whom they have no meaning are not obliged to go to them. It is possible to be a Hindu without entering a temple, let alone going on pilgrimage; the cave of the heart is also a sacred place.

Teaching Ideas

Early Years

(a) Journeys. Turn the case study into a simple story of a pilgrimage journey, bringing details to the fore which would interest younger children e.g. some of the characters, the country and its climate, modes of transport, the time the journey took. Use the story to introduce simply some of the reasons why the pilgrims made the journey and incorporate an account of some of their devotions. Activities can be selected from those listed on pp. 35–6.

(b) Buildings. Begin from pupils' own experience (if any) of places of worship, collecting information about the places and anecdotes about what children did and felt during visits. A Hindu temple in Britain can be introduced visually using slides and/or pictures, for example, from the resource pack *The Hindu Mandir*.

Middle Years

(a) Water. Possibilities for the inclusion of material from Hinduism in a topic on water have already been mentioned (p. 8). Material on the association of pilgrimages with rivers and with the sea and on the myth of the descent of the Ganges can be incorporated into this work (pp. 146–7). Appropriate passages can be simplified and used as on pp. 31–2. The example used on p. 32 is also on the subject of pilgrimage.

(b) Places of Worship. A visit to a Hindu temple can be followed up by children's responses in poetry and art-work. These can express the theme of 'sacred place' very effectively. See pp. 44–55 for details of organising a visit to a Hindu temple. Audio-visual material is second best to a visit, but nevertheless can be effective if used imaginatively (see pp. 27–30). Examples of audio-visual materials dealing with pilgrimage and temples are given below.

Adolescence and Post-16

(a) Pilgrimage, reasons and motives. Using our case study, preferably in conjunction with the Open University video *Pilgrimage in the Hindu Tradition*, ask groups to list the main reasons and motives the pilgrims had for making their journey. Some of these will centre round the fulfilment of vows, others are concerned with life-cycle rites, with giving thanks or asking for blessing. Note the significance of *darshana*, experiencing the presence of the divine through seeing an image of a god or saint, or visiting his *samādhi*. Observe how various activities are concerned with the accumulation of merit or the removal of sin. Note too the importance of experiencing the presence of fellow devotees as well as the special opportunity, in this case, for women and for members of lower castes to take an important part in devotions. These reasons and motives can be used as a checklist when looking at another

example of Hindu pilgrimage, e.g. the Central Television programme *Pilgrimage* in the 'Believe It Or Not' Series.
(b) Pilgrimage in two traditions. Groups can compare Hindu
pilgrimage with pilgrimage in one other religious tradition. Are
there any common patterns e.g. association with vows and with
'practical' goals? Are there any common issues, e.g. the paradox of
having a sacred place and yet believing in the omnipresence of
God (see p. 150, p. 180)? What features are distinctive to pilgrimage in the Hindu tradition and in the other religion being studied?
(c) Sacred place: symbol and myth. Material from pp. 148–9 can
be used to examine the symbolism of the Hindu temple and its
association with mythology. Das, *Temples of India* introduces
sixteen major Hindu temples in India, together with their mythology. Many of these are important pilgrimage centres. Groups
can take a particular site and assemble information and visual
material on its myths. There is scope here for artwork and poetry
and for audio-tape 'documentary' programmes. Pupils may be
able to share knowledge of the mythology of place from other
societies.

Resources

Pupils' Books
Yogeshananda, *The Way of the Hindu*; Bennett, *Buildings*, 'Explor-
ing Religion' series, Bailey, *Religious Buildings and Festivals*, 'Reli-
gion in Life' series; Collinson and Miller, *Believers: Worship in a
Multifaith Community*; Mayled, *Pilgrimage, Buildings*, 'Religious
Topics' series; Das, *Temples of India* (Echo Books); Bahree, *Hindu
World* and *Hinduism*.

Audio-Visual

Slides: see various sets on temples listed under the Bury Peerless
Collection p. 219; *Hindu Worship* (Slide Centre); Pilgrimage to
Vārānasī, (Farmington).
Audio-tape/radio: *The Hindu Temple* (Open University); *Coventry's
Square Mile* (BBC Radiovision); *Places of Worship* (BBC Radio-
vision); *Places of Pilgrimage* (BBC audio-tape); Resource Pack *The
Hindu Mandir*, Avon.
Video: *Pilgrimage in the Hindu Tradition* (Open University); *Aspects*

of Hinduism, (Videotext); *Pilgrimage,* 'Believe It Or Not' (Central TV).
Film: *An Indian Pilgrimage: Ramdevra* (University of Wisconsin). Distributed by Scottish Central Film Library.

Further reading

Michell (1977); Killingley (1984); Binford (1976); Knott (1986a).

Note

1   The pilgrimage described here can be seen in the film *An Indian Pilgrimage: Ramdevra,* made by University of Wisconsin South Asia Film Project, distributed by Scottish Central Film Library (p. 236). Excerpts from the film are included in the Open University video cassette *Pilgrimage in the Hindu Tradition.*

12

Sacred Literature

We have referred to Hindu literature several times already, since rules of behaviour are described in the literature of dharma, myths are told in the epics, purānas and other texts, and texts are recited in ritual. There is, however, no single body of literature which can be called the 'Bible' of Hinduism; different Hindus are familiar with quite different texts. It would have been misleading to begin the study of Hinduism by discussing texts, as this would have suggested that the texts laid down the norms for all Hindus.

We shall approach the subject of Hindu literature through the autobiography of someone whose experience was partly shaped by the literature known to him, but who also helped to shape today's attitudes to that literature (Gandhi, 1927).

Case study: Mohandas Gandhi

Mohandās Gāndhi (1869–1948) – later known, against his will, as the Mahātmā ('great-souled') – was born in the Kathiāwār peninsula of Gujarat in Western India. As the name Mohan-dās, meaning 'servant of the charmer (Krishna)', implies, his family were Vaishnavas. They were of a merchant caste[1] but his father and grandfather served the rulers of the small state of Porbandar, on the Kathiawar coast, as Dewan. The term *dewan* can refer to the prime minister of a ruler, or to a wealthy person's business manager; in a small state such as Porbandar, whose affairs were largely controlled by a British official, the Political Agent, the Dewan's functions were something between the two. When Mohandas was seven, his father was appointed as assessor to a court set up to settle disputes between rulers and their tenants. For this appointment he had to move to Rājkot, a larger town, where Mohandas went to school, and where he was also married at the age of thirteen.

English was the main medium of instruction in the upper part of the school, and there was a choice between learning Sanskrit and learning Persian. Many of the boys chose Persian because it was easier and the teacher more lenient. Mohandas found the amount of rote-learning needed for Sanskrit too burdensome and started to switch to Persian, but the Sanskrit teacher, Krishnashankar Pāndya, persuaded him to continue, saying: 'How can you forget that you are the son of a Vaishnava father? Won't you learn the language of your own religion?' He promised to help him through the difficulties, and told him it would become interesting later on. Mohandas persevered with Sanskrit, though he never became proficient in it and would be the last to claim that he had. He remembered Krishnashankar with gratitude in his autobiography, for he valued his teaching as an introduction to Hindu sacred literature, and considered Sanskrit the key to a knowledge of the Indo-Aryan vernaculars, such as Bengali, Gujarati, Hindi and Marathi.

Even without the Sanskrit classes, he would have had some superficial acquaintance with Sanskrit literature since many Sanskrit words are used in the vernaculars also, the texts he heard recited would not have been totally meaningless to him. His father, though having little formal education, took up the recitation of the *Bhagavad-Gītā* towards the end of his life, on the advice of a learned Brahmin friend; but Mohandas did not learn it till much later. In the Rajkot house, on the 11th of each half-month (p. 135), part of the *Bhāgavata Purāna* was recited – a text filled with devotion to Krishna. Mohandas, however, did not find the reciter inspiring.

What did inspire him was the epic of Rāma, in the Hindi version by Tulsī Dās, which was recited by a famous devotee of Rāma during his father's last illness. Later, the orderly character of Rāma appealed to him far more than the capricious Krishna. He also learnt from his nurse to recite the name of Rāma as a protection against ghosts and spirits (p. 108). This laid the foundation of his habit of reciting the name of Rāma at moments of personal crisis, including his own death. Before he was seven he had learnt a prayer, the *Rāma Rakshā* ('Rāma's protection'), and recited it every morning after his bath; but he wrote later that the reason was not faith in the prayer so much as pride in his pronunciation. Besides the story of Rāma, he was deeply moved by the Puranic story of Harishchandra, which he saw performed as a play, and by the story of Shravana, who was so devoted to his blind parents that he carried them on a pilgrimage (p. 117, p. 164).

He also tells us that he found the *Laws of Manu* among his father's books. This book begins with a mythological chapter on the origin of the world, and goes on to describe the dharma – the nature and duties – of various kinds of people according to their varna and stage of life (p. 78, p. 97). He found the mythology incredible, and was puzzled by the differences between the rules on diet in the book and the practices with which he was familiar. A cousin whom he consulted on these problems merely told him he would understand when he grew up.

It was not from books that Mohandas had his grounding in Hinduism, but from the people round him: his stern father, his pious mother who visited the temple daily, his cousins, and friends of the family. Temple worship did not appeal to him, however; its glitter and pomp, and the imagery of love and beauty used in the Pushti-Mārga form of Vaishnavism (p. 188), were contrary to his ascetic temperament. His religious development was a lone quest for a faith which would match his moral convictions; and though his early life presented him with many guides, he never became an unquestioning follower of any of them.

It was when he was a twenty-year-old law student in London that Gandhi first read the *Bhagavad-Gītā*, the text that he was later to call his spiritual reference book. He read it not in Sanskrit or Gujarati but in English, in Sir Edwin Arnold's verse translation which remained his favourite. In England, and later in South Africa, he met people interested in Hinduism who assumed that he was familiar with its scriptures, and who asked him to explain them; he had to admit that he knew very little of them, even in translation, and was unable to read them in Sanskrit. As a lawyer in Johannesburg in 1903, he took up the study of the *Bhagavad-Gītā* in earnest, sticking verses from it on to the bathroom wall so that he could learn it while washing. In 1929, after studying the book in prison, he published a Gujarati translation, with a simple introduction and notes, in a very cheap edition. This helped to make the *Bhagavad-Gītā* into one of the best-known Hindu texts. What impressed him most about it was its teaching that salvation is to be found in a life of selfless action in the service of others, performed as a sacrifice to God, and without desire for its rewards.

While in South Africa he also studied the Upanishads, again in English, but made the most of his small knowledge of Sanskrit to compare the translations with the originals. Among these, his favourite passage was the first verse of the *Īsha Upanishad*, which may be translated:

> The universe, whatever moves in the world, is to be dwelt in by God. Enjoy it by renouncing it; do not covet anyone's wealth.[2]

In a speech in 1937, Gandhi said that if all other Hindu texts were reduced to ashes, and this one verse was remembered by Hindus, Hinduism would live for ever.

By selecting this verse, Gandhi declared that true Hinduism was directed outwards to the world, rather than inwards to the God who is hidden in the cave of the heart. Hindu literature is vast, and its meaning is not always plain; those who expound it must select and interpret, and may find very different messages in it.

The variety of Hindu literature

Mohandas Gandhi was an exceptional person in many ways, but his early experience of Hindu literature was not untypical. He was familiar with the sound of Sanskrit recitation, and was aware of some of the great Sanskrit texts; but it was from plays and recitations in vernacular languages that he learnt many of the traditional themes. There is no sharp divide for Hindus between sacred and secular literature, and traditional ideas and stories are transmitted by troupes of actors as well as by reciters and storytellers. It is not so much the written texts as the sound of them, spoken or sung, that counts most in the experience of Hindus, and to know them thoroughly is to memorise them, as Mohandas did the *Bhagavad-Gītā*. Most texts are in verse, the rhythms of which are recognisable even to those who do not know the language in which they are composed.

The literature of Hinduism is endless, since some texts have been current since the second millennium BCE and others are quite recent, while more are no doubt still being added by vernacular poets. Vernacular texts are little known outside the region where their language is spoken, though Tulsī Dās' poem of Rāma, in Hindi, is famous enough to have been heard by Gandhi in Gujarat. Some of the Sanskrit literature, on the other hand, is known in all regions, though only to a few, mainly Brahmins; this literature is also the source of many of the ideas, words and stories current in the vernacular languages, helping to give unity to the multilingual tradition.

Shruti and smriti

The Sanskrit literature of Hinduism is traditionally divided into *shruti*, 'hearing', and *smriti*, 'memory, tradition'. The shruti texts are the Veda, which is said to be eternal, breathed out by God at the beginning of each cosmic day (p. 137). They thus have no authors, according to tradition; the ancient sages or rishis did not compose them but received them thanks to their supranormal insight, and then passed them on to others by reciting them. The texts were handed on from one generation of reciters to another orally, the pupil repeating the words and their intonation exactly as he heard them from the teacher. Though writing has been known in India from the last few centuries BCE (to say nothing of the Harappan writing system of pre-Vedic times, before about 1500 BCE), it has always been considered better to recite a Vedic text from memory, not from a written page. Even if we do not accept the idea that the Veda is eternal, we can understand why these texts should be called shruti, 'hearing': for thousands of years they have been received and preserved in the form of sound.

The smriti texts, unlike the Veda, are not eternal. They embody traditions that have been current at various times; but legend attributes them to authors with superhuman powers of knowledge, which gives them very high authority.

The Veda

Historians generally attribute the Veda to the Āryans who invaded north-west India in the second millennium BCE, and their descendants who extended their culture over northern India, becoming increasingly integrated with the indigenous population. Its composition took about a thousand years. It is sometimes referred to as the Four Vedas, since it consists of four collections, the *Rig-Veda, Yajur-Veda, Sāma-Veda* and *Atharva-Veda*; sometimes only three Vedas are counted, the last being omitted. The word *veda* means 'knowledge', and the collections provided different classes of priests with the knowledge they needed for their functions in the increasingly elaborate Aryan ritual. The *Rig-Veda* contains the hymns recited by the principal priest; the *Yajur-Veda* contains verses and prose formulae spoken by the priest who carried out the manual work of the ritual; and the *Sāma-Veda* contains verses with tunes, to be sung by a specialist in chant. The *Atharva-Veda* was learnt by a class of priests who conducted rituals for private purposes, such as cures, curses, or success in enterprises; these were outside the main ritual, which is why the *Atharva-Veda* is not always counted. These four collections of *mantras*, words to be spoken or sung in the ritual, mainly in verse, constitute the earliest layer of the Veda.

In time, each of the Vedas came to include discussions of the ritual and its purpose. These discussions, called *brāhmanas*, constitute a second layer of the Veda. A third layer, the *Āranyakas*, contains more advanced discussion of ritual matters, and a fourth, the *Upanishads*, is largely concerned with the quest for knowledge, which often involves a rejection of ritual. Besides these four layers, each Veda has its *sūtras*, brief notes on how the ritual is to be performed.

Vedic ritual is rarely performed today, but this does not make the Veda obsolete. There are still Brahmins who recite it from memory, since knowledge of the Veda is valued in itself. Some parts of it are still used, such as the Gāyatrī Mantra (p. 96), or this verse from a hymn describing the marriage of Sūryā, the daughter of the sun god, to the fire god Agni, which is used in the marriage ceremony:

> To you they first escorted Sūryā with her retinue;
> Again, Agni, give the wife to the husband, with offspring
> (*Rig-Veda* 10, 85, 38).[3]

According to the texts on dharma, only the twice-born (p. 78) are permitted to hear the Veda, and Vedic mantras are not used in the life-cycle rituals of other castes. Initiation with the sacred thread (p. 91; p. 95) is the prerequisite for learning it, though it is usually only Brahmins, and not even many of them, who learn much more than the Gāyatrī Mantra. Since knowledge of the Veda is restricted, it cannot be an effective authority for more than a very few. It is quite absent from Mohandas Gandhi's early experience.

Moreover, historians and traditional Hindus agree that the conditions presupposed by the Veda no longer apply. In the historical view, the oldest layer of the Veda was composed in north-west India among a semi-nomadic cattle-herding people, long before the growth of the city-based kingdoms of the Ganges basin which transformed North Indian culture around the sixth century BCE. In the traditional view, the Veda can only be completely followed in the first, perfect age (p. 136); in the present fallen age many of its practices can no longer be followed, and some (such as animal sacrifice) are actually forbidden. Many of the gods mentioned in the Veda, even the warrior god Indra who is the one most frequently worshipped in the hymns, are little worshipped today.

However, some of the ideas expressed in the Veda still prevail. The idea that man is a microcosm whose parts correspond to parts of the cosmos is found in one of the best-known Vedic hymns, in which man is made the origin of the world:

> The moon was born from his mind, the sun was born from his eye;
> From his mouth Indra and fire; from his breath the wind was born.
> (*Rig-Veda* 10, 90, 13)[4]

This idea, elaborated in the Brāhmanas and Upanishads, is continued in the Tantric practices, which seek to identify the initiate with the cosmos (p. 162; p. 189). Related to it is the idea, common in the Brāhmanas, that the aim of ritual is to build a person a new body; this aim is found in the funeral rites, and in the building of a temple (p. 97; p. 149). The most pervasive contribution of the Veda to Hindu thought is the idea that all phenomena are manifestations of one original conscious being:

> In the beginning the world was only a self, in the form of a man
> (*Brihadāranyaka Upanishad* 1, 4, 1)[5]

In the Upanishads and later, the One which is the source of all is often called *Brahman* (p. 173), a word which can also refer to the Vedic ritual and to the Veda itself.

Smriti literature

Among the smriti or traditional texts, the longest and most widely influential is the *Mahābhārata*. It is the longest poem in the world, in nearly 100,000 verses. Its core is the story of a dynastic war between two branches of the descendants of King Bharata, at the beginning of the Kali Age (p. 136). Most of the poem, however, is not directly concerned with this heroic theme. Characters in the main story tell further stories, and stories within stories; and besides these stories there are discourses on morality, statecraft, religion and other matters. The poem seems to have grown, over a period of centuries – perhaps 400 BCE to 400 CE – into an encyclopaedia of ancient Indian traditions.

Many passages in the *Mahābhārata* are substantial pieces of literature in their own right; the most famous of them is the

Bhagavad-Gītā. The *Gītā*, as it is often called, comes at a dramatic point in the story, where one of the heroes, Arjuna, realising that he is about to fight against his own kinsmen and elders, lays down his weapons. His charioteer Krishna, who is also God in human form (p. 119), persuades him to fight: at first by appealing to his dharma as a Kshatriya, but afterwards by placing Arjuna's problem in a wider, cosmic context. All action, he explains, belongs not to us but to God; it is not for us to decide what to do or what not to do, but to act according to our dharma and to make each action a sacrifice to God. The most dramatic part of the poem is the vision of the whole universe in Krishna's body, which fills Arjuna with awe and then terror. This vision, Krishna explains, can only be won by devotion such as Arjuna has for him. The *Bhagavad-Gītā* soon became one of the most important texts, and commentaries were written on it from various points of view. In the twentieth century it has won fresh popularity through translations and commentaries in many languages, including English, of which Mohandas Gandhi's is one. Its ideal of selfless action inspired the movement for Indian independence, and it is often used as a class text for instruction in Hinduism.

Another epic, the *Rāmāyana*, tells the story of Rāma, who went into voluntary exile to fulfil his father's rash promise, followed by his wife Sītā. The story has been retold in many languages, and performed by actors and puppets in many versions in India and South-East Asia (p. 34). Part of its significance lies in the fact that Rāma is not only a supremely righteous prince but an avatāra of Vishnu, and is worshipped by many Hindus as their chosen deity (p. 119).

Also classed as smriti are the eighteen Purānas, which contain mythology, legendary history, instructions on dharma and ritual, and hymns in praise of the gods. Among them, the *Bhāgavata Purāna* or *Shrīmad Bhāgavata* is the most influential, as it is the scripture of many worshippers of Krishna; *bhagavat*, 'bountiful', is an epithet of Krishna and of Vishnu. There are another eighteen secondary Purānas, and numerous local Purānas, in vernacular languages as well as Sanskrit, telling the myths of particular sacred places.

The term *smriti* is applied particularly to texts on dharma, such as the *Laws of Manu*. These cover not only criminal and personal law, but ritual, varna (p. 78), the four stages of life (p. 97), and rules of purity (pp. 66–8); these topics are also dealt with in the *Mahābhārata* and Purānas. Mohandas was not the first to note the discrepancy between these texts and current practice; over the centuries commentaries have been written which re-interpret and elaborate their meaning in the light of prevailing ideas (p. 82).

Other Sanskrit texts

There are numerous texts called *Tantras*, which teach ways of reaching freedom through a mystical understanding of the body and its relation to the universe (p. 189); many of them also teach the worship of the Goddess (p. 121). There are hymns to various gods and goddesses, such as the one recited at Mr Dutt's pūjā (pp. 103–5), and a wealth of philosophical and theological literature (pp. 176–7). Nor should we forget the commentaries which have been written on virtually all the texts we have mentioned, narrowing or widening their meaning, bringing them up to date, and interpreting them according to particular systems of thought. Since ideas in the Indian traditions are valued for their antiquity, not their novelty, the time-honoured way to promulgate one's views is to write a commentary showing that they are taught in some ancient text. Most commentaries have not been translated into English, but translators have often followed commentaries in interpreting Sanskrit texts.

Vernacular literature

Sanskrit texts can only be directly understood by a few, though the ideas in them have a far wider influence. Most Hindus are familiar with vernacular texts, whether through reading, through hearing and joining in devotional singing, or through the simple songs of wandering devotees. Literature does not always depend on literacy (p. 341).

Tamil has the longest literary tradition of India's vernaculars, and devotional poetry has been composed in it from the seventh century CE. Poets, who are also revered as saints, composed poems to both Vishnu and Shiva, showing an intense longing for God which is different from earlier devotion, and justifies the *Bhāgavata Purāna*'s claim that bhakti was born in the south. The poets, both men and women, often express their feelings in terms of a girl's longing for her lover:

> Our Krishna dark as rain cloud
>   has stolen my heart

and it has gone away with him
    all by itself. (Ramanujan 1981: 34)[6]

The art of devotional poetry was taken up in other regions, giving every Hindu a means of addressing and understanding God. The use of the vernaculars made worshippers independent of Sanskrit-speaking Brahmins, and bhakti poetry often expressly rejects the claims of ritual and of learning. Kabīr (p. 186) said:

Reading book after book the whole world died
    and none ever became learned . . .
He who can decipher just a syllable of 'Love',
    is the true Pandit! (Vaudeville 1974: 308)

Several bhakti poets were of low castes, and several were women.

Vernacular literature also includes mythology, lives of saints, and religious instruction. Some works are of regional origin; others are versions of Sanskrit texts, including the many popular versions of the story of Rāma. The most popular of these is the *Rām Charit Mānas* by Tulsī Dās, which Gandhi heard.

Devotional poetry is still heard in temples and in homes. In modern cities, both in India and in Britain, Hindus meet in houses and temples for bhajans, kīrtans or satsangs – meetings for the singing of devotional songs (p. 141; p. 182; Singer 1972: 199–241). Some of the songs are by the great bhakti saints; others are easy choruses for everyone to join in. One such chorus, which was a favourite of Gāndhi, is popular among British Hindus; it calls on God by various names, beginning with some names of Rāma:

Raghupati Rāghava Rājā Rām . . . (Mahadevan 1956: 274).

The fifth Veda

While the Veda is little known and rarely understood, other texts are often said to have as much authority, or even to convey the same meaning. The *Mahābhārata* is called the fifth Veda, as it contains instructions for all human duties in the present fallen age (p. 136). In the *Laws of Manu* we read:

Any duty of any person that is laid down by Manu is fully described in the Veda, since the Veda contains all knowledge (*Manu* 2, 7).

It is believed that only a fraction of the Veda is known in the present age; anything in Manu that is not found in the current Veda, therefore, must be in the lost part.

Many texts, such as the *Bhāgavata Purāna* and the *Rāmāyana*, are said to contain the true meaning of the Veda in an easier form. The poems of the Tamil Vaishnava saints are called the Tamil Veda. The folk-memory of women, which contains the intricacies of household ritual, is called the fifth Veda (Stevenson 1920: xiii). Hindu teachers often say: 'It says in the Veda', without being able to quote chapter and verse; whatever they feel to be true, must be part of that eternal store of knowledge.

Knowledge of the words of the Veda is not always prized. To humble those who prided themselves on their learning, the Marathi saint Jñānadeva or Dnyāndev[7] miraculously taught a buffalo to recite the Veda. Besides, the Veda itself says that true wisdom is not to be found in knowledge of words. An Upanishad, speaking of the person who seeks true wisdom, says:

> Let him not ponder many words, for that wears out the voice
> (*Brihadāranyaka Upanishad* 4, 4, 21)[8].

Teaching Ideas

Early Years

Hindu religious literature is best introduced through stories. See pp. 126–7 for sources of Hindu stories and p. 123 for teaching ideas. See also pp. 35–6 for a suggested cycle of children's activities for use in working with story. Sources for two stories which inspired Gandhi as a child are as follows: Harishchandra: Amar Chitra Katha No. 17, *Harischandra*; Gavin, *Stories from the Hindu World*, 1986.
Shravana: 'The Pilgrims' in Awasty, R., *Stories of Valour*, Nehru Library for Children 16, New Delhi, National Book Trust, India.

Middle Years

(a) The topic is best approached through story, though the names of major texts from which stories are selected can be introduced. (See pp. 126–7 for sources and pp. 35–6 and p. 124 for teaching ideas.) The following sources are also suggested. O'Flaherty, *Hindu Myths* is a rich source, though teachers will need to modify stories for use with children. For example, the myth of the dismemberment of Purusha (the primeval man) in order to create the four varnās ('classes') of society (p. 78) (O'Flaherty, 1975: 27f) can be adapted as an example of material from the Veda. Amar

Chitra Katha No. 20, *The Mahabharata* gives a brief outline of the epic while Rao, *The Mahabharata*, is a good condensed version of parts of the text. Amar Chitra Katha No. 127, *The Gita*, gives the storyline of the book in comic strip format. Sources for *Rāmāyana* stories are given in Chapter 9. The Amar Chitra Katha series (p. 206) includes a selection of myths from Puranic sources, e.g. No. 29 *Shiva Pārvatī*; No. 89 *Ganesha*; No. 160 *Tales of Vishnu*). See also the Bala books (p. 207).

(b) Drama can be employed to highlight some of the uses and functions of Hindu scripture. Incidents from selected stories can be dramatised and linked together by a paurānika (see Chapter 9) in order to bring out points such as:

(i)   the *sound* of the text is itself edifying
(ii) stories can have both an entertainment and a spiritual value
(iii) stories can be interpreted in order to meet the moral and religious needs of the listeners (pp. 114–6).

Adolescence and Post-16

(a) GCSE syllabuses in Hinduism require pupils to know the main divisions (a mnemonic: s*h*ruti, '*h*earing'; s*m*riti, '*m*emory') of Hindu religious literature and the names and themes of the major texts. This information is provided above. It is important that students are not given the impression that most Hindus are likely to want or need to be familiar with the full range of sacred literature in their own tradition. In this connection the account of Gandhi's experience of Hindu religious literature (pp. 154–7) should be useful.

(b) The use of sacred literature in devotional practice can be illustrated by using audio-visual material. Videotext's *Aspects of Hinduism* (p. 229) includes domestic and temple worship and a wedding. Emphasis can be placed on the oral transmission and use of sacred literature in devotional practice as well as on the reading of texts. The importance of devotional hymns (bhajans) can also be noted. The filmstrip and audio-tape *A Hindu Pūjā* includes extracts (in Sanskrit and English) from Hindu literature used in pūjā (p. 223).

(c) Older pupils may enjoy reading and discussing extracts from Hindu texts. Especially recommended are Wendy O'Flaherty's selections published by Penguin – *Hindu Myths* (1975) and *The Rig Veda* (1981). Penguin also publish a selection from the *Upanishads* freely translated by Juan Mascaró (1965). The Upanishads are also translated by R. E. Hume, *The Thirteen Principal Upanishads*, London, OUP, 1921. There are plenty of English translations of the *Bhagavad Gita* including those by Mascaró (Penguin, 1962), Swami Prabhavananda and Christopher Isherwood (entitled *The Song of God*, Mentor, 1954), R. C. Zaehner in *Hindu Scriptures*, F. Edgerton, *The Bhagavad Gītā*, and A. C. Bhaktivedanta Swami Prabhupada (entitled *Bhagavad-gītā as it is*, abridged edition, Bhaktivedanta Book Trust, 1968/1975). Many of the sources of Epic and Puranic literature aimed at younger children can also be enjoyed by older students and adults (p. 161; pp. 126–7).

Three good collections of bhakti poetry are *Speaking of Shiva* (Ramanujan 1973) (Lingāyat), *Hymns for the Drowning* (Ramanujan, 1981) (Tamil Vaishnava) and *In Praise of Krishna* (Dimock and Levertov 1968) (Bengali Vaishnava).

Donald Butler's *Many Lights* (p. 217) includes a useful anthology of Hindu literature ('versions' rather than translations).

Further reading

Gandhi (1927); Ramanujan (1973); Zaehner (1966); O'Flaherty (1981).

Notes

1   The word *gāndhi* means a dealer in perfumes or spices, and is a common surname in Gujarat. The Prime Ministers Indira Gandhi (1917–1984) and her son Rajiv Gandhi (b.1944) take their surname from the former's husband, a Parsi, and are not related to Mohandas.

2   For a full translation of this short Upanishad see Zaehner (1966: 165–7); Hume (1921: 362–5).

3   For the full hymn see O'Flaherty (1981: 267–71).

4   For the full hymn see O'Flaherty (1981: 30f.); Zaehner (1966: 8–10). This hymn contains the earliest mention of the four varnas.

5   For the full passage see Zaehner (1966: 35–9); Hume (1921: 81–6).

6   Ramanujan uses the name Kannan, the Tamil form of Krishna's name; we have replaced it with well-known Sanskrit form.

7 The spelling Dny- gives a clearer idea of the initial sound, but Jñ- is more usual in Western publications.

8 See Zaehner (1966: 73); Hume (1921: 143).

13

Theology and Philosophy

For most Hindus, ideas such as brahman (p. 122) or moksha (p. 15) do not need to be argued about or justified. Nevertheless, in Hinduism as in other religious traditions, there are those who specialise in discussing such ideas. We can call them Hindu theologians, if by 'theology' we understand the presentation of received religious ideas in a systematic manner. On the other hand, since such specialists rely where appropriate on reason and knowledge which is available to all, we may call them Hindu philosophers. The distinction between theology and philosophy is a Western one, and not part of the Indian tradition; many Hindus prefer to speak of philosophy rather than theology, feeling that 'theology' implies uncritical acceptance of tradition.

We begin this chapter with a person who has spent his life studying Hindu thought and interpreting it both to Hindus and to Westerners. His selection and interpretation of ideas is based on one particularly influential school of Hindu thought, which is accepted by many Hindus though not by all (Mahadevan 1956).[1]

Case study: T. M. P. Mahadevan

Professor T. M. P. Mahadevan was a distinguished academic philosopher. He was educated at a school in Madras run by the Ramakrishna Mission (p. 190), graduated in Madras University, and spent his teaching career there. His philosophical commitment was to the Hindu school known as Advaita Vedānta, which the Ramakrishna Mission seeks to propagate.

Vedānta is the name of a branch of thought which is devoted to interpreting the Upanishads (p. 159; p. 177); the word *vedānta*, meaning 'end of the Veda', can also refer to the Upanishads themselves, since they represent the culmination of Vedic thinking. The central topic of the Upanishads is Brahman, the ultimate cause of the universe. Mahadevan describes Brahman as the 'one all-pervading and all-transcending spirit which is the basic reality – the source and ground of all things' (Mahadevan 1956: 22–3). He further explains that while the wise realise Brahman as the impersonal Absolute, Brahman is also referred to as God – conventionally spoken of as masculine, though it is as appropriate to call God Mother as Father. Vedānta is concerned with understanding Brahman.

There are several schools of Vedānta, which attempt to answer questions about Brahman which the Upanishads leave obscure. Advaita Vedānta, the school to which Mahadevan and many other modern Hindu teachers belong, is the oldest extant, and the most influential; it was formulated by Shankara around 700 CE,[2] and elaborated by his successors.

Shankara takes his stand on certain statements in the Upanishads, which identify Brahman with the universe, and also with the self which is the underlying conscious principle in each of us. It is because he holds that nothing besides Brahman has any reality of its own that his system is called Advaita, 'without duality'.

Mahadevan often sums up Advaita Vedānta by quoting a line of Sanskrit verse which he translates:

> Brahman is real; the world is an illusory appearance; the individual soul is Brahman alone, not other (Mahadevan 1956: 141).

To call the world an illusory appearance does not mean that it is just like a dream; as Shankara points out, dreams are inconsistent, while the world follows consistent laws. But it is finite and changeable, and our knowledge of it is finite and liable to contradiction. The one knowledge which cannot be contradicted, and which never changes, is our knowledge of our own existence; each one of us is intuitively aware of himself or herself. Our knowledge of ourselves is partially false, however, because we identify ourselves with a particular body and personality which are subject to birth, death and other changes. If we could get rid of this false way of viewing ourselves, we would be intuitively aware of the pure, unchanging self which is not other than Brahman. As well as analysing the way in which the world appears to exist, Advaita Vedānta shows how we can free ourselves from the world and reach this intuitive awareness of Brahman. Such knowledge is moksha (salvation or release), since it is only our false knowledge that binds us to the round of rebirth (samsāra) (p. 15; p. 173).

Mahadevan's commitment to Advaita Vendānta was in no sense merely academic. He not only studied it as a subject but lived it as a way of life and a spiritual discipline; he regarded it not as a theory but as the experience of the highest truth. 'Strictly speaking', he says,

> Advaita is not a system in the sense of a set of 'closed' doctrines. Its primary aim is to break through all limited views of reality and lead the aspirant to the plenary experience of the Absolute which is limitless (Mahadevan 1956: 141).

The experience of the oneness of all things, including one's own self, is for him the final goal of Advaita, and also the ultimate confirmation of its truth.

His commitment also carried him outside academic work, in which his achievement is considerable, into popularisation. He was the author of many books for the general public, including *Outlines of Hinduism*, written originally for Indian students; a contribution to the collection *Vedānta for Modern Man*, published in New York; and a series of translations from Shankara published annually on Shankara's birthday. He also founded a centre in Madras which organises talks and meditation classes.

Mahadevan's work of popularisation bears witness to his belief that Advaita is not just for an intellectual élite. Ideas about the essential unity of all things, and explanations of how the world presents an appearance of multiplicity despite this unity, may seem difficult when presented as theories. But Mahadevan holds that Advaita itself is 'the highest experience and not a theory' (Mahadevan 1977: 151). In other words, the oneness of all things can be known intuitively, without elaborate thought.

As an example of one who has had this experience, Mahadevan points to Shankara himself, whom he describes as an 'expert physician of the soul', who taught the unifying knowledge of Brahman which was as desperately needed in his own troubled time as in ours (Mahadevan 1961: 77). Some think that Advaita Vedanta turns away from worldly problems in its search for saving knowledge, but Mahadevan is convinced that such knowledge is essential for the well-being of society.

Shankara is remote from us in time, and known only through his Sanskrit writings. But Mahadevan also points to a teacher of our own time, Ramana Maharshi (1879–1950). Ramana (the title Maharshi means 'great sage') lived on the holy mountain of

Arunāchala or Tiruvannāmalai (p. 147) from the age of seven-
teen. Mahadevan met him several times, and found that he had
realised the truth of Advaita Vedānta without being taught by
anyone. In one of his accounts of Ramana he comments:

> It is not often that a spiritual genius of the magnitude of Srī Ramana
> Maharshi visits this earth. But when such an event occurs, the entire
> humanity gets benefited and a new era of hope opens before it
> (Mahadevan 1961: 117).

It is remarkable that the professor who devoted much of his life
to the detailed study of the complex arguments of Shankara and
other teachers of Advaita should pay such tribute to an untaught
holy man, especially as Shankara himself stresses the importance
of Vedic learning and the guidance of a guru, both of which
Ramana lacked. It is consistent, however, with Mahadevan's
view that Advaita Vedānta is not a theory but a way to what he
refers to as 'realisation', that is, the intuitive experience of the
oneness of the self with Brahman. Ramana was able to reach that
realisation unaided.

Mahadevan's *Outlines of Hinduism* presents Hindu ideas rather
than practice, and sees these ideas as culminating in Advaita
Vedanta. A third of the book is on 'The Philosophies' and, while
this section surveys a wide range of Hindu ideas, it is Advaita
which receives the longest treatment. Mahadevan reveals his
commitment at the outset in his statement that 'the summit of
religious experience is the intuition of unity' (Mahadevan, 1956:
p. 4). He also values the experience of a personal relationship with
God, and includes accounts of six Tamil devotional poets in his
book *Ten Saints of India* (Mahadevan 1961).

The vocabulary of Hindu thought

Not all Hindus accept Advaita. A follower of Chaitanya, for
instance, believes that the universe is caused and ruled by Krishna, and would not agree with Mahadevan's belief that a personal
view of God is less true than the impersonal Brahman (p. 173).
Nevertheless, there are some ideas running through the Hindu
systems which have to be understood if one is to appreciate any of
them fully, and some key terms or sets of terms which are used,
with modifications, by many or all schools. Some of these ideas
and terms date from the Veda, especially the Upanishads; others
were developed later. The following is a brief survey.

Agent and experiencer

A person[3] is related to the world in two ways: as agent and experiencer. That is, one has an output of actions which affect one's surroundings, and at the same time one receives an input of experiences, pleasant and unpleasant. As agent, one's actions (*karma*) affect not only one's surroundings but one's own character and destiny, since they give rise to good or evil fruit in this life or a future one (p. 16). Similarly, as experiencer one receives pleasant and unpleasant experiences not at random, but as the fruit of good and evil actions done in the past, whether since one's most recent birth or long before. This succession of cause and effect requires each individual to pass through an infinite series of lives, which may be in any form, human or non-human, from the god Brahmā, father of the gods (p. 121), down to a tuft of grass; even the gods are involved in the round of rebirth. The form of each embodiment is determined by previous action, not necessarily done in the immediately preceding life.

In the course of one human lifetime, one may perform actions which result in several different births, since their fruits cannot all be experienced in the same body. A simple example is the story of Bharata, a king who retired to the forest and made great progress in yoga. While doing so, however, he looked after a motherless fawn, and became so anxious about it that he was distracted from his yoga, and when he died was reborn as a fawn himself. But his earlier progress in yoga could not be fruitless, so when his life as a deer was over he was reborn as a Brahmin who knew the whole truth of Advaita without being taught – like Ramana Maharshi (*Vishnu Purāna* 2, 13; Wilson 1961: 197–203). This answers a question which is often asked by non-Hindus: how can the actions of a plant determine its future birth? It is not the actions of the plant that shape its destiny; this has been shaped already by actions in some earlier, human body.

This process of acting and experiencing, perpetuated by rebirth, is called *samsāra*. However pleasant it may be some of the time, the wise regard it as bondage, and the ultimate aim of Hindu thought is to show the way of escape from it. But this is not one's only aim.

The four aims

A person has three aims in this world: the lowest is *kāma*, meaning pleasure, the satisfaction of desires; next is *artha*, wealth and worldly power, and above that is *dharma*, the fulfilment of one's duties as determined by varna, stage of life, and other factors (p. 16; p. 78; p. 97). All these aims are legitimate, but the lower must be subordinated to the higher, so that one does not lose one's wealth in pursuit of pleasure, or gain power wrongfully. Much of a Hindu's behaviour, like anyone else's, can be accounted for by these three aims; this applies to religious as well as other behaviour. Mr Dutt's pūjā (pp. 103–5) was motivated by artha as well as dharma; the pilgrims to Rāmdevrā (pp. 141–5) expected to have fun as well as benefits such as success in business, and some came as a duty, for instance in fulfilment of a vow. They, and Mr Dutt, were also motivated by devotion (bhakti), though this is not one of the standard list of aims.

Overriding these three worldly aims is the transcendent aim of *moksha* – release from samsāra, salvation. The state is described differently by different schools, though it always includes freedom from the bondage resulting from one's previous deeds. In Advaita Vedānta, moksha is knowledge of the unity of the self and Brahman; Mahadevan calls it 'the realisation of the soul's identity with the Absolute Spirit' (Mahadevan 1956: 256). On the other hand, those sects and schools which emphasise devotion think of salvation as an eternal relationship between the self and God. The Chaitanya sect (p. 188) goes so far as to make devotion a fifth aim of man, beyond even salvation.

God, selves and nature

All existence can be summed up in three terms: God, selves and nature. Even in Advaita Vedānta, where the distinction between these terms is ultimately false, they are useful nevertheless in describing the false world in which we find ourselves.

God

God can be referred to by various names: Brahman, the Lord (*īshvara*), the Self-existent (*svayambhū*). Shaivas regard Shiva as God, Vaishnavas Vishnu. Advaita has two ways of understanding Brahman: in relation to the world, where terms such as 'Lord' are appropriate, and as it is in itself, where any implication of personality is out of place. God is related to the world in three ways: as the cause of its origin, continuance, and cessation

(p. 123). A point of difference between the schools is whether or not God is the substance out of which things are made, as pots are made of clay (their material cause), as well as that which brings them into existence, as pots are made by a potter (their efficient cause). Advaita insists that since nothing truly is except Brahman, it must be the material as well as the efficient cause, although it does not undergo any real change. On the other hand Madhva held that nature, the material cause, is eternally separate from God (p. 187).

Selves

The self (*ātman*) in each of us is that which receives the input from all our senses, and also causes our output of actions. Whether it is pictured as a little man the size of a thumb living inside the heart (*Katha Upanishad* 6, 17), or whether it is thought of as pervading the body, it is instantly aware of whatever happens to our head or our toes. Awareness or knowledge is the essential characteristic of the self; *Brihadāranyaka Upanishad* 4, 3, 19–33 claims that even in dreamless sleep it is still aware, though it is aware of nothing but itself.

The self is also eternal and changeless; it does not undergo birth or death, as is graphically described in the *Bhagavad-Gītā*:

> Unborn, eternal, everlasting, ancient, it is not killed when the body is
> killed . . .
> Just as a man abandons his old clothes and puts on new ones,
> The embodied self abandons its old bodies and goes to new ones
> (*Bhagavad-Gītā* 2, 20; 2, 22)

The self is, however, or at least appears to be, involved in the round of birth and death through its connection with a body. Even when the body dies, the self is not thereby released, since, in its passage from one gross body – the body in the ordinary sense – to another, it carries with it some invisible luggage called the subtle body. This consists of the psychological apparatus which we shall describe under the heading of 'nature'. Through this subtle body the self experiences pleasure, pain, change, and the bondage of karma.

One question which the early texts leave uncertain is whether there are really many selves (as common sense indicates) or one. Since Advaita Vedānta holds that the self is really Brahman, it follows that there can only be one self; the common sense view is an error resulting from our connection with a multitude of false bodies. Most other systems hold that there are many selves: some in bondage, some seeking salvation, and some already in eternal communion with God.

Nature

While God and the self are beyond change, we constantly observe things that are changeable and perishable, including our own experiences and states of mind. All these are parts of what is called *prakriti* meaning roughly 'nature'.

Hindu thought is interested in the world primarily as something that impinges on our consciousness, rather than as existing out there by itself. Our surroundings are known to us through our five sense faculties: hearing, touch, sight, taste and smell. Nature is accordingly divided into five elements, each of which is the carrier of a particular sensation: ether carries sound, wind carries tactile sensations, fire (in the form of light) carries visual sensations, water carries flavour, and earth carries odour. Together with our five sense faculties, these elements and sensations make up the mechanism which gives us our input of experience. The output is provided by our five faculties of action:[4] speech, manipulation, locomotion, reproduction and excretion – a less obvious list than the five sense faculties, but one which is intended to sum up the ways we act on our surroundings.

Controlling the action faculties, and putting together the input received from the sense faculties, is the mind (*manas*).[5] Beyond that is the intellect (*buddhi*), which makes decisions. There is also the peculiar faculty which makes us aware of our own existence, enabling us to refer to ourselves as 'I' – the I-faculty or egoism (*ahamkāra*).

Our intellect, I-faculty, mind, sense faculties and action faculties make up our subtle body or personality, and this, together with our gross body made of the five elements, keeps us in bondage. But these can also be our means of escape from bondage, if we discipline our subtle and gross bodies and bring them under the control of the self, instead of letting them be distracted by desire or loathing for the various objects surrounding us.

This discipline or control is called *yoga*, a word originally referring to the harnessing of horses, and cognate with the English 'yoke'. The reason for using such a word is apparent from an Upanishadic passage which speaks of the self as riding in a chariot, which is the body, driven by the intellect; the mind is the reins, and the faculties are the horses. If the intellect is skilled in controlling the faculties through the mind, the self will be brought to the journey's end – salvation; but if it fails to do this, the faculties will run out of control and the self will return to the round of rebirth (*Katha Upanishad* 3, 3–9).

Nature is not uniform; it consists of three strands (*guna*), which combine in various proportions, like contrasting threads in a piece of cloth, to give the variety of phenomena which we observe, and the characters of different people. The three strands are goodness (*sattva*), which predominates in whatever is pure and clear, and in enlightened people; passion (*rajas*) in active things, and in impetuous people; and darkness (*tamas*) in heavy things, and in lazy and stupid people. Detailed descriptions of them can be found in *Bhagavad-Gīta* 14, 5–18; 17, 2–22; 18, 7–9; 18, 20–39.

The six systems

Though many of the above terms can be found in common Hindu discourse, their full meaning was worked out by exponents of various highly developed systems.

A system of thought which explains our condition and shows us the way to release from it is called a *darshana*, a view or way of seeing (the same word is used for the experience of seeing a deity, p. 106). Some systems, such as Buddhism, Jainism and materialism (all three of which existed in ancient India from about 500 BCE or earlier) reject the Veda (pp. 158–60) and are therefore called unbelieving or unorthodox (*nāstika*). There is a traditional list of six systems which are believing or orthodox (*āstika*), though they do not all make equal use of the Veda as a source of knowledge. Each of them has a basic text, composed some time in the early centuries CE, followed by centuries of commentary and development.

Two of the six, *Nyāya* (logic) and *Vaisheshika* (atomism) are effectively one system; Nyaya providing a method of enquiry and Vaisheshika providing an analysis of the world into various substances, the self being one of them. Another pair, *Sāmkhya* and *Yoga*, are also similar to each other. Sāmkhya ('reckoning, reason') usually dispenses with the concept of God, and accounts for each person's experience as an encounter between a self (which it calls *purusha*, 'man') and nature. Since we all have different experiences, and perform different actions whose fruits we receive, there must be a multitude of selves. The self is essentially conscious but not active, while nature is active but not conscious, and is analysed into the elements and the constituents of personality described above (p. 175). The highest aim of the self is to free itself from nature, and to remain conscious of nothing but itself.

The Yoga school elaborates the methods by which this freedom can be achieved. These are built on the basic idea of yoga as discipline and control; posture, breath control and meditation are used to make the body a tranquil environment for the self. Most forms of the yoga taught in the West are based on this system. Yoga admits the idea of God; not as cause of the world, as in Nyāya-Vaisheshika or Vedānta, but as an object of meditation.

The remaining two schools are both sometimes called *Mīmāmsā*, 'exegesis', since they are both concerned with interpreting the meaning of the Veda. *Pūrva-Mīmāmsā*, 'earlier exegesis', is often called simply Mīmāmsa; it interprets the Veda as a set of prescriptions for ritual. *Uttara-Mīmāmsa*, 'later exegesis', is more commonly called *Vedānta* (p. 168); it approaches the Veda as a source of knowledge about the true nature of reality and the way to salvation, and consequently is interested in the Upanishads (p. 159) far more than in the earlier layers of the Veda.

The ground-rules for the interpretation of the Upanishads are contained in the *Vedānta-Sūtra* or *Brahma-Sūtra*; but, as this consists only of brief notes, it is open to various interpretations. The Upanishads, *Vedāntā-Sutra* and *Bhagavad-Gītā* are called the three foundations of Vedānta.

There are several schools of Vedānta. Besides Advaita, which we have already looked at (p. 169), forms of Vedānta were formulated by Rāmānuja, Madhva, Vallabha (p. 187) and others, including Baladeva, a follower of Chaitanya. All these stress the personal nature of God, and man's dependence on him.

Vedānta in its various forms has prevailed over and largely absorbed the other systems, drawing its method of interpreting texts from Pūrva-Mīmāmsā, its logic from Nyāya, its analysis of nature from Sāmkhya, and its programme of discipline from Yoga.

Outside Vedānta, other schools have given systematic accounts of our relation to God and of the way to salvation. The Tamil Shaiva Siddhānta ('the system of the followers of Shiva') sees Shiva as God, on whom the selves and nature depend though he remains distinct from them; in the Kashmir school of Shaivism, on the other hand, the selves and nature are ultimately identical with Shiva.

Hindus do not necessarily subscribe to any of these schools, though some of the schools provide the doctrinal basis for major sects (pp. 187–9). All the schools apply intellectual methods to interpret texts and our condition in the world; even the anti-rationalistic Vedānta of the Chaitanya sect is based on the argument that since the Veda tells us that God has infinite powers, it is impossible for us to think about him. None of them, however, says that we can reach salvation by cultivating knowledge alone; for, without the right behaviour and affective attitudes, we cannot develop the right knowledge.

The three ways (mārga)

Modern expositions of Hinduism often refer to a set of three ways (*mārga*) to salvation: the way of action (*karma-mārga*), the way of devotion (*bhakti-mārga*) and the way of knowledge (*jñana-mārga*) (p. 116). The idea of three ways, or three yogas, is traditionally used in commentaries on the *Bhagavad-Gītā*, though they are not listed in the text itself. Different schools evaluate them differently. In Advaita Vedānta the way of action (which refers especially to ritual action) is essentially a preparation which purifies the mind, and devotion is a way of directing the mind towards God; salvation itself can only be reached by knowledge, since for the true knower action and devotion have no value. In Rāmānuja's school, action and knowledge are both preparatory to devotion, since the self finds its true meaning by devoting itself to God's service. Madhva, Baladeva and many other thinkers similarly give devotion the highest place.

Modern thinkers stress public service rather than ritual in their interpretation of the way of action. They also often think of the three ways as different paths to the same goal for people of different temperaments. Mahadevan thinks of them all as parts of the same journey (Mahadevan 1956: 84).

Hindu thought, like any other religious thought, is not static; it is constantly being adapted as ideas about ourselves and the world around us change. Modern Hindu thinkers are fascinated by scientific developments such as evolution, which corroborates the idea of a scale of being from Brahmā down to a tuft of grass (p. 172), or nuclear physics, which points to new ways of understanding nature (p. 175). Systems of thought are also to be tested by our experience; they are not there to be learnt as an intellectual exercise, but to put into practice, as ways leading out of the limitations of our worldly existence.

Teaching ideas

What we have called Hindu theology and philosophy are not explicitly part of the religious lives of most Hindus. Many of the concepts and some of the claims are implicit in popular Hindu practice, however, and some of the doctrinal positions adopted by the philosophical schools (especially the different forms of Vedānta) are mediated to ordinary people through the teachings of sects (pp.182–92). We have used some of the ideas from the chapter to relate to issues that are likely to be of more general concern to some older students.

Adolescence and post-16

(a) Who am I? An examination of views of the nature of the person in different religions and ideologies. The Hindu contribution could include the following.
(i)   All living things have indestructible souls (*ātman*), essentially equal but differentiated through *karma*, the effects of previous deeds.
(ii) The soul is limited both by the gross body and the subtle body. Release (*moksha*) is from *samsāra* – the process of acting and experiencing perpetuated by rebirth. The soul is released from both the gross and the subtle bodies.
(iii) During ordinary human life, a person has a series of legitimate goals – pleasure (*kāma*), material prosperity (*artha*), duty (*dharma*) and release (*moksha*) – which are of ascending importance and are related to some extent to the stage of life that person has reached (p. 97). In order to pursue the goal of *moksha*, a person may emphasise a particular technique or combination of techniques (see the three mārgas, p. 178).
(iv) The current state of a person (rich or poor; well or sick; happy or miserable, and so on) is consequent on conduct in previous lives.
(v)   Although each person is essentially an individual, life in society carries with it a whole range of obligations to others which are related to family, caste, stage of life (p. 63; pp. 76–80; p. 97) etc.
(vi) Advaita Vedānta (and other monistic schools) ultimately sees the individual soul as being part of Brahman, the one ultimate reality, while other schools qualify this position, some to the extent of making a logical distinction between God and the rest (nature and selves) parallel to that made in

the Semitic religions (Judaism, Christianity and Islam).

(b) Ideas of God. Groups of older students can attempt a defini-
tion of God, and then discuss the adequacy of the definitions and
issues arising from them.

(i)　If, for example, God is deemed to have personal characteristics, would these not be limiting? Can the greatest conceivable being have such limitations and still be the greatest
conceivable being?

(ii)　If God is essentially beyond human understanding, language used to speak of God must be non-literal – perhaps
metaphorical or symbolic. If this is so, why should that
language not use female imagery as well as male, or animal
as well as human? The question of whether, and in what
senses, Hinduism is polytheistic can be discussed (pp. 110–
11; p. 112; pp. 122–3).

(iii)　Is there a logical distinction between God and all else that is?
The Semitic religions (Judaism, Christianity, Islam) make
this distinction, as do the theistic schools of Vedanta.
Advaita Vedānta, however, argues the essential oneness of
the individual self and of Ultimate Reality – a oneness that is
perceived spiritually, rather than grasped logically. Is the
distinction between the two positions as clear as it seems to
be? Doesn't the Christian idea of the omnipresence of God,
for example, have a pantheistic ring about it (see p. 150)?
Also, at one level, many Advaita Vedāntists are theists,
happy to regard God as personal and as an object of worship
(p. 169). Advaita also holds that Brahman is totally *other*
than all that we observe – it is not an object of knowledge, not
subject to samsāra, not limited, not divisible, not multiple,
etc.

(c) The problem of suffering. Older students can compare ways in
which different religions attempt to explain the problem of
apparently undeserved human suffering. Care should be taken
not to be too simplistic, for the religions generally encompass
several views. Furthermore, the ideas of theologians and philosophers may not always totally agree with the experience of
ordinary religious believers.

(d) Life after death. Groups can list reasons why they think many
religious people believe that life continues after physical death.
These can be compared with reasons given from within the
religions and with those given by critics of religion. Material from
the Hindu tradition can be included, showing its essential plural-

ism as well as the main concepts and tendencies (see p. 91; p. 97).
(e) Food and philosophy. Students may be interested to know that
Hindu views of diet, food handling and cookery are influenced by
philosophical ideas about the nature of matter (p.38).

Further reading

One or more introductions to the philosophy of religion would be
useful as resources for teachers and for able pupils. One well-
written text which discusses ideas from Eastern as well as Western
religion is John Hick, *The Philosophy of Religion* (1973). Other
useful texts include T. M. P. Mahadevan, *Outlines of Hinduism*
(1956); Geoffrey Parrinder, *The Indestructible Soul* (1973); P. T.
Raju, *The Philosophical Traditions of India* (1971); Ninian Smart,
Doctrine and Argument in Indian Philosophy (1964) and R. C. Zaehner,
Hinduism (1962).

Notes

1   Much of the biographical material has been taken from an
    unpublished paper by Dr Jacqueline Suthren Hirst.

2   Mahadevan, in common with many scholars since the late
    nineteenth century, gives 788–820 as Shankara's dates. Re-
    cent research, however, places him about a century earlier.

3   Traditional writing uses the Sanskrit word *purusha*, which,
    though often translated as 'person', actually means 'man', as
    opposed to 'woman'; Hindu philosophical and theological
    writing is almost all the work of men, and reflects a masculine
    outlook. However, since modern Hindu thought recognizes
    the importance of women's experience and activity, we use
    inclusive terms here.

4   We use the word 'faculty' to translate Sanskrit *indriya*. Most
    writers in English use 'sense', which is inappropriate in
    referring to the faculties of action.

5   'Mind' in Western philosophy has a different meaning; it is
    essentially conscious, which *manas* is not, and corresponds
    approximately to the self and subtle body together.

14

Sects and Movements

The term 'sect' is somewhat loosely used with reference to Hinduism. The three broad groupings of Vaishnavas, Shaivas and Shāktas (p. 122) are sometimes called sects, but as each of these includes people following widely differing beliefs and practices, this usage is misleading. Vaishnavas, for instance, include worshippers of Vishnu himself (mainly in South India), of Krishna (mainly in the west and north-east), and of Rāma (mainly in the north). What we mean by a sect here is a group of people following a distinct set of doctrines and practices, and looking to a particular person, living or dead, as their teacher, as their authority in the interpretation of tradition, or as a manifestation of God.[1]

Our case study is based on a British Hindu who played a leading part in the rise in this country of a movement whose central figure is still living. From its own point of view, this movement is not a sect, nor is it Hindu; it brings a revelation of God to the whole world. However, it shows many features of a Hindu sect.[2]

Case study: Mr Sitaram

Mr Sītārām was a Brahmin from Tamil Nadu who had a successful career as an accountant in Burma from 1926 onwards. He and Mrs Sitaram were Shaivas, but they also took part in devotional meetings at which hymns (bhajans) to Krishna were sung. When Mr Sitaram retired from his Rangoon practice in 1963, they came to Britain and settled in Pinner, North London. There, they maintained contact with India by corresponding with friends and subscribing to Indian magazines; they also held bhajan meetings in their own home. Such meetings are popular among the urban middle class to which the Sitarams belonged, as a way of keeping in touch with tradition (p. 116; p. 163); they are also a common form of religious expression among British Hindus.

One day in 1966, Mr Sitaram read something in an Indian magazine that changed his life. It was a reivew of the first volume of the biography of a contemporary Hindu saint in Āndhra Pradesh, born in 1926, who from the age of fourteen had been recognised by an increasing number of followers as an incarnation of an earlier saint, Sāi Bābā (1868–1918), known as Shirdi Sāi Bābā from the town of Shirdi in Maharashtra where he had lived. Shirdi Sai Baba (1866–1918) had combined elements of Hindu and Muslim practice; he claimed to be an incarnation of the fifteenth-century poet-saint Kabīr, whom both Hindus and Muslims claim as their own (p. 186). The present saint, who changed his name from Sathyanārāyan to Sathya Sāi Bābā[3] to mark his oneness with his earlier manifestation, is Hindu in his forms of expression, though he recognises other religions as ways to God. He claims also to be an incarnation of Shiva-Shakti, that is, God himself, who is both male as Shiva and female as Shiva's wife or Shakti (p. 12).

From the brief review which Mr and Mrs Sitaram read, they saw that Sathya Sai Baba was a holy man, and longed to worship him by doing puja to his picture (p. 109; p. 111). They therefore wrote to a friend in Madras, asking for a picture of him. This friend did not have a picture himself, but his neighbour had just been to Sathya Sai Baba's āshram, Prasānthi Nilayam ('abode of peace') in Āndhra Pradesh, and had brought back a photograph of the saint – a man in orange robes whose kindly, smiling face was framed in a great halo of curly black hair. Moreover, the neighbour said spontaneously that she wanted this photograph to be sent to Mr and Mrs Sitaram, without even being told that they wanted one. The photograph was duly sent, and arrived in time for Sathya Sai Baba's birthday on 23 November; it was on that day that Mr and Mrs Sitaram performed their first pūjā to him, using the photograph which they had obtained in this miraculous way.

The bhajan group which met at their home soon learnt of Sathya Sai Baba, and made him its object of devotion. Within five years there were three hundred devotees in the group instead of twenty, so that Mr Sitaram had to hire a hall for bhajans, and through contact with its members, other groups took up the worship of Sathya Sai Baba. This was the beginning in Britain of what is now a well-established movement, with centres through-

out the country which attract not only South Indians like Mr and
Mrs Sitaram and Sathya Sai Baba himself, but other Hindus, and
also non-Hindus. It includes a Society for Education in Human
Values.

In 1968, Mr and Mrs Sitaram revisited India, and went to a
conference of Sathya Sai Baba's devotees in Madras. Although
they had not made any formal approach to the conference, they
were accepted as the official London delegation, and allowed to
have darshan of the saint himself. He asked them whether they
had received the photograph he had sent them – further confirmation of the miraculous nature of its acquisition.

In 1975 the expanding British movement was formally organised as a branch of the World Council of Srī Sāi Sevā ('service')
Organisations, with Mr Sitaram as its first president. He died in
1986, on Sathya Sai Baba's sixtieth birthday, while on a visit to
Prasanthi Nilayam, the world headquarters of the movement.
Shortly before he died, he told a friend that Sathya Sai Baba had
come to him, looked into his eyes and given him a final darshan
and blessing.

The guru

We have noticed that there is no single sacred place common to all
Hindus, nor a single pattern of behaviour, nor a single set of
beliefs. Neither is there a single source of authority which all
Hindus look to; different Hindus, even in the same place, follow
different authorities with different teachings on practice and
belief. Mr and Mrs Sitaram took as their authority a living
teacher, with whom they established a personal relationship
although they lived in a distant country. This relationship was
made possible by the use of photographs and the postal system,
which enabled them to have darshan of Sathya Sai Baba in his
physical absence; but this would not have come about if Sathya
Sai Baba himself had not had the power to perceive and influence
distant events.

Hindus have always respected the guru, the teacher who
imparts not merely knowledge but spiritual qualities, enabling his
pupils to perform their functions in this world, and ultimately to
reach moksha (p. 173). Since knowledge in ancient times was
handed on orally, not taken from books, the teacher was vital to
the pupil's development, and himself embodied the knowledge
and the qualities which he taught. The word *guru* has the same

origin as Latin *gravis* (whence *gravity*); both words mean 'heavy', and, in a moral sense, 'weighty, important, grave'. It is applied not only to teachers but to elder relations, as these too are worthy of the highest respect. A popular explanation of the word says that *gu* represents darkness and *ru* either light or restraint: the teacher leads from darkness to light, or restrains darkness. Another term for 'teacher' is *āchārya* literally 'man of conduct', since the teacher's function includes teaching good behaviour, to which he has to adhere himself.

One of the guru's functions is to initiate the pupil by teaching a mantra. Besides the initiation with the sacred thread, in which the Gāyatrī mantra is learnt (p. 96) various sects have their own initiations, each with an appropriate mantra; many of these are open to women and to people outside the twice-born castes.

The pupil's welfare, in this life and beyond, depends on the guru. The guru provides a way to God, and he can even be regarded as an avatāra (p. 119; p. 183). An old verse says:

> There are many gurus who will relieve a pupil of his wealth; it is hard to find the true guru who will relieve a pupil of his affliction.

To merit a pupil's trust, a guru must show evidence of his authority. This authority may be evident simply from his own personal qualities, or it may result from his having been initiated and taught by a reliable guru, and so on in a line of pupils and teachers going back to some teacher whose authority is widely accepted.

Sects

Such a succession of teachers is called a *sampradāya*, 'handing on, tradition'. This is the nearest term in Indian languages to 'sect' in the sense used here; for it is through the gurus of a particular sampradāya that the members of a sect are linked to its founder and learn its beliefs and practices.

Members of sects often mark their foreheads, especially during worship, with the mark of their sect, given at their initiation by the guru. Shaivas mark themselves with three horizontal lines, made with the fingers dipped in ashes; Vaishnavas make a U-shaped mark in a kind of white clay, with a red line down the middle. The exact form of the mark varies with different Shaiva and Vaishnava sects. This should not be confused with the *tilak* or *chāndlo* made on the foreheads of worshippers by someone performing pūjā

(p. 107), or the *tika* or *bindi* worn by women; all these are sometimes wrongly called 'caste marks'.

Some sects can only be entered through a formal initiation given by a member of a strict succession of gurus. Others are less tightly organized; it is possible to become a devotee of Sathya Sai Baba merely by accepting his miracles, even if one belongs to a religion other than Hinduism. What counts is a personal relationship with him, even at a distance, rather than any formal act or membership of an organisation. A similar relationship is enjoyed by devotees of Rāmdev (pp. 141–5), who need no initiation and no succession of gurus.

Charismatic sects

The Sai movement which Mr and Mrs Sitaram joined is formed around the supranormal personal qualities of its central figure, which sociologists call his 'charisma'. Many sects have a founder of this charismatic type, and see him as an incarnation of God or as having an unusually close relationship with God.

We have already mentioned Kabīr, of whom Shirdi Sai Baba claimed to be an incarnation. Kabīr is believed by Hindus to have been a Hindu, and by Muslims to have been a Muslim; little is certain about his life, and he is known mainly from the verses attributed to him, in a simple form of early Hindi. Many of these verses reject the claims of both Hindu and Muslim teachers, and all forms of ritual, in favour of the worship of God, whom he calls Hari or Rām, who is to be sought in the heart and not at any temple or holy place (p. 150). These verses are widely known, and some of them are included in the *Guru Granth Sahib*, the holy book of the Sikhs. Besides being generally revered as a holy man by Hindus, Muslims and Sikhs, Kabīr has a particular following, the Kabīr-panthīs, or 'people of the path of Kabīr', who say he is an avatāra of Vishnu (p. 119); one is initiated as a Kabīr-panthī by receiving a mantra from the mouth of a guru.

A sect of more recent origin is the Rādhā Soāmī Satsang. The first guru, Shiva Dayāl Singh (1818–78), who lived in Agra, is believed to be a manifestation of God. He himself is called Soāmī (an unusual spelling of *svāmī* 'master'), and his wife is called Rādhā, the name of Krishna's favourite among the cowherd girls (p. 120). *Rādhā-svāmī* can also mean 'husband of Rādhā', referring to Krishna, and the name Rādhā Soāmī is used by the sect as a name of God, and also represents the eternal sound which can be received by its devotees under the guidance of a guru. Initiates must be over twenty-five years old, and strict vegetarians; they are also selected by the guru personally. The guru is believed to be one of an endless succession of masters sent by God to lead people to himself. The sect flourishes in the Panjab, and also outside India; its spread has been facilitated by the use of English, introduced by the second and third gurus.

Charismatic sects have a special appeal for urban and overseas Hindus, especially if the charismatic figure is still living. However, continuity with the past is important to Hindus, and besides his charisma the guru may have a link with previous gurus. Sathya Sai Baba is a reincarnation of Shirdi Sai Baba, who in turn was a reincarnation of Kabīr. Kabīr is believed by Hindus to have been taught by an earlier saint Rāmānanda. The Rādhā Soāmī sect uses the poems of Kabīr, and its founder was initiated by a Vaishnava guru, although being already fully enlightened, he did not need to learn from him.

Doctrinal sects

Some sects or sampradāyas are based on a founder whose authority lies in his ability to give reliable expositions of received teachings and to refute rival interpretations of them, rather than in charisma – though he may possess this quality also. One such teacher was Rāmānuja (c. 1050–1137), a Tamil Brahmin who was one of a line of teachers devoted to Vishnu. He developed the doctrine that intense devotion (bhakti) to Vishnu is man's highest aim. His teachings were handed down by his pupils and their pupils to the present day. As priest in charge of the temple of Vishnu at Shrīrangam, he established a pattern of worship led by Brahmins but including Shūdra participants. His form of Vaishnavism, which stresses the devotees' dependence on God, and God's grace in making himself accessible to them, owes much of its inspiration to the Tamil bhakti poets. But his own writings were in Sanskrit, and strove to show, through quotations from the Upanishads, that Vaishnavism is the true message of the Veda (p. 177). Further north, in Karnātaka, Madhva established another Vaishnava sect in the thirteenth century (p. 177). Besides bhakti, he placed great importance in the guru. Since, in his view, individual souls differ from one another, the guru's role is essential in prescribing for each person their particular way to salvation.

In the sixteenth century, two Vaishnava teachers in the tradition of Madhva formed independent sects. In Bengal, Chaitanya (1485–1533) was so devoted to Krishna that he would spend days dancing in ecstasy and reciting the names of his God; his family considered him mad, but his followers accepted him as an avatāra of Krishna himself. Chaitanya was thus a charismatic guru; the doctrines of the sect (p. 177) were formed by his successors. Authority in the sect since his time has lain with the Gosains or Goswāmīs, Brahmin descendants of Chaitanya's companions; it was brought to the West by A. C. Bhaktivedānta Swāmī (p. 191).

Chaitanya's contemporary Vallabha (1479–1531) is also claimed as an avatāra of Krishna. His sect, the Vallabha sampradaya, is often known as Pushti-Margā, 'path of grace' (or more literally 'path of nourishment or prosperity'), referring to its distinctive doctrine that the highest devotion can only be experienced through God's grace, which is only available to initiates. The authorities and channels of grace in this sect are Vallabha's descendants, known as Mahārājas ('great kings'); initiation is granted by a Mahārāja or by a guru deputed by him. The sect's followers are mainly from the merchant castes of Gujarat; it sees no conflict between spiritual and material well-being.

A very different form of Vaishnavism which is also prevalent in Gujarat is the Swāmi Nārāyana sect. Swāmi Nārāyana is a name given to the founder, Sahajānand (1780–1830), implying that he himself is the supreme God, one of whose names is Nārāyana (p. 122). Unlike the Pushti-Mārga, this sect sets great value on asceticism; the founder was a sannyāsī (p. 83), and so are his successors. For this reason there is no hereditary succession, and there are now several rival branches. Nevertheless it is highly disciplined, and has prospered among Gujaratis in East Africa and Britain as well as India.

Shaivism also has its sects. In South India, besides the traditions handed on by Shaiva Brahmins who conduct worship in the great temples, there are the largely non-Brahmin followers of the Shaiva Siddhanta sect (p. 177). This school, inspired by Shaiva poetry in Tamil, offers salvation through the grace of Shiva, working through a guru. The gurus are non-Brahmins who have progressed through four grades of initiation.

A distinctive Shaiva community in Karnātaka, the Lingāyats, or Vīra-Shaivas, also has its own non-Brahmin gurus, and looks down on Brahmins. Vīra-Shaiva rituals are centred on the linga (p. 109), and a small linga, worn in a case hung round the neck, is given in an initiation ritual soon after birth. The gurus, called *jangamas*, are organised in a hierarchy, and each acts for a group of families.

While membership of Shaiva Siddhānta and Vīra-Shaivism is mainly hereditary, there are also numerous groups of Shaiva sannyāsīs and yogīs, which are entered voluntarily by individuals who place themselves under a guru of their choice. There are also Tantric groups, which are entered by initiation and place great importance on the initiate's relationship with the guru. These follow the Sanskrit texts called *Tantras* (p. 162), which give instruction in a particular type of ritual aimed at freeing the initiate from the limitations of worldly existence and gaining mastery of the world and the body, through a combination of yoga and worship of the Goddess, the wife of Shiva. The methods of Tantrism include the recitation of mantras, some of which are in the form of single syllables charged with mystical power, and meditation on geometrical diagrams called *yantras*. Since the universe originates from the sexual activity of Shiva and the Goddess, sexual symbolism is important in Tantrism; and a sense of indifference to polarities such as purity and pollution, life and death, or male and female, is developed through a systematic flouting of the ritual rules which obtain outside the circle of initiates.

Reform movements

From the beginning of the nineteenth century printed books, periodicals, public lectures and educational institutions began to rival the guru-pupil relationship as ways of transmitting ideas. Hindu ideas were also influenced by contact with the West, especially in Calcutta, which at that time was the main seat of British power in India. The Brāhmo Samāj, or Theistic Society, was founded in Calcutta in 1828 by the Bengali Brahmin Rāmmohun Roy (1772–1833), and considerably transformed by Debendranāth Tāgore (1817–1905) and Keshub Chunder Sen (1838–84). Rammohun believed that true religion consisted of the rational contemplation of God as the author of the universe, and benevolence towards mankind; he held that this religion was taught in the Veda and other Hindu literature, but had been obscured by unnecessary doctrines and rituals. The Brahmo Samaj was intended to restore it, and to combat false and degenerate forms of Hinduism. It acted as a forum for the exchange of traditional and modern ideas, and promoted social reform, especially the rights of women. Its influence spread beyond Bengal, and led to the founding of similar societies elsewhere.

Rammohun claimed neither charisma nor the authority of a succession of teachers; he appealed only to common sense and the Sanskrit texts. A similar appeal was made by Dayānanda Saravastī (1824–83), though to very different effect. Dayānanda, a wandering sannyāsī from Gujarat, with a deep knowledge of the Sanskrit tradition and an indirect acquaintance with modern ideas, held that the Vedas were revealed truth, but had been wrongly interpreted; they taught the worship of one God, not many, and encouraged commercial and military enterprise and a scientific outlook. Dayananda ridiculed the authority of Brahmins, and said that according to the Veda society should be divided not into many hereditary castes, but into four varnas (p. 78), membership of which should depend on merit, not birth. In 1875 Dayananda formed the Ārya Samāj. This, like the Brāhmo Samaj, opposed image worship and caste, and used lectures, publications and educational projects to disseminate its views; it had far more popular appeal, especially in the Panjab. Its main form of worship is the havan, the Vedic offering in fire (p. 105; p. 108). Part of its appeal lies in the fact that its rituals, particularly for marriage, are far simpler and less costly than more traditional ones.

There are many other movements which combine religious and social reform, and present ancient ideas in forms acceptable in the modern world. Among them, the Rāmakrishna Mission, founded by Swāmī Vivekānanda (1862–1902), is dedicated to teaching Advaita Vedānta (p. 169; p. 177) world-wide, and to charitable work in India. It has centres around the world, each headed by a swāmī. The swāmīs are members of a highly trained and organised body of sannyāsīs, with their headquarters near Calcutta. Followers, both Hindus by birth and others, are attracted to the swamīs' lectures and to the pūjās which they perform to Hindu gods and to Vivekānanda's master, the Bengali saint Rāmakrishna (1836–86).

Missions to the West

Though Dayananda intended to bring true Hinduism to the whole world, the Ramakrishna Mission was the first organisation to attempt this in practice. Since then, and especially since the 1960s, Hindu missions have appealed to Westerners seeking alternatives to Christianity and materialism. Transcendental Meditation is a form of yoga presented as a means to individual happiness and the welfare of society, in which a mantra is learnt in a Hindu ritual setting from a teacher. While the movement's leader, Māharishi Mahesh Yogī is a much publicised figure, he is also a member of a line of gurus going back to Shankara (p. 169). Bhaktivedānta Swāmī (1896–1977), the founder of the International Society for Krishna Consciousness (ISKCON), was in a different line of gurus, and used modern methods to teach the doctrines of Chaitanya (p. 188; Knott 1986b; Carey in Burghart 1987: 81–99).

Charismatic movements such as Sathya Sai Baba and the Radha Soami Satsang are also active in the West. The Divine Light Mission has had some following in Britain, among Hindus and others, since the visit of the fourteen-year-old Guru Mahārāj Ji in 1971; devotees mediate on him as a manifestation of the divine light.

The place of sects in Hinduism

Some Hindus follow more than one sect; others do not belong to any. The latter sometimes describe themselves as *sanātanī* Hindus, meaning followers of *sanātana dharma*, the eternal norms. Sect members, on the other hand, may claim that theirs is the real *sanātana dharma*.

A sect may try to keep itself separate from outsiders, while outsiders may equally keep aloof from the sect members. If this leads to avoidance of intermarriage, the sect can become a caste, like the Kabīr-panthīs (p. 186), or a group of castes, like the Vīra-Shaivas (p. 188). Conversely a caste can become a sect if all its members accept the same guru; this happened when a Panjabi leatherworking caste became Ravidāsīs, followers of Ravidās or Raidās, a teacher in the same tradition as Kabīr. The Sikhs (meaning 'disciple') originated as a Hindu sect; their first guru, Nānak (1469–1539) had a similar outlook to Kabīr (p. 59). Like many other sects, the Sikhs eat together regardless of caste, and this, together with their opposition to image worship, has combined with political developments to separate them from Hinduism.

Besides the sects we have mentioned, there is a class of Brahmins called *Smārta*, meaning those who follow the smriti or tradition (p. 161). Rather than a single god, they worship a representative group of five gods: Vishnu, Shiva, the goddess Durgā, the elephant-headed Ganesha, and Sūrya, the sun. This rule is attributed to Shankara (p. 169), who is also said to have established five gurus, each appointing and initiating his successor, in different parts of India: at Bādrīnāth in the north, Shringerī and Kānchī in the south, Dwārakā in the west, and Purī in the east. Those gurus, who are all named Shankarāchārya ('the teacher Shankara') after their founder, are appealed to by Smārtas on questions of practice. They are the nearest approximation in Hinduism to a central authority, and the practices of the Smārtas are sometimes referred to as Hindu orthodoxy. In some ways, however, the Smārtas are themselves a sect.

Teaching ideas

Given the tendency by some parts of the press to group all modern religious movements together as potentially dangerous cults, it is important that groups such as the International Society for Krishna Consciousness or the Sathya Sai Baba organisation – even though they have western members – are understood as a legitimate part of the Hindu tradition. The following ideas concentrate on groups familiar in the West, but could be extended to include other movements.

Middle years

Leaders. Founders and leaders of sectarian groups and modern movements within Hinduism generally have interesting biographies and their stories – showing their spiritual qualities as well as their teachings – are likely to raise a variety of questions for discussion. A simple profile of one or more such characters can be made and the Indian roots of each of their sects or movements can be traced, e.g. Sathya Sai Baba – Shirdi Sai Baba – Kabīr; ISKCON – A.C. Bhaktivedanta Swami – the Gosains/Goswāmīs – Chaitanya).

Bala books publish *The Life Story of His Divine Grace A. C. Bhaktivedanta Swami Prabhupada* by Satsvarupa dasa Goswami. This is a 'comic book' account that could be used by children as a resource. A full list of Bala books (written for children of various ages) is available from The Bhaktivedanta Book Trust (see p. 236).

The Amar Chitra Katha series includes a 'comic book' version of the life of Sathya Sai Baba (p. 207). The Sri Sathya Sai Education and Publication Foundation have published *Divine Album : Sathya Sai Pictures*, an illustrated, highly devotional account for children of Sathya Sai Baba's life. Christina Walker, *Sai Baba Picture Book*, Element Books. Bury Peerless' collection of visual material includes a set of 24 slides taken at Sathya Sai Baba's ashram in Andhra Pradesh.

A life of Swami Vivekananda, founder of the Ramakrishna Mission, is included in the Amar Chitra Katha children's series (No. 146) and further material is available from the Ramakrishna Vedanta Centre. Lists of currently available books and audio tapes will be sent on request (enclose S.A.E).

Adolescence and Post-16

(a) Values. One or more sects or movements can be studied with a view to identifying the group's key moral and spiritual values. The exercise is a useful one in gaining examples of different Hindu perspectives on moral issues (as required by some GCSE syllabuses) and can help students to understand how particular moral values are integral to religious ways of life.

One approach is to get students to compare values or moral beliefs of a sect or movement with their own, noting similarities and differences. If any values coincide, then the reasons for holding the beliefs can be compared. For example, a student who is a vegetarian could compare his or her reasons with those of a Hindu movement, such as Krishna Consciousness. Several groups produce their own literature which is available in Britain. Older students could profitably use some of this as source material, though teachers will need to make a preliminary selection.

(i)   The Sathya Sai Baba movement is committed to promoting the values of Truth, Righteous Conduct, Peace, Love and Non-Violence. These values are explored and taught at classes for children organised by the movement and in the movement's literature (published for teachers and for children). The following are among texts used in Bal Vikas (child blossoming) classes and are published by the Sri Sathya Sai Bal Vikas Education Trust, Prasanthi Nilayam, India : *Curriculum and Methodology for Integrating Human Values in Education* (international edition) and *Teacher's Handbook for the Course in Human Values* are written for teachers, while

Education in Human Values : Primer I, II, *Pathfinder* I, II and *Stories for Children* I, II are produced for pupils. These texts are not available through booksellers but are available from some Sathya Sai Baba groups. The monthly newspaper, the *Sai World Gazette,* is another useful source of material.

(ii)   Krishna Consciousness. Kim Knott's *My Sweet Lord* (Aquarian Press, 1986) places ISKCON in its wider Hindu context. The movement itself publishes a wide range of books for adults and children. One moral issue on which the movement takes a stand is that of vegetarianism in particular and non-violence in general. Adiraja dasa, *The Hare Krishna Book of Vegetarian Cooking* (Bhaktivedanta Book Trust, 1984) is a richly illustrated collection of Indian vegetarian recipes. The introduction is a clear statement of the movement's position on vegetarianism, pointing to issues of health and world economics and drawing on the philosophy of the Hindu scriptures.

(b) Sects and their philosophies. Sects and organised movements are often the mediators of philosophical ideas to a wider audience. The theological and philosophical ideas of one or more sects or movements could be studied, using the movements' own publications as source material. The Ramakrishna movement advocates the monistic philosophy of Advaita Vedānta – having its roots in the philosophy of Shankara – while ISKCON's theistic views can be traced back via Chaitanya to Madhva. Publications (including audio tapes) expounding Advaita Vedānta philosophy are available from the Ramakrishna Vedanta Centre. Send SAE for current lists. Lists of ISKCON's materials are available from the Bhaktivedanta Book Trust. See also pp. 179–81.

Further reading

Pocock (1973); Knott (1986b); Burghart (1987); Farquhar (1914); Roy (1982).

Notes

1   This use of the word 'sect' should not be taken as implying rejection of the authority of a church; indeed, in Hinduism no such authority exists apart from the sects themselves.

2   Material from an unpublished paper by Dr D. Taylor. See also his paper in Burghart (1987).

3   *Satya* means 'truth' in Sanskrit; the sound which we spell *t* is often spelt *th* in South India. *Bābā*, 'father' is a title of respect given to old men and to holy men (p. 64). *Sāi* is explained by the sect as meaning 'mother', so that the name Sāi Bābā represents God as Shiva and Shakti.

4   Quoted in Roy (1982: 29).

Part Three

Resources for Teaching About Hinduism

Resources

References

Some references in Parts 1 and 2 are to teachers' books and pupils' books listed on pp. 199–218. This bibliography includes only these books which are not listed there but which are referred to in Parts 1 and 2.

Adiraja dasa, 1984: *The Hare Krishna Book of Vegetarian Cooking* (Letchmore Heath: Bhaktivedanta Book Trust).

Archer, W. G., 1958: *The Loves of Krishna* (London: Allen and Unwin).

Babb, L. A., 1975: *The Divine Hierarchy* (New York: Columbia University Press).

Basham, A. L., 1967: *The Wonder that was India* (London: Sidgwick and Jackson).

Berkshire, 1982: *Religious Heritage and Personal Quest*, Guidelines for Religious Education (Berkshire Education Authority).

Bhagavad-Gita: See Edgerton (1972), Zaehner (1966), (1969).

Bhaktivedanta Swami, A. C., 1975: *Bhagavad-Gita as it is* (Letchmore Heath: Bhaktivedanta Book Trust).

Bhardwaj, S. M., 1973: *Hindu Places of Pilgrimage in India: A Study in Cultural Geography* (Berkeley: University of California Press).

Binford, Mira Reym, 1976: 'Mixing in the color of Rām of Rānujā: a folk pilgrimage to the grave of a Rajput hero-saint', in Bardwell L. Smith (ed.), *Hinduism : New Essays in the History of Religions* (Leiden: Brill).

Birmingham, 1975: *Agreed Syllabus of Religious Instruction* (City of Birmingham Education Committee).

Bowen, D. G. (ed.) 1981: *Hinduism in England* (Bradford College).

Dumont, Louis, 1970: *Homo Hierarchicus* (London: Weidenfeld and Nicholson, reprinted Paladin, 1972).

Durham, 1970: *The Fourth R – The Durham Report on Religious Education* (London: National Society and SPCK).

Durrans, R. and Knox, R., 1982: *India : Past Into Present* (London: British Museum Publications).

Eck, D. L. 1983: *Banaras, City of Light* (London: Routledge and Kegan Paul).

Edgerton, Franklin, 1972: The *Bhagavad Gita* (Cambridge, Mass, USA: Harvard University Press).

Farquhar, J. N., 1914: *Modern Religious Movements in India* (Oxford University Press, reprinted Delhi, Munshiram Manoharlal, 1967).

Gandhi, Mohandas Karamchand, 1927: *An Autobiography : The Story of my Experiments with Truth* (Ahmedabad: Navjivan).

Hampshire, 1978: *Religious Education in Hampshire Schools* (Hampshire Education Authority).

Hick, John, 1973: *The Philosophy of Religion* (Englewood Cliffs: Prentice Hall).

Holm, Jean, 1984: 'Growing up in Hinduism', *British Journal of Religious Education*, Vol 6, No 3, pp.116–20.

Hume, R. E., 1921: *The Thirteen Principal Upanishads* (London: OUP; reprinted New York, 1971).

ILEA, 1984: *Religious Education for Our Children* (Agreed Syllabus for the Inner London Education Authority).

Ions, V., 1967: *Indian Mythology* (London: Hamlyn).

Jackson, R., 1981: 'The Shree Krishna Temple and the Gujarati Hindu Community in Coventry' in Bowen (1981) pp.61–85.

Jackson, R. (ed.) 1982: *Approaching World Religions* (London: John Murray).

Jackson, R. 1985: 'Hinduism in Britain : Religious Nurture and Religious Education', *British Journal of Religious Education*, Vol 7, No 2, Spring, pp.68–75.

Jackson, R. and Nesbitt, E., 1986: 'Sketches of Formal Hindu Nurture', *World Religions in Education 1986*, Journal of the Shap Working Party, pp.25–29.

Jaffrey, Madhur, 1978: *An Invitation to Indian Cooking* (Harmondsworth: Penguin)

Jaffrey, Madhur, 1985: *A Taste of India* (London: Pavilion).

Karve, Iravati, 1961: *Hindu Society: An Interpretation* (Poona: Deccan College).

Knott, K., 1986a: *Hinduism in Leeds: A Study of Religious Practice in the Indian Hindu Community and in Hindu-Related Groups* (Leeds: Department of Theology and Religious Studies, University of Leeds).

Knott, K., 1986b: *My Sweet Lord* (Wellingborough: Aquarian Press).

Mahadevan, T. M. P., 1977: *Outlines of Hinduism* (Bombay: Chetana).

Mahadevan, T. M. P., 1961: *Ten Saints of India* (Bombay: Bharatiya Vidya Bhavan).

Mahadevan, T. M. P., 1977: *Ramana Maharshi: The Sage of Arunachala* (London: Allen and Unwin).

Mahar, J. M., 1972: *The Untouchables in Contemporary India* (Tucson: University of Arizona Press).

Mandelbaum, D. G., 1970: *Society in India*, 2 Vols. (Berkeley: University of California Press).

Manu (legendary author): *The Laws of Manu* (tr. Georg Bühler) (Oxford: Clarendon Press, 1886).

Mascaró, Juan, 1962: *The Bhagavad-Gītā* (Harmondsworth: Penguin).

Mascaró, Juan, 1965: *The Upanishads* (Harmondsworth: Penguin).

Mayer, A., 1960: *Caste and Kinship in Central India* (London: Routledge & Kegan Paul).

Michell, George, 1977: *The Hindu Temple: An Introduction to its Meaning and Forms* (London: Paul Elek).

Minority Rights Group, 1982: *The Untouchables of India* (London: Minority Rights Group Report No. 26).

Narayan, R. K., 1965: *Gods, Demons and Others* (London: Heinemann).

O'Flaherty, W. D., 1975: *Hindu Myths* (Harmondsworth: Penguin).

O'Flaherty, W. D., 1981: *The Rig Veda* (Harmondsworth: Penguin).

Opie, Iona and Peter, 1959: *The Lore and Language of School Children* (Oxford: OUP).

Pandey, Raj Bali, 1969: *Hindu Samskaras*, (Delhi: Motilal Banarsidass).

Parrinder, E. G., 1973: *The Indestructible Soul* (London: Allen and Unwin).

Pocock, D. F., 1973: *Mind, Body and Wealth: A Study of Belief and Practice in an Indian Village* (Oxford: Blackwell).

Prabharananda, Swami and Isherwood, C., 1954: *The Song of God: Bhagavad-Gita* (New York: Mentor).

Price, Merlin, 1985: 'Religious Story in the Primary School', *Resource*, Vol. 7, No 3, Summer 1985.

Raju, P. T., 1971: *The Philosophical Traditions of India* (London: Allen and Unwin).

Ramanujan, A. K., 1973: *Speaking of Shiva* (Harmondsworth: Penguin).

Ramanujan, A. K., 1981: *Hymns for the Drowning*, (Princeton University Press).

Roy, Rammohan, 1982: *The Only True God* (tr. D. H. Killingley) (Newcastle upon Tyne: Grevatt and Grevatt).

Santa Maria, Jack, 1973: *Indian Vegetarian Cookery* (London: Rider).

Santa Maria, Jack, 1979: *Indian Sweet Cookery* (London: Rider).

Schools Council, 1971: *Religious Education in Secondary Schools*, Schools Council Working Paper 36 (London: Evans/ Methuen).

Shackle, C. (ed), 1985: *South Asian Languages: a Handbook* (London: External Services Division, School of Oriental and African Studies).

Shap Calendar of Festivals, distributed annually by the Shap Working Party, 7 Alderbrook Road, Solihull, W. Midlands.

Sharma, Ursula, 1971: *Rampal and His Family* (London: Collins).

Singer, Milton, 1972a: *When a Great Tradition Modernises: An Anthropological Approach to Indian Civilisation* (London: Pall Mall Press).

Singer, Milton, (ed.), 1972b: *Krishna: Myths, Rites and Attitudes*. (Chicago: University of Chicago Press).

Singh, Dharamjit, 1970: *Indian Cookery* (Harmondsworth: Penguin).

Smart, Ninian, 1964: *Doctrine and Argument in Indian Philosophy* (London: Allen and Unwin).

Smith, W. C., 1978: *The Meaning and End of Religion* (London: SPCK).

Srinivas, M. N., 1976: *The Remembered Village* (Berkeley: University of California Press).

Stevenson, Mrs Sinclair (Margaret Stevenson), 1920: *The Rites of the Twice-born* (London: OUP, reprinted in Delhi).

Stutley, M. and J., 1977: *A Dictionary of Hinduism* (London: Routledge & Kegan Paul).

Tandon, Prakash, 1961: *Punjabi Century : 1857–1947* (London: Chatto and Windus, and New Delhi, Orient Paperbacks).

Taylor, J. H., 1976: *The Half-Way Generation* (Slough: National Foundation for Educational Research).

Upanishads: See Hume (1921), Zaehner (1966).

Vaudeville, Charlotte, *Kabīr*, 2 vols. (Oxford: Clarendon Press).

Veda: see O'Flaherty (1975), Zaehner (1966).

Vishnu Purāna: See Wilson (1961).

Warwickshire, 1985: *Religious Education in Warwickshire Schools and Colleges* (Warwickshire Education Authority).

Weightman, Simon, 1978a: 'Hinduism and Religious Education' in R. Jackson (ed.), *Perspectives on World Religions*, (London: School of Oriental and African Studies).

Weightman, Simon, 1978b: *Hinduism in the Village Setting* (Milton Keynes: Open University).

Weightman, Simon, 1984: 'Hinduism' in J. R. Hinnells (ed.), *A Handbook of Living Religions* (London: Penguin).

West Riding, 1947: *Syllabus of Religious Instruction* (County Council of the West Riding of Yorkshire Education Department).

West Riding, 1966: *Suggestions for Religious Education, West Riding Agreed Syllabus* (County Council of the West Riding of Yorkshire Education Department).

Wilson, H. H., 1961: *The Vishnu Purana: A System of Hindu Mythology and Tradition* (Calcutta: Punthi Pustak).

Zaehner, R. C., 1962: *Hinduism* (London: OUP).

Zaehner, R. C., 1966: *Hindu Scriptures* (London: Dent).

Zaehner, R. C., 1969: *The Bhagavad Gita* (Oxford: Clarendon Press).

Teachers' Books

Bahree, Patricia, 1982: *India, Pakistan and Bangladesh: A Handbook for Teachers* (London: School of Oriental and African Studies). Available from SOAS, ISBN 0 7134 3654 9.
A considerable amount of background and resource material on history, geography, religion and art.

Brown, Alan (ed.) 1986: *Festivals in World Religions* (London: Longman ISBN 0 5823 6196 6.
This volume, written by members of the Shap Working Party, includes a chapter on Hindu festivals introducing Hindu calendars as well as offering information on pan-Indian festivals and a wide selection of regional festivals from different parts of India. A few local festivals are described to illustrate some of the general themes which tend to recur in India's countless village celebrations.

Burghart, Richard (ed.) 1987: *Hinduism in Great Britain: The Perpetuation of Religion in an Alien Cultural Milieu* (London: Tavistock). ISBN 0 4226 0910 2.
This covers many aspects of Hinduism in Britain, one chapter being devoted to a discussion of the different ways in which Hinduism has been portrayed in religious education literature and textbooks in the United Kingdom.

Cole, W. O. (ed.) 1983: *Religion in the Multifaith School* (Amersham: Hulton). ISBN 0 7175 1159 6.
Especially relevant are sections dealing with the religious upbringing of a Hindu child, Teaching Hinduism, Indian writers in English and an anthology of Hindu stories.

Hayward, Mary (ed.) 1985: *Understanding the Hindu Tradition.* Available from The York RE Centre, The College of Ripon and York St. John, Lord Mayor's Walk, York, YO3 7EX.
Papers from the 1985 York Shap conference for teachers on Hinduism. Subjects include 'Unity and Diversity', 'Story and Symbol', 'Hindus in Britain', 'Rites of Passage', 'Hindu Society', 'Indian Dance', 'Worship', and 'Teaching about Hinduism'.

Hinnells, J. R. and Sharpe E. J. (eds.), 1972: *Hinduism*, (Newcastle: Oriel Press) (London: Routledge & Kegan Paul). ISBN 0 8536 2137 3.
This substantial introduction is divided into three parts: Hinduism Past and Present, The Teaching of Hinduism, and Appendices (including language and pronunciation, the calendar, bibliography and glossary). Part One represents a brave attempt at the difficult problem of introducing Hinduism impartially and in a way that would not overwhelm newcomers to the study of religion. The last nine (of forty two) chapters cover practice, although the philosophies and mythologies are not tied in with it. The best chapter in Part Two is by Donald Butler, on teaching Hinduism in secondary schools.

Hull, J. (ed.) *British Journal of Religious Education* Vol. 6 No. 3, Summer 1984. Available from CEM, Lancaster House, Borough Road, Isleworth, Middlesex, TW7 5DU.
The whole issue, called *Teaching Hinduism Today*, is devoted to teaching about the Hindu tradition.

Jackson, R. (ed.), 1978: *Perspectives on World Religions* (London: School of Oriental and African Studies). ISBN 0 7286 0055 2. Available from SOAS.
This includes Simon Weightman's essay on 'Hinduism and Religious Education' as well as material by Helen Kanitkar on 'Social Aspects of Hinduism', John Marr on 'Popular Hinduism in South India' and David Taylor on 'Religion and Politics in India'.

Kanitkar, Helen A. and Jackson, R., 1982: *Hindus in Britain*, Occasional Paper VI (London: School of Oriental and African Studies). ISBN 0 7286 0106 0. (Available from SOAS).
Some background information on Hindu practice in Britain, with a section on teaching ideas, books and A.V. resources.

Kanitkar, V. P. (Hemant), 1984: *Hindu Festivals and Sacraments*. (New Barnet: the author). ISBN 0 9477 3400 7. Available from Arthur Probsthain, Oriental Booksellers, 41 Great Russell St., London WC1B 3PN.
Written by a Maharashtrian Hindu author who has worked in London as a teacher for 25 years. The author introduces 28 Hindu festivals and the 16 principal samskāras or 'sacraments'. A clearly written text illustrated by 45 line drawings. Note that much of the data is based on textual sources, and that the number and details of the samskāras varies considerably in practice.

Killingley, Dermot (ed.), 1984: *A Handbook of Hinduism for Teachers* (Newcastle upon Tyne: Grevatt and Grevatt). 9 Rectory Drive, Newcastle upon Tyne. NE3 1XT. ISBN 0 9507 9186 5.

This volume has useful material for both primary and secondary teachers, including an anthology of Hindu stories for younger children. Other sections cover Hindu practices, Hindu society, the gods, Hindu ideas, Hindu literature, historical background and biographical sketches of eminent Hindus. The emphasis is on what Hindus do and think, both in Britain and in India.

Mitchell, A. G., 1982: *Hindu Gods and Goddesses* (London: HMSO). ISBN 0 1129 0372 X.

Information on many deities and their iconography. Black and white photographs illustrate the Victoria and Albert Museum's collection of bronzes.

Scottish Working Party on Religions of the World in Education, 1984: *Knowing and Teaching about Hinduism*. Available from Helen Montgomery, 60 Forest Rd., Aberdeen, Scotland AB2 4BP.

A useful booklet produced by Shap's sister organisation in Scotland. The first section introduces the Hindu tradition while Part Two is a compilation of teaching schemes and material.

Pupils' Books (Single Faith)

Aggarwal, Manju, 1984: *I am a Hindu*. (London: Franklin Watts). ISBN 0 8631 3168 9.

The text is simple and well-written. It introduces various aspects of Hindu practice and faith in Britain through the experience of eleven-year-old Gaytri Devi Goswami and her family. Thirty six colour photographs break up the text and engage the reader's interest. Suitable for junior and middle school children.

Amar Chitra Katha series.

Comic book versions of many Hindu myths and stories that can be used directly or adapted for use with children. The booklets are imported from India and are available from Asian booksellers and general stores. The following is a useful selection. *Krishna* (No.11), *Rama* (No.15), *Hanuman* (No.19), *Mahabharata* (No.20), *Shiva Parvati* (No.29), *Prahlad* (No.38), *Ganesha* (No.89), *The Gita* (No.127), *Tales of Vishnu* (No.160), *Tales of Shiva* (No.164), *Tales of Durga* (No.176), *Hanuman to the Rescue* (No.254).

Bahree, Patricia, 1982: *The Hindu World* (London: Macdonald Education). ISBN 0 3560 7521 4.

Excellent colour illustrations and a straightforward text. Hinduism is presented as a dynamic, colourful and varied amalgam of practice and belief and the various sections of the book, through text and picture, reinforce the idea of Hinduism as a living tradition. Older juniors and lower secondary.

Bahree, Patricia, 1984: *Hinduism, Dictionaries of World Religions* series (London: Batsford). ISBN 0 7134 3654 9.
A very good blend of short articles including entries on key concepts and personalities. Excellent black and white illustrations. Class library: top junior upwards.

Bala Books series.
Well-produced versions of classic Hindu tales, published by the International Society for Krishna Consciousness. Titles include *Krishna, Master of All Mystics*; *Prahlad*; *Colouring Book of the Incarnations*; *Krishna's Birth*; *Krishna*; *Krishna and the Demons*. A full list is available from the Bhaktivedanta Book Trust.

Bennett, Olivia, 1986: *Festival ! Diwali* (Basingstoke: Macmillan Education). ISBN 0 3333 7899 7.
Middle school level text with alternate colour and black and white photographic spreads. The text is well written and captures the diversity of the festival and its mythology in India and abroad.

Bennett, Olivia, 1987: *Holi, Hindu Festival of Spring* (London: Hamish Hamilton). ISBN 0 2411 1986 3.
Manisha, a Hindu girl from Coventry, is followed through school, home and temple as she explores Holī's mythology through dance, and then participates in the festival with her family. Well-written text and excellent colour photographs. Junior level.

Bolwell, Laurie, 1985: *A Journey Down the Ganges* (Hove: Wayland). ISBN 0 8507 8498 0.
A book for Junior/Middle pupils which traces a journey down the River Ganges from source to mouth. Unfortunately the text perpetuates old errors, and an unfortunate imperialist flavour pervades the text, with recurrent reference to India's and Bangladesh's poverty. Not recommended.

Bonnici, Peter, 1984: *The First Rains* and *The Festival, Arjuna's Family* series (London: Bell and Hyman).
Designed for the young reader, these two stories are set in an Indian context and introduce Indian life to western readers. *The First Rains* (ISBN 0 7135 1457 4) shows the young boy Arjuna

waiting in the sticky heat for the monsoon rains, while *The Festival* (ISBN 0 7135 1458 2) has Arjuna participating in a local festival of a south Indian village temple. There are coloured pictures on each double spread.

Bridger, P., 1969: *A Hindu Family in Britain* (Religious Education Press).
The book traces the migration of the Shah family to England from Gujarat. Contents include the main points of religious belief, a summary of the Rāmāyana, a festival, life-cycle rites, caste, the status of women, and how the Shahs get on in England. There is some romanticism about marriage, and especially about caste and varna. The best chapter is on 'Customs and Behaviour'. Aimed at lower secondary. The book has now been replaced by a completely new volume with the same title, but by a Hindu author Sauresh Ray (see below).

Butler, Donald, 1980: *Life Among Hindus, Friends and Neighbours* series (London: Edward Arnold).
A collection of eight short plays covering life in a Hindu home, worship, festivals, marriage and death. Two Hindu children, Kanju (aged 12) and Yasoda (aged 13), introduce aspects of their life and culture to Susan (13) and Peter (12). They are joined occasionally by Isaac, who brings in a Jewish viewpoint.

Candappa, Beulah, 1984: *Tales of South Asia* (Aylesbury: Ginn, 1984). ISBN 0 6022 2634 1 (set).
Part of the *Traditional Tales from Around the World* series. This set of four books, with teachers' notes, contains folk tales, legends, poems and songs which reflect the culture of South Asia. Material is arranged under the titles *Out of the World*, *Fools or Wise Men*, *Legendary Creatures* and *How Things Began*. The geographical area covered includes Pakistan, Burma, Bangladesh and Sri Lanka as well as India, and only a portion of the stories is from Hindu sources.

Candappa, Beulah, 1985: *Diwali, Celebrations* series (Aylesbury: Ginn). ISBN 0 6022 2688 0 (set).
Most of this booklet is a well told version of the Rāma and Sītā story, attractively illustrated in colour. Six pages on the festival follow, illustrated with nine colour photographs. Published as part of a set of six books with teachers' notes (Ginn Reading level 10).

Cole, W. O., 1987: *Meeting Hinduism* (London: Longman). ISBN 0 5822 2385 7.

Aimed at the secondary age range (with a particular eye to GCSE) this text introduces Hinduism as a living way of life and belief. It arose from a study visit to India by the author in 1983. Chapter headings include 'Hindu Villages', 'Caste', 'Festivals and Pilgrimages' and 'Hinduism in Britain'.

Constant, Audrey, 1985: *Man of Peace: The Story of Mahatma Gandhi* (Exeter: Religious and Moral Education Press).

One of the *Faith in Action* series aimed at middle and secondary pupils. The text, illustrated in black and white, examines the Mahatma's life and influence, though it gives insufficient detail to some of the more controversial issues and events.

Crompton, Y., 1971: *Hinduism* (London: Ward Lock). ISBN 0 7062 3598 3.

Written by a Western convert to Hinduism, the book is idiosyncratic in parts, e.g., his account of the teachings of Hinduism and of caste. The book could be used selectively by teachers as a resource, but not as an accurate general introduction to the tradition nor as a pupils' book. Illustrated with black and white photographs.

Deshpande, Chris, 1985: *Diwali, Celebrations* series (London: A. and C. Black). ISBN 0 7136 2643 7.

Thirty four colour photographs, showing Diwālī at school, home and temple, illustrate a simple text suitable for infants and lower juniors.

Echo Books series.

This series, published by India Book House Education Trust, Bombay, includes several valuable anthologies of Hindu stories. These include Keskar, S., *Tales the Ramayana Tells*; Manjeshwar, S., *Krishna and the Pandavas* and *Birth of the Gods*; D'Souza, N., *Hanuman and Jatayu*; Balse, M., *Of Gods and Demons* and *Of Gods and Goddesses*; Dayal, R., *Legends from the Puranas*; Boothalingam, S., *The Legends of Lord Ganesha*. Das, M., *Temples of India*; Rau, I. B. M., *Easy Stories from the Mahabharata*; Sreenivasan, V., *Indian Myths*.

Ewan, John, 1977: *Understanding Your Hindu Neighbour* (London: Lutterworth). ISBN 0 7188 1800 8.

The framework is a year in the life of the Patel family, during which major festivals are covered. There is a birth, a marriage and a death in the family (so the *Samskāras* are treated as they happen). Temple worship, including ārati and pūjā in the home are both described in some detail. Junior and lower secondary.

Ewan, John and Pancholi, N., 1981: *A Hindu Home* (London: CEM). ISBN 0 7188 1800 8.

A short booklet with sections on welcome, the family, worship and meditation, special occasions in life, festivals in the home and what Hindus believe.

Gavin, Jamila, 1986: *Stories from the Hindu World* (London: Macdonald). ISBN 0 3561 1509 7.

Twelve stories sensitively and economically retold from Hindu sacred texts. The selection includes 'How Lord Shiva Became Blue-throated', 'Manu's Ark', 'The Birth of Lord Krishna', 'The Story of Rama and Sita' and 'How the River Ganga came to Earth'. There are lively colour illustrations and brief notes at the end of the book helpfully augment each story. Junior level.

Hannaford, Janice, 1983: *Holi*, *Living Festivals* series (Exeter: RMEP). ISBN 0 8029 283 6.

An inexpensive booklet, suitable for secondary pupils and illustrated in black and white, does not do full justice to the variety of forms in which this festival appears.

Hardy, Aruna, 1980: *Ravi of India* (London: Lutterworth). ISBN 0 7188 2419 9.

Part of the *How They Live Now* series, this book introduces a wealth of detail about a child's view of Indian life. The author draws sensitively on her own experience as a Hindu from the state of Maharashtra. It is a pity that the publishers did not use photographs: the rather poor colour illustrations lack the realism of the text.

Harrison, Steve, 1986: *Daksa and Arun : Two Hindu Children Visit India* (Basingstoke: Macmillan Education). ISBN 0 3333 8609 4.

Part of a series aimed at 8–14 year olds which explore and explain the everyday experiences of second generation children from various ethnic backgrounds. Daksa and Arun Patel visit the Gujarati village where their father grew up and experience customs and practices that their parents brought to England, but in their original setting. There are alternate colour and black and white photographic spreads. One of the pictures on p. 18 shows children learning Bengali, not Gujarati. Older juniors upwards.

Jackson, Robert, 1988: *Religions through Festivals : Hinduism* (London: Longman). ISBN 0 5823 1788 6.

The text is written for 11 to 13-year-olds and there is an emphasis on active learning methods. There are quotations from British

Hindu children and their parents, talking about their own experiences of festivals in India, East Africa and Britain. Illustrated with colour and black and white photographs.

Jaffrey, Madhur, 1985: *Seasons of Splendor* (London: Pavilion). ISBN 0 9075 1658 0.

A selection of delightfully told Hindu stories, beautifully illustrated (by Michael Foreman), set in the context of the festival cycle and including some of the author's childhood reminiscences. Includes the birth of Krishna, Rāma and Sītā, how Ganesh got his elephant's head and many others.

Kanitkar, V. P. (Hemant), 1986: *Hindu Stories* (Hove: Wayland). ISBN 0 8507 8863 3.

Designed for top infants and juniors and illustrated in colour. The stories are entitled: 'Ganesha'; 'Damayanti and the Swan'; 'Krishna's escape'; 'Krishna tames Kaliya'; 'Prince Rama'.

Kanitkar V. P. (Hemant), 1986: *Hinduism* (Hove: Wayland). ISBN 0 8507 8687 8.

This book describes the origins of Hinduism and the tradition's central beliefs, explaining the Hindu idea of God, rites of passage, family life, holy places and shrines, festivals and the purpose of life. Illustrated with colour photographs. The statement (on p. 5) 'Hindus do not eat with people who are not of their caste' needs modification.

Kanitkar, V. P. (Hemant), 1986: *Indian Food and Drink* (Hove: Wayland). ISBN 0 8507 8897 8.

A useful resource book covering nutritional and geographical material as well as religious aspects of food. Illustrated with attractive colour photographs. Older junior and lower secondary.

Kerven, Rosalind, 1986: *Festival! Diwali: Teacher's Notes and Pupils' Worksheets* (Basingstoke: Macmillan Education). ISBN 0 3333 7903 9.

This material is designed to accompany the pupils' book of the same title written by Olivia Bennett. The information is well-researched and the notes and worksheets cover many aspects of India's culture and history that go far beyond the Diwālī festival. A very useful publication, with good ideas for junior and lower secondary children.

Khanna, G. S., 1983: *The Story of Diwali, The Festival of Lights*, privately published, available from Virdee Brothers, 102 The Green, Southall, Middlesex UB2 4BQ.

A retelling of the Rāma and Sītā stories, illustrated with line-drawings. Older juniors.

Knutsson, B. and Arlemahm E., 1983: *Hinduism, Life and Faith* series, (Hulton).
Translated from the Swedish, this colour-illustrated booklet is aimed at the younger reader. Although attractive colour photographs are reproduced, the text contains several inaccuracies and over-simplifications and is not recommended as it stands. The publishers are planning a second edition with a revised text.

Lefever, Henry, 1973: *One Man and His Dog* (London: Lutterworth). ISBN 0 7188 205 8.
An anthology of 11 Hindu and 9 Buddhist stories retold for children. Includes the story of Manu, the birth of Krishna, Nala and Damayantī, Rāma and Sītā, with black and white illustrations. Suitable for reading to the junior age range.

Marsh, Howard, 1982: *Divali, Living Festivals* series (Exeter: RMEP). ISBN 0 0802 7874 4.
A well balanced introduction to the festival, showing various emphases in some different parts of India. Some Hindus have found the poor illustrations of Lakshmī (p. 16) and Vishnu (p. 21) offensive.

Mayled, John, 1985: *Hindu Worship, Holt World Religions* series (Eastbourne: Holt, Rinehart and Winston). ISBN 0 0391 0581 4.
Covers much more than worship. This is a pity since the condensed treatment of Hinduism leads to a number of imbalances, confusions and misleading comparisons with Christianity. A more detailed account of 'worship', including interviews with worshippers, would have been more useful. Aimed at secondary age range.

MGSS, *How a Hindu Prays* (Coventry Education Authority). Available from MGSS, Southfields Old School, South Street, Coventry.
Cheaply produced illustrated booklet describing pūjā at a Hindu temple.

MGSS 1983: *The Story of Divali* (Coventry: MGSS). Available in English and Hindi from MGSS (p. 236).
The Rāma and Sītā story is *a* rather than *the* story of Diwālī. This budget-priced illustrated version retells the story simply. An

assembly pack on Diwālī is also available, of which this booklet forms a part.

Mitter, Partha and Swasti, 1982: *Hindus and Hinduism* (Hove: Wayland). ISBN 0 8534 0908 0.
A clear introduction to Hinduism suitable for middle and lower secondary pupils, illustrated with nearly fifty black and white photographs. Teachers will need to point out to pupils that the account of Durgā Pūjā (p. 31) refers to the festival as celebrated by Bengalis. Unfortunately pictures of Sikhs, not Hindus, are shown on pp. 53–54 without comment or clarification. Otherwise this is a useful introduction.

Mitter, Swasti, 1985: *Hindu Festivals* (Hove: Wayland). ISBN 0 8507 8571 5.
An attractively produced middle school text especially valuable for its chapter on the celebration of Diwālī in different regions of India. Copiously illustrated with very good colour photographs, many by Bury Peerless.

Nehru Library for Children
This series, published in New Delhi by the National Book Trust, India, includes several good story books including No. 16, *Stories of Valour* (includes the story of Shravana) and No. 30 *The Prince of Ayodhya* (Rāma and Sītā). Available through Indian booksellers (see pp. 236–7).

Nivedita, Sister, 1968: *Cradle Tales of Hinduism* (Calcutta: Advaita Ashrama).
An anthology of Hindu stories (including Shiva, the cycle of the *Rāmāyana*, the cycle of Krishna) retold by a Western member of the Ramakrishna order. Available from the Ramakrishna Vedanta Centre.

Perry, Tony, 1978: *Our Hindu Friends* (National Christian Education Council: Denholm House Press). ISBN 0 8521 3167 4.
Rather dated format, written from a Christian perspective.

Peterborough, 1981: *Divali and Other Aspects of Hinduism*, (Resource Centre for Multi-racial Education) 165A Cromwell Road, Peterborough PE1 2EL.
An example of useful, locally produced resource material.

Ramachandran, A., 1979: *Hanuman* (London: A. and C. Black). ISBN 0 7136 1923 6.
A simple version of one of the myths about the monkey god

Hanuman. Illustrated with vivid modern Indian pictures (presumably by the author), this book is suitable for reading aloud to infants and lower junior children.

Rao, Shanta Rameshwar, 1986: *The Mahabharata* (London: Sangam Books). ISBN 0 8613 1607 X.
This is a well-produced, beautifully illustrated abridgement of one of India's two great epics. The text is rather densely written in parts but older juniors upwards should enjoy selections from it. There are notes on main characters and on illustrations. Inevitably, such an attractively produced book is expensive.

Ray, Sauresh, 1986: *A Hindu Family in Britain* (Exeter: RMEP). ISBN 0 0803 1782 0.
Replaces the volume with the same title written by Peter Bridger (see above). An English girl makes friends with fellow pupils at her school who are Hindus and gradually learns about their way of life. Readers are introduced to Hinduism Bengali style; it is good to have one of Britain's smaller Hindu communities represented. The material is detailed and wide ranging, including topics of community relations and historical interest as well as many aspects of Hindu religion. Illustrated with over 60 b/w photographs. Upper secondary.

Ray, Sauresh, 1985: *Saraswati Puja*, *Living Festivals* series (Exeter: RMEP). ISBN 0 0803 1745 6.
Written by a Bengali Hindu author who is also head of a London primary school. Includes some black and white illustrations reproduced from photographs. The best parts of the text draw on the author's own experiences and memories. Middle and secondary.

Schools Council, 1978: *The Hindu Way*, *Journeys into Religion* series, Schools Council Religious Education in Secondary Schools Project (St. Albans: Hart Davis).
Emphasises practice rather than belief, encourages pupils to enter imaginatively into the Hindu way of life and gives them the opportunity to investigate and discover for themselves. Illustrated with black and white photographs. A more balanced treatment than many other school books though the authors' admirable attempts to be sympathetic occasionally lead to a degree of romanticism, e.g., about caste and marriage. Upper secondary.

Sharma, D., 1984: *Hindu Belief and Practice* (London: Edward Arnold). ISBN 0 7131 0943 2.
It is valuable to have books available written from inside the

tradition, but it is important that pupils should realise that this textbook is written from a particular stance within Hinduism. The author's position is pantheistic rather than monotheistic; personified forms of God are treated briefly under the heading 'popular deities', and the glossary of Sanskrit words includes neither *bhakti* (devotion) nor *Bhagwān*, the commonest monotheistic term for God. The chapter on Hindu women is devoted to marriage and the status of women, but ignores domestic rites and fasts. Nevertheless the text is useful for older secondary students as an introduction to a position which favours the 'way of knowledge', rather than the ways of works and of devotion (p. 178).

Sharpe, Eric, 1971: *Thinking About Hinduism* (London: Lutterworth). ISBN 0 7188 1822 9.

Although the book over-emphasises belief and tends to give the impression that theory and practice are not closely connected this is a thorough and clearly written short introduction. Older secondary pupils.

Singh, Gurdip, *Ten Stories From Hinduism*, privately published n.d., available from Mrs J. Kaur, 22 Haselbech Road, Coventry, West Midlands.

Includes three Krishna stories and the story of Prahlāda, which is associated with the Holī festival. Older juniors.

Singh, Rani, 1984: *The Indian Storybook* (London: Heinemann). ISBN 0 4349 6330 5.

Eight well-told stories from the Hindu tradition (including stories of Vishnu, Hanuman and Krishna) illustrated in black and white and colour by Bryan Orion. Suitable for upper juniors, but could be read to younger children.

Solomon, Joan, 1984: *Sweet-tooth Sunil* (London: Hamish Hamilton). ISBN 0 2411 1201 X.

The text, illustrated with colour photographs, describes the celebration of Diwālī in a British Hindu family, giving a child's perspective on the adults' devotions to Lakshmī, the goddess of wealth. Suitable for infants and lower juniors.

Solomon, Joan, 1981: *Wedding Day* (London: Hamish Hamilton). ISBN 0 2411 0552 8.

An attractively-written account of a Hindu wedding in Britain seen through the eyes of a Hindu girl and her non-Hindu friend. Fully illustrated with colour photographs. Suitable for reading to infants and lower juniors and as a reader for juniors.

Thompson, Brian, 1980: *The Story of Prince Rama* (London: Kestrel Books). ISBN 0 7226 5684 X.
An attractive retelling of the Rāma and Sītā story with beautiful colour illustrations, some traditional and some by the contemporary painter Jeroo Roy. Junior and lower secondary.

Thompson, Ruth, 1986: *My Class at Diwālī* (London: Franklin Watts). ISBN 0 8631 3425 4.
An account of Diwālī celebrations, including a dramatisation of the Rāma and Sītā story, at a predominantly white primary school. Fully illustrated with colour photographs by Chris Fairclough. Infants and lower juniors.

Troughton, Joanna, 1975: *The Story of Rama and Sita* (Glasgow: Blackie). ISBN 0 2168 9895 1.
A junior level retelling of the story, illustrated attractively in black and white by the author. Confusingly, only the monkey king Sugrīva, and not the more important Hanuman, is mentioned as a major character in the tale.

West London Institute, 1985: *Hindu Gods*, available from RE Centre, West London Institute of Higher Education, Borough Road, Isleworth, Middlesex.
A useful 'duplicated' booklet, produced by young people on an MSC project. Line drawings and explanatory notes covering the ten avatāras of Vishnu, Lakshmī Shiva, Pārvatī, Ganesha and Kārttikeya (Skanda).

Yogeshananda, Swami, 1973: *The Way of the Hindu* (Amersham: Hulton). ISBN 0 7175 0626 6.
Combines a practising Hindu's insights with a commendable sense of balance and detachment. A range of topics, including some often ignored in schoolbook presentations of Hinduism (South India; time), is arranged around the central theme of pilgrimage. Lower secondary.

Pupils' Books (Thematic)

Several books which deal with religions thematically contain material on Hinduism. These include the following:

Bailey, John, *Religious Buildings and Festivals* (1984) ISBN 0 7217 3033 7; *Founders, Prophets and Sacred Books* (1985)

ISBN 0 7217 3034 5; *Worship, Ceremonial and Rites of Passage* (1986) ISBN 0 7217 3035 3. *Religion in Life* series (Huddersfield: Schofield and Sims).

This series for secondary pupils emphasises religion in contemporary Britain. The books are well illustrated with colour photographs and include questions at the end of each unit of work to encourage discussion. The first book deals with two themes and covers five religions. Books 2 and 3 deal with three themes, and religions are covered separately (one religion per unit). The brief discussion of Hinduism inevitably leads to imbalances and a superficial treatment. *Religious Buildings and Festivals*, for example, fails to stress the diversity of the tradition e.g. p. 101 does not mention the great range of Navarātri/Dasahrā celebrations. The list of gods on p. 63 includes Nandi, Shiva's vehicle, as a deity. The description of Kālī as the 'goddess of motherhood' is odd – *all* forms of the goddess are referred to as Mā (mother).

Bennett, Olivia, 1984: *Exploring Religion* series (London: Bell and Hyman).

Festivals (ISBN 0 7135 2330 1) is an appealing and well-illustrated book covering four festivals including the Hindu festival of Diwālī *Buildings* (ISBN 0 7135 2330 1) covers a Christian church, a Jewish synagogue and a Hindu temple. *Signs and Symbols* (ISBN 0 7135 2329 8) deals with Christian, Jewish and Hindu symbolism. Good text, illustrations and teachers' notes. This very good series is aimed at the junior/middle range.

Brown, Alan, (ed.) 1987: *Religions* (London: Longman). ISBN 0 5822 2341 5.

Written for GCSE students, this volume includes a chapter by the editor on Hinduism. Useful basic information, but needs to be supplemented with further material that draws on Hinduism as a living tradition.

Butler D. G., 1975: *Many Lights* (London: Geoffrey Chapman). Versions rather than translations of passages from religious texts, including a selection of Hindu scriptures. The extracts are selected both because of their importance in the various traditions and because of their relevance and interest to children of varying abilities aged 11–15.

Cole, W. O., (1981) 1985: *Six Religions in the Twentieth Century* (Amersham: Hulton). ISBN 0 7175 1290 8.

Aimed at GCSE candidates primarily, though a useful general introduction for non-specialist adults. Hinduism is one of the faiths covered in six chapters dealing with the themes 'Messengers', 'Scriptures', 'Worship', 'Pilgrimage', 'Festivals' and 'The Coming Together of Religions'.

Cole, W. O. (ed.), 1982: *Comparative Religions* (Poole: Blandford Press). ISBN 0 7137 1266 X.
Includes a chapter by a Hindu author, which is both Vaishnava and Gujarati in its emphasis. Suitable for sixth formers and as a teachers' resource.

Collinson, C. and Miller, C., 1981: *Believers : Worship in a Multi-Faith Community* (London: Edward Arnold). ISBN 0 7131 0525 9.
Includes material on Hinduism in Wolverhampton (good black and white photographs) and deals with places of worship, sacred books in worship and prayer in worship. Older secondary.

Collinson, C. and Miller, C., 1984: *Milestones: Rites of Passage in a Multi-Faith Community* (London: Edward Arnold). ISBN 0 7131 0961 0.
Includes material on 'birth ceremonies', 'ceremonies of commitment', 'marriage ceremonies' and 'death'. A useful selection of black and white photographs. As is often the case in books which deal with initiation ceremonies, there is undue emphasis on the sacred thread ceremony. Suitable for upper secondary work.

Davies, R, 1981: *Holy Books*, 'The Religious Dimension' series (London: Longman).
A rather dull presentation, with some over-simplifications. Nevertheless a useful source of basic information about texts.

Mayled, John, 1986, 1987: *Religious Topics* series (Hove: Wayland). *Initiation Rites* (ISBN 0 8507 8767 X), *Pilgrimage* (ISBN 0 8507 8768 8), *Marriage Customs* (ISBN 0 8507 8718 1), *Death Customs* (ISBN 0 8507 8719 X), *Feasting and Fasting* (ISBN 0 8507 8769 6), *Religious Buildings* (ISBN 0 8507 8952 4), *Family Life* (ISBN 0 8507, 8722, 6).
Each of these hardback thematically-organised information books has about four pages devoted to Hinduism, each page having an attractive colour photograph and a short simple, passage in large type. There are some false assumptions (e.g. most Hindus do not pass through sixteen *saṃskāras* during their life), plus occasional factual errors and inclusion of unnecessary technical terms. Suitable for juniors, but should be supplemented with other material.

Parrinder E. G., 1961: *Worship in the World's Religions* (London: Faber).
Sections on mythology, ritual (almost half the book) and biography (famous teachers and mystics) include selective coverage of Hinduism. Includes material on the Goddess, various Brahmin rituals, an account of pūjā as performed by a non-sectarian household priest. Also deals with temple worship in some detail, and introduces festivals, places of pilgrimage and cremation ritual. Secondary.

Wigley, B. and Pitcher, R., 1972: *Faith Looks Outwards, The Developing World: Religion Three* (London: Longman).
The overall presentation is sketchy and disjointed and although at first glance the text seems to offer a liberal plea for reformed Hinduism, the book's negative and eccentric comparisons between Hinduism and aspects of Christianity seem designed to undermine the former. Examples of inaccurate and misleading claims include the assertion on p. 52 that only five per cent 'of all Holy Men' are genuine gurus, and the suggestion on p. 48 that Hindu vegetarianism (especially the refusal to kill cows) is a cause of poverty in India. This book and others in this series – *From Fear to Faith* and *Paths to Faith* are not recommended.

Audio-visual resources

Slides

The Bury Peerless Collection

Slides of a very good quality, each set accompanied by brief explanatory notes, are produced by Ann and Bury Peerless (p. 237), and distributed by them. Note that Bury Peerless regularly revises his material, adding new slides and notes as appropriate and he will provide up-to-date lists on request (enclose SAE). The following sets, grouped here thematically, were available at the time of writing.

(i) HINDU MYTHOLOGY

Hindu Mythology : 36 slides and notes.
Sculptures and miniature paintings of the main gods. Useful slides on the Krishna legend, on Rāma and Sītā, and on the avatāras of Vishnu.

Gods and Goddesses of the Hindus : 12 slides and notes.

The main concern here is with Brahmā, Vishnu and Shiva.

The Ten Incarnations of Vishnu : 12 slides and notes.
The avatāras shown from sculpture or miniature paintings with detailed notes on each.

Rama and Scenes from the Ramayana : 20 slides and notes.
The notes give a resume of the story of the *Rāmāyana*, focusing particularly on the Rāma and Sītā element; the slides are again a combination of sculptures and miniature paintings.

The Krishna Legend : 24 slides and notes.
A collection based on miniature paintings and drawing largely on the Purānic accounts of Krishna's birth, childhood and youthful exploits in Vrindāvan. The sequence ends with the lesser known story of Krishna's marriage to Rukmini and usefully with the Krishna of the Gītā accompanying Arjuna at Kurukshetra.

Shiva, his many different forms and aspects : 24 slides and notes.
The stories surrounding Shiva are probably less familiar in this country than those concerning Krishna or Rāma. This slide set is useful therefore in highlighting varying iconographic representations of Shiva and pointing to some of the mythology which surrounds him – though the notes tend to be a little 'thin'.

(ii)   FESTIVALS

Durga Puja : 24 slides and notes.
This festival (above, p. 132) is a celebration of Durgā, one of the forms of Pārvatī Shiva's consort. The slides show the celebration of Durgā Pūjā in a Bengali community in Delhi.

Ramlila : 24 slides and notes.
Rāmlīlā – literally the 'play of Rāma' – comprises an acting out of the story of Rāma and Sītā. The plays form part of the larger celebrations surrounding the Durgā Pūjā/Dasahrā festival in some parts of India. The studies show Rāmlīlā celebrations in Delhi.

Saraswati Puja : 24 slides and notes.
Slides of the festival as celebrated in rural West Bengal. Cf Ray (1985).

(iii)   TEMPLES AND RELIGIOUS CEREMONIES

Hindu Temples : Meenakshi and Brihadeesvara : 12 slides and notes.
Slides of two famous south Indian temples, useful for highlighting some key features of temples, e.g. Gopuram, Shikhara, Mandapa.

Lakshmi Narayan Temple, Delhi : 24 slides and notes.
Slides of the temple funded by the Indian industrialist, Birla.

A Hindu Temple including puja : 12 slides and notes.
Slides taken in the Jagdīsh Temple in Udaipur, devoted to the worship of Vishnu; briefly shows individuals at the shrines and circumambulation as well as some significant temple features.

Hindu Shrines : act of worship including a wedding ceremony : 12 slides and notes.
A collection which shows a variety of shrines – temple, wayside, school and home. Includes 2 wedding slides which are really marginal to the set as a whole.

The following slide sets show various aspects of temple sculpture, architecture and art. Numbers of slides are given in brackets.

Ellora Cave Temples (12)

Elephanta Cave : Sanctuary of the God Siva (12)

The Shore Temple and rock sculpture, Mahabalipuram (12)

Chennakesava Temple, Belur (12)

Hoysala Temple, Halebid (40)

Kesava Temple, Somnathpur (28)

Chandella Temples, Khajuraho (40)

Terra-cotta Temples of Vishnupur, W.Bengal (40)

Hindu Funeral and Cremation : 12 slides and notes.
Interesting slides mainly of the funeral of a Rajput Queen of Mewār – a former princely state – in Rajasthan. The notes here are slight, providing only a 'caption' for each slide.

Hinduism in India : A pilgrimage to Tirupati : 24 slides and notes.
Tirupati is one of the most famous places of pilgrimage in South India, the focus of worship being Vishnu in the form of Lord Venkateswara – an example of a modern Hindu revival movement.

A Pilgrimage to the Holy City of Benares : 40 slides and notes.

Kali Worship : 12 slides and notes.
Slides taken in Calcutta, Kalighat and Dakshineswar.

Temple Car Procession in Udupi : 24 slides and notes.
This set of slides relates to religious festivities in Udupi some sixty miles north of Mangalore in South West India. Krishna is the focus of worship and according to legend his image was installed in Udupi by Srī Madhvāchārya or Madhva (above, p. 177; p. 187). The slides show a temple car procession, and the installation of a boy Swāmī a tradition going back to Srī Madhvāchārya.

(iv)   PEOPLE AND PLACES

Hindu Holy Men and Holy Places : 24 slides and notes.
These slides take the viewer to 7 holy places of India, including for example the birthplaces of Rāma and Krishna. They also depict various types of holy men – and end with the memorial temple to Gandhi at Cape Comorin.

Mahatma Gandhi : 12 slides and notes.
The notes here offer a biographical sketch of Gandhi, whilst the slides focus on places associated with Gandhi, and where he is remembered today – especially his birthplace, Porbandar.

Religious Reformers : Kabir and Ramakrishna : 20 slides and notes.

Sathya Sai Baba : 24 slides and notes on a currently popular Hindu sectarian movement.

Hinduism in Malaysia : 24 slides and notes.

Ancient Cults : 50 slides and notes.
A collection including village deities, snake stones, effigies in ghost houses etc. South India.

Slides from Other Sources

Slide Centre Ltd. *Hindu Worship* : 24 slides and notes, (Slidefolio : S1415) 1980.
One of a recent series which looks at worship in different religious traditions. The pūjā shown on the slides is in a mandir in Leicester.

Slide Centre Ltd. *Search for Meaning: Who is my neighbour?* 12 slides and notes. (Slidefolio : S1079) 1976.
Slides designed to complement the *Search for Meaning* series of books published by Denholm House Press. The slides are concerned with *Holi in Coventry*, Holī being a Spring festival celebrated in many parts of India.

Slide Centre Ltd. *A Hindu Wedding*: 24 slides and notes. (Slidefolio : S1526), 1986.
The slides illustrate the main steps in the wedding ritual and were photographed during a wedding ceremony in Britain.

Slide Centre Ltd. *The Hindu Temple and its Symbols.* (Slidefolio : S1525), 1986.
Covers some aspects of iconography as well as more abstract symbolism (e.g. swastika, yantra). The photographs were taken in Hindu temples in Britain.

MGSS. Divali Slides : 31 slides with notes.
A delightful sequence in which children from Pridmore Infants'
School Coventry act out the story of Rāma and Sītā 'on location'
in the grounds of a local stately home. Available from MGSS
(p. 236).

Farmington Institute, *A Christian Approach to Hinduism* : 12 slides
and notes, suggestions for use and audio cassette.
This kit concentrates on the life and teaching of Srī Ramana, used
as 'an example of Hinduism in practice', (Slides 1 – 6) and on one
particular Christian response to Hinduism that represented by
the Christian āshram in Pune (Slides 7 – 12). The tape includes a
play about an imaginary visit to the Srī Ramana āshram (in order
to highlight 'possible western reactions') and material relating to
the āshram. The life of the Christian āshram is also described and
discussion material is provided. Available from The Farmington
Institute, 4 Park Town, Oxford.

Farmington Institute, *Pilgrimage to Varanasi*, 1984.
12 slides with full notes, plus suggestions for work with secondary
pupils. Available from The Farmington Institute, 4 Park Town,
Oxford.

Diwali : 28 slides and notes.
The set is about the festival but tells of it through dance. Available
from Dancevision (below).

Storyteller : 46 slides and notes.
An extensive set looking at Indian Dance and its links, for
example, with natural forms and temple sculptures. Available from
Dancevision, Natya-Padam, 1 Alfred Road, London, SE25 5LE.

Filmstrips

A Hindu Puja, Educational Productions, 1979, (Filmstrip No.
C6820)
This filmstrip of 15 frames explores pūjā in the home; it offers a
clear and sound set of notes, but the detail to which they draw
attention is not always clearly visible in the pictures. (See also
Hindu Puja p. 225).

The following filmstrips are now dated, but are nevertheless
still useful if selected frames are used and the notes updated:
Hinduism in India, CMS; *Hinduism*, Concordia; *Hinduism*, Education Productions; *India – Religion*, Gateway Educational Films
Ltd.

Posters and Photographs

Pictorial Charts Educational Trust, 27 Kirchen Road, West
   Ealing, London W13 OUD.
This trust has in recent years produced material on world religions. The following sets are those which include a poster
relating to the Hindu tradition:

E700 Creation Stories I, E720 Birth Rites, E722 Marriage Rites,
E724 Holy Places, E725 Holy Writings, E727 Holy Books II,
E729 Days of Worship.

Pictorial Charts Educational Trust, *Hindu Festivals* (E 748) 1982.
A set of four colourful and informative charts, covering six Hindu
festivals that are important in India and central to the calendar of
those Hindus in Britain whose families came originally from
Gujarat. The festivals covered are Mahā-Shivarātri, Holī, Rāma,
Navamī and Janmāshtamī (Rāma and Krishna's birthdays respectively), Navarātri and Diwālī. A set of notes accompanies the
charts.

Pictorial Charts Educational Trust, *Hindu Gods* (E 731) 1985.
Beautifully reproduced colour pictures of Brahmā, Shiva and
Pārvatī, Hanuman, Vishnu and Lakshmī, Rāma and Sītā,
Ganesha, Krishna and Rādhā, Durgā. The notes, however, con-
tain some oversimplifications and should be augmented with
reliable material on Hindu iconography.

Pictorial Charts Educational Trust, *Indian Musical Instruments*
   (R744), 1986.
Eight 25 × 38cm photographs and notes.

Pictorial Charts Educational Trust, *Indian Dance, The Story of
   Diwali* (R754), 1986.
Eight 25 × 38cm photographs and notes.

Argus, *Major World Religions Series*, Poster 42905.
Picture of a shikhara with Vaishnavite devotees and caption
   'Truth is what is – and what is the beauty of it.'

Argus, *Major World Religions Series*, Poster 42917.
Seven posters in this series offer graphic representations of sym-
bols with a quotation relevant to the faith in question. The
Hinduism poster shows the syllable *Om*.

The Bhaktivedanta Book Trust offers a wide range of posters
including pictures of Hindu deities. A list is available from the
Trust (p. 236).

Ann and Bury Peerless, *Durga Puja*.

Large colour print of the placing of the image of the goddess in a river at the end of the celebrations (see p. 237 for address).

Slough Intercultural Services, Thomas Gray Centre, Slough SL1 3QW., *Symbols of Faith.*
One poster in the set is given to Hinduism : each poster shows one or more symbols and gives explanatory comments or a 'text' from the tradition. The set was prepared by Slough Intercultural Services and Berkshire Advisory Service.

Dancevision Natya-Padam : *Bharatanatyam : The Classical Dance of South India.*
12 photographs (colour and b/w) with notes introducing aspects of Indian Dance (see p. 223 for address).

Audio-tapes and Radio Broadcasts

Audio-Tapes

W. Owen Cole, *A Hindu Puja*, Educational Productions 1975.
The tape was originally available in conjunction with the film-strip). The tape discusses the term 'Hinduism', comments on the nature of pūjā and goes on to look at some extracts from Hindu scriptures used in pūjā; they are chanted in Sanskrit and then spoken in English. The notes provide a translation of the texts and suggestions for activities.

Ninian Smart, *The Indian Religious Experience*, Living Parish Tapes. A one hour tape, in which the origins and developments of Hinduism and Buddhism are examined, together with their interaction with existing cultural patterns.

Open University, *AD 208 Man's Religious Quest*: 02/05 Devotional Hinduism/A Hindu Testimony : 06 The Hindu Temple.
Each sequence lasts 20 minutes. *Devotional Hinduism* examines some devotional chants in relation to the bhakti tradition, whilst its reverse side offers insight from a priest and teacher in the Hindu community on his childhood in India. *The Hindu Temple* discusses the kinds of motive a Hindu might have in visiting a temple.

Sussex Tapes, MP11, *'Mahatma' Gandhi*, 1982
The speakers on this tape – Richard Tames, Peter Robb and David Taylor (all of SOAS) – describe Gandhi's development as a political figure and a thinker and assess his impact within India. Teachers notes include a summary of the cassette, questions for discussion, topics for research and a bibliography. Sixth-form level.

Radio broadcasts

The following programmes have all been broadcast on BBC Radio 4. Many Teachers' Centres stock copies of the programmes, which can either be borrowed or copied for use in schools. Most of the programmes are repeated from time to time and it is worth checking the annual list of programmes published by the BBC. An increasing number of past broadcasts and Radiovision filmstrips will become available in the future from the BBC School Radio Shop (p. 236). The free catalogue is constantly being expanded. The series *Quest* was aimed at the 9–12 range but since 1986 has been aimed at lower secondary pupils. *Religious Education* covers the 13–16 age range, and *Religion and Life* (no longer being broadcast) was aimed primarily at 6th formers. The dates listed below indicate when programmes were first broadcast.

Festivals: *Hindu* (Religious Education, January 1976). Holī in Coventry as celebrated by Gujarati and Punjabi Hindus.

Coventry's Square Mile (Radiovision – 'Religion and Life'). Shows arati at the Shree Krishna Temple, Coventry. For fifth and sixth form now available as a pack from BBC School Radio Shop.

Holi (Quest, 23rd February, 1977). Describes a visit to the festival at the Shree Krishna Temple, Coventry, and includes a drama based on the story of Prahlāda and Holikā.

Navaratri: (Radiovision – *Quest*, October 1977). Includes Hindu children talking about the festival of Navarātri at the Shree Krishna Temple, Coventry, and a drama connected with the goddess Saraswatī.

A Hindu Community in Britain (*Religion and Life*, October 1979). Includes a celebration of the festival of Rāma Navamī at the Shree Krishna Temple, Coventry, and a visit to a Hindu wedding.

Signs of Life (Radiovision – *Quest*, October 1979). Three frames on the sacred thread ceremony with commentary by a Maharashtrian Hindu who lives in England.

The Problem of Suffering: *The Hindu View* (*Religious Education* 1981).

Celebration Meals: (Radiovision – *Quest*, March 1980). Frames showing prasāda during ārati at the festival of Navarātri, Shree Krishna Temple, Coventry.

Sacred Books (Radiovision), (*Quest* and *Religious Education*, March, 1982). Includes frames showing the *Rāmāyana* during worship at the Shree Krishna Temple, Coventry, during the month of Chaitra, 1981.

Finding Out About Hinduism, Quest, 1981. Includes a dramatised version of a story from the Panchatantra, recordings of bhajans at the Shree Krishna temple in Coventry and an interview with a member of the Shree Krishna temple congregation.

Places of Worship (Radiovision), *Quest* and *Religious Education*, 1984.

Celebrating Diwali, Contact 1983 (8–12 age range).

A Hindu Tale, Contact, 1983 (8–12 age range).

Places of Pilgrimage (Religious Education). Audio cassette available from the BBC School Radio Shop (p. 236). One side describes a Hindu pilgrimage to Vārānasī Secondary.

Death, Religious Education. Includes material on Hindu ideas and beliefs associated with death. Secondary.

Hindus and Sikhs in Britain, Quest, a radiovision programme illustrating family life, beliefs, worship and customs. (Spring 1987). Lower secondary.

Hinduism – the Festival of Holi, Quest. The programme uses the festival to consider a number of issues including the meaning and function of myth. (Spring 1987). Lower secondary.

Hinduism – the Festival of Navaratri, Quest. As well as dealing with the festival, Hindu ideas of the Divine are considered. (Spring 1987). Lower secondary.

Hinduism – the Festival of Divali, Quest. Diwālī's New Year theme is used as a springboard to consider 'sacred time' in the Hindu tradition (Spring 1987). Lower secondary.

Multi Media Kits

Argus, *Religion in Human Culture : The Hindu Tradition*, 1978. This kit consists of A Teachers Guide; A Reader; Two filmstrips with cassettes and guides (*Introduction to Hinduism* and *Hindu Rituals*); Set of 4 Blackline Masters (Word Associations, Major Historical periods in the development of Hinduism, Snakes and Ladders Game, Goal of Life in Hinduism.)
The kit provides a clearly structured programme for a study of Hinduism, with a sound background resource in the Reader.

Time Life, *The World's Great Religions : Hinduism*, 1973.

The kit consists of A Teachers' Guide to Hinduism; Two film-strips (Hinduism Parts I & II); Two audio cassettes (Hinduism Parts I & II); *Life* magazine reprint on Hinduism; Three spirit masters – 'exercises' on Hinduism. The Teachers' Guide consists largely of suggested objectives, questions for class discussion and the text of the tapes. Part I attempts to trace the development of Hinduism, touching on scriptures and key concepts : Brahman, samsāra, karma, yoga, caste and the dharma of varna and āshrama (p. 78; p. 97). Part II turns to Hinduism's rich myth-ology, but also has some reference to death and to Gandhi.

Mary Glasgow Publications, *Festivals*, 1984
One of the 5 filmstrips in this multi-media pack is on *Diwālī*; it is accompanied by well organised notes and a cassette tape and looks at the festival as celebrated by a Hindu family in Birming-ham.

Thomas S. Klise Co., *Great World Religions Series : My Soul is Brahman : the story of the Hindus*, 1981. (Filmstrip, audio cassette and notes).

This is one of a set of six soundstrips introducing world faiths, each intended to cover the development of a religion and its main duties and beliefs. The visuals depend heavily on artists' impress-ions and are subservient to a text which does not always lend itself to illustration. The subtitle, the 'Story of the Hindus' indicates a fundamental problem with this sound-strip: its tendency to systematise and thus to obscure the reality of many 'stories', indeed of many 'Hinduisms'.

Resource packs

Vida Barnett et al, *Diwali*.
An inexpensively produced pack planned with the primary school in mind. Prepared by teachers for teachers, assisted by Shap Working Party's Information Officer. Available from Mrs V Barnett, 81 St Mary's Road, Huyton, Merseyside, L36 55R.

S Y Killingley and D Killingley, *Hinduism Iconography Pack*. Avail-able from Grevatt and Grevatt, 9 Rectory Drive, Newcastle upon Tyne, NE3 1XT.
A4 size line drawings of Ganesha, Vishnu, Lakshmī and Sarasvatī supplemented by short explanatory notes.

Avon, *The Hindu Mandir*, 1984.
A resource pack including Teachers' Guide, pupil materials and a

slide set with commentary. An inexpensively produced pack introducing a Hindu temple in Britain. Available from Resources for Learning Development Unit, Bishop Road, Bishopston, Bristol, BS7 8LS.

Minority Group Support Service, Coventry Education Authority. The following resource packs are all available from MGSS (p. 236).

Divali Pack: aimed at the junior age range. Includes 'Happy Diwālī' posters in English, Punjabi, Hindi and Gujarati; a Diwālī card; a version of the Rāma and Sītā story; floor patterns (*alpanā* and *rangoli*).

Holi Pack: aimed at the junior age range. Includes background information on the festival; the story of Prahlāda, with illustrations for colouring; a contemporary account of the festival as told by a schoolboy; two Krishna stories with illustrations for colouring.

Gandhi Assembly Pack. Teachers' notes and overhead projector transparencies. Available in 'Junior' and 'Secondary' versions.

The Story of Mohenjo Daro: aimed at the 10–14 age range. This detailed project includes a Teachers' Guide, a booklet for pupils, a pupils' pack and a colour poster. The approach emphasises historical material and there is a limited amount of information on religion, not all of it accurate.

Invitation to a Wedding: Flexibly produced so that it can be adapted for use by several age-groups (junior-adult). Six accounts of weddings, one of them Hindu, and all with a Coventry connection. Includes a teachers' book, a pupils' book and a set of work cards.

Video Material and Television Broadcasts

Videos

CEM, *Hinduism through the eyes of young Hindus*.
Looks particularly at worship in home and temple, the idea of God, music and dance as expressions of worship, symbolism, Hindu cooking and food. A pupil booklet is to accompany the tape. Available from CEM Video, Lancaster House, Borough Road, Isleworth, Middlesex, TW7 5DU.

Videotext/Exmouth School, *Aspects of Hinduism*.
Fourth in the Videotext World Religions Series. Distinguished by its deliberate omission of spoken commentaries, this series

attempts to provide 'cameos' of religious traditions rather than 'tours'. The onus is on the teacher to *use* the material. This video looks at worship in the home and in the temple; the features of the temple; Diwālī; New Year; it offers interviews under the title 'Some Personal Views of Hinduism' and concludes with a wedding ceremony.

Open University, *Pilgrimage in the Hindu Tradition.*
Includes extracts from the film *An Indian Pilgrimage : Ramdevra,* used as the basis for the case study on pp. 141–5 above.

Television broadcasts

Among the television series for schools that have included material on Hinduism are the following. These programmes are likely to be repeated periodically.

Believe It Or Not : Central Television. Up to Summer 1986 the series included 'Hinduism', a programme featuring Hindus in Leicester, and 'Festivals', a thematic programme including material on Diwālī. Programmes for 1987 included material filmed in India especially for the series. They are 'Hinduism', 'Hinduism in India', 'Death', 'Pilgrimage' and 'One God?' Further details from The Education Officer, Central Independent Television plc, Central House, Broad Street, Birmingham, B1 2JP.

Theatre Box : Granada. 'The Prince and The Demons' (dramatisation of the Rāma and Sītā story).

Watch : BBC. Diwālī (6–8 years), October 1981.

Why? Because . . . : BBC 2. 'But Is It True?' A programme on the *Rāmāyana*, 1986.

Films

An Indian Pilgrimage : Ramdevra. University of Wisconsin South Asia Film Project. This film is the basis for the case study of pilgrimage in Chapter 12 of this book. Distributed by Scottish Central Film Library (p. 237).

Hindu Artefacts

The following items are available from specialist Asian shops, some of which are listed on pp. 236–7 (See pp. 27–8 on using artefacts and pp. 103–13 for information on worship). For worship (pūjā) booklets containing prayers and ritual instruction are often used. Such items as water, milk, rice grains, flower petals, fruit, coconuts and certain nuts all play a part as they are often offered to the deity and distributed among worshippers.

Thālī: Round steel tray (the sort used as a plate for meals too) on which other items used in pūjā are placed.

Katorī: Small round steel bowl in which e.g. coins or red powder might be placed. This stands on the thālī.

Spoon or *ladle*: For giving a spoonful of e.g. holy water or milk to each participant as formal worship ends.

Bell: Rung vigorously while the āratī hymn is sung and the thālī is moved in front of the deity.

Dīvā, dīpa: Earthenware lamp in which cotton-wool wick, soaked in clarified butter, is lit. Used in daily worship and particularly at Diwālī.

Pānchāratī: Metal lamp held in right hand and circled in front of the deity during āratī, after which it is proffered to each worshipper in turn and each wafts the light from the flames to his/her eyes and head.

Incense Sticks: Made from fragrant substances such as sandalwood, burned during worship especially. Brass holders for the sticks are also available.

Har: A garland, a means of showing honour. A gold tinsel one could be used to festoon bride and bridegroom during the marriage. A silver tinsel garland could decorate a religious picture. A photograph of a deceased relative is garlanded with a fragrant hār made of sandalwood shavings.

Toran: A decorative hanging made of red fabric, beadwork or leaves. Gujaratis in particular hang a toran over the doorway on propitious occasions and above their shrines.

Manjīrā: A pair of cymbals played as rhythmic accompaniment to bhajans (hymns).

Janeu (Gujarati), *Yajnopavīta* (Sanskrit), *Poita* (Bengali): Sacred cotton thread with which brahmin boys are still sometimes initiated. It is worn over the left shoulder diagonally across the chest (p. 91).

Maulī (Panjabi), *Mangal Sūtra* (Hindi), *Kumbhanaru* (Gujarati): Red cotton thread used in religious ceremonies e.g. it is tied around a coconut or around the right wrist of someone performing a pūjā or around bride's and bridegroom's right wrist.

Rākhī: A decorative thread tied by a girl or woman around a brother's right wrist on Rakshā-bandhana day (p. 130).

Wicks: Made by twisting raw cotton (cotton wool). These are used in a dɪva or pancharatɪ and are soaked in clarified butter.

Diwali cards: Contain greetings in English and Gujarati or another Indian language for the festival of Diwālī (usually in November) (p. 130).

Kumkum (Hindi), *Kanku* (Gujarati): Scarlet powder for use in worship e.g. for tracing a sacred motif such as the Swastika on the thālī used in āratī It is also applied to worshippers' foreheads as a red dot and worn in a women's hairparting to show she is married.

Mālā: A rosary – of white wood beads, or the multi-faceted *rudrāksha* seeds (these are expensive) or *tulsī* (basil) stems (worn particularly by devotees of Vishnu/Krishna such as members of ISKCON). Rosaries are used in meditation on God's name or a mantra (p. 108).

Gujarati calendar: 'Block' type calendars are available showing both the Gujarati lunar calendar and Western calendar months. Festivals and fasts are indicated.

Images (mūrti) of deities: These are usually available in plaster of paris, plastic or brass. Images of the major deities are readily available. They should, of course, be treated with great respect.

Hinduism in the General Certificate of Secondary Education

All five English and Welsh GCSE Examining Groups have one or more Religious Studies syllabuses which include Hinduism. A summary of the Hinduism components of the syllabuses for 1988 is given below. In all cases assessment is by both written examination and course work. Further details are available from each Examining Group (addresses below).

London and East Anglia Group

Syllabus B Candidates study two out of eleven units on offer, one of which is Hinduism.

Part 1 – The development of Hinduism

A Historical context: (The Indus Valley people and the Aryan invaders; The Vedic and Upanishad periods; The emergence of the caste system; Modern movements and people).

B Traditions and beliefs: (An outline of the literature; God; Basic concepts of existence and release).

Part 2 – Hindu practice

A Worship and ritual: (Puja; Festivals; Rites of passage; Sacred places).
B Application: (Stages of life; Expression of belief in daily life; Ahimsa; Social order and expression; Multi-cultural dimension).
Further details from Schools Examination Board, London University, Stewart House, 32 Russell Square, London WC1.

Midland Examining Group

Syllabus A Candidates study two out of seven options, one of which is Hinduism. The aim of the syllabus is to promote an understanding of the range and diversity of beliefs and practices within contemporary Hinduism.
1 Worship: Places of Worship (The Temple; Community Worship; Private/Individual Worship).
2 Special occasions: Fasts; Festivals; Life-cycle rituals (samskāras).
3 Pilgrimage
4 Sacred writings
5 Beliefs and values

Syllabus B A thematic study from *three* of: Christianity, Hinduism, Islam, Judaism, Sikhism. The topics are arranged under three sections. Section one is compulsory. In addition, candidates do *either* section two *or* three. Section three is assessed entirely by course work.
Section 1 Encounter with Religions: (Sacred buildings and places of worship; Worship; Festivals, Special days and fasts; Holy books; Beliefs; Moral values/precepts and qualities).
Section 2 Religious Practices: (Rites of passage; Major divisions and sects; Pilgrimages and special places).
Section 3 Religion in the Everyday World. (Candidates submit six assignments, two based on each of the three themes in this section. Each assignment must be based on a single topic within each theme, and must cover two religions. The six assignments as a whole must demonstrate some degree of achievement in all three of the religions studied.)
Theme One – Personal experience
  Topics : Friendship, marriage, divorce, family relationships, wealth

Theme Two – Community experience
Topics : Work, leisure, crime and punishment, author-
ity and government, people who need caring
for.
Theme Three – Inter Community Experience
Topics : International relations, poverty, planet earth,
human rights and prejudice.
Further details from Midland Examining Group, Syndicate
Buildings, 1 Hills Road, Cambridge CB1 2EU.

Northern Examining Association

Syllabus A   Dimensions of Religion. Candidates study two options, one of which may be Hinduism. They are expected to be
aware of the common ground that all Hindus share, as well as to
appreciate the great variety of practices found in Hinduism. They
will be expected to know and understand the proper terms for
aspects of the Hindu faith and practice which form part of the
subject content.
1 Practice
Worship in the home; Temples and shrines; Rites of passage
(life-cycle rituals): Pilgrimages; The major religious sects.
2 Central Beliefs
Scriptures and Religious Literature (outline only) (the Vedas,
Epics, Puranas); Ideas about the nature of God; Beliefs about life
after death.
3 Hinduism in Society
The origins of Hinduism in pre-Aryan and Aryan culture; The
caste system; The four stages of life; The important of Hinduism
as a way of life, in India and in Britain.

Syllabus B   Themes from Three World Religions. Candidates
study specified themes from *either* Section One : Buddhism,
Hinduism and Sikhism *or* Section Two : Christianity, Islam and
Judaism.
Hinduism
1 The Expression of Religious Belief in Practice
    (a) Religious lifestyles i.e. ways in which religious faith is
        expressed as a way of living.
        Among the lay/ordinary people (the four stages of life).
        Among holy men (brahmins; gurus; yogis; rishis).
    (b) Activities and rituals which express religious faith

(c) Expressions of religious belief on special occasions and in special places: (Festival of Diwālī Benares (Vārānasī), Hindu temples and shrines).

2 Central beliefs (Brahman/atman; karma and samsara; Moksha and rebirth; caste).

3 Scriptures: their nature, role and importance: (The Vedas)

4 Moral Values in the Modern World:

    (a) General values e.g. dharma, varna (p. 78) and āshram (p. 97), ahimsā 'non-injury'.

    (b) Particular issues (The role of women; family relationships; social equality).

Further details from NEA, Joint Matriculation Board, Manchester M15 6EU.

Southern Examining Group

Syllabus A   Two out of eight options, including Hinduism.

1 *Geographical and Historical Background*

2 *The Sacred Writings*: Candidates should be familiar with the name, authorship and origins, general outline of content of the following sacred writings and show an understanding of their importance in public and private devotions: The Vedas, The Upanishads, The *Rāmāyana*, The *Mahābhārata* (with special reference to the *Bhagavad-Gītā*, The Purānas.

3 *Beliefs*: In studying these beliefs, their application to everyday life and ethical issues should be considered. Brahman, the gods and humankind; life and liberation (samsara; class and caste; dharma; karma; reincarnation; moksha; samskāra; dietary laws; ahimsā (non-violence)).

4 *Worship, Festivals and Pilgrimage*

5 *Rites of Passage* (life-cycle rituals)

Syllabus B   Personal and Social Ethics in a Religious Context.
The syllabus considers three areas of ethical concern – marriage and the family; peace and conflict; humankind and nature – in the light of three world religions (Christianity, Hinduism, Islam) and a secular response where appropriate.

Syllabus C   A thematic study of any *three* of Buddhism, Christianity, Hinduism, Islam, Judaism and Sikhism.
The syllabus is in three parts (reference is made here to Hinduism only).

1 Sacred Buildings and Places of Pilgrimage.

2 Worship, Festivals and Ceremonies (life-cycle rituals).
3 Sacred Writings.
Further details from South Western Examining Board, 23–29 Marsh Street, Bristol B51 4BP.

Welsh Joint Education Committee

There are nine options arranged in three groups of three. Candidates must study one option from each of any two groups. Hinduism is an option in group two. The Hinduism option provides for a study of the diversity of Hinduism and what it means to be a Hindu today. This involves: knowledge of the historical background of Hinduism; a study of its main beliefs and practices; and of representative personalities and movements in modern Hinduism.
Material is studied under the following headings:
What does it mean to be a Hindu?; Principal Hindu beliefs; Worship and celebration; Customs and rites; Sacred writings; Hinduism in the modern world. Further details are available from the Welsh Joint Education Committee, 245 Western Avenue, Cardiff CF5 2YX.

Addresses

Articles of Faith, 123 Neville Road, Salford, M7 0PP. Tel. 061–792–6212 (Suppliers of religious artefacts).

BBC Schools Radio Shop, Centre for Educational Technology, Civic Centre, Mold, Clwyd, CH7 1YA.

Bhaktivedanta Book Trust, Croome House, Sandown Rd., Watford, Herts., WD2A 4XA.

Element Books, 23 All Saints Villas Road, Cheltenham, Glos., GL52 2HB. Tel. (0242) 516273. (Distributor of Sathya Sai Baba books and other books on Hinduism).

Gohil Emporium, Stratford Road, Birmingham, B11. Tel. 021–449–7827 (Supplier of artefacts).

International Society for Krishna Consciousness (ISKCON) Bhaktivedanta Manor, Letchmore Heath, Nr. Watford, WD2 8EP, Herts. Tel. Radlett 7244.

MGSS (Minority Group Support Service, Coventry Education

Authority), Southfields Old School, South St., Coventry, CV1 5ET.

National Council of Hindu Temples (UK), The Secretary, Shree Sanantan Mandir, Weymouth Street, Leicester, LE4 6FP.

Patel, Manubhai C., Sri Sathya Sai Centre of Wembley, 35 Clifton Avenue, Middlesex. Tel. 01–903–0886. (Supplier of books about Sathya Sai Baba and Bal Vikas books).

Peerless, Ann and Bury, 22 King's Avenue, Minnis Bay, Birchington, Kent, CT7 9QL. (Suppliers of slides).

Pictorial Charts Educational Trust, 27 Kirchen Road, West Ealing, London, W13 0UD.

Printrite Co., Mr. Harbans Singh, 18 Queen Victoria Road, Coventry. Tel. (0203) 278803. (Suppliers of Calendars).

Ramakrishna Vedanta Centre, Blind Lane, Bourne End, Buckinghamshire, SL8 5LG.

Sai World Gazette, The Editor, Devereux House, 50 Longley Road, London, SW17 9LL.

Scottish Central Film Library, Dowanhill, 74 Victoria Crescent Road, Glasgow, G12 9JN. (Distributor of a selection of films on Hinduism).

Shah Pan House, Mr. Suresh Shah, 523 Foleshill Road, Coventry. Tel. (0203) 665277. (Suppliers of books and artefacts).

The Slide Centre Ltd, 143 Chatham Road, London, SW11 5BR. (Suppliers of slides).

SOAS (School of Oriental and African Studies), External Services Division, Malet St., London WC1E 7HP.

Soma Books, 38 Kensington Lane, London, SE11 4LS.

Shreeram Vidyarthi, Books from India, 45 Museum Street, London, WC1A 1LR. Tel. 01–405–7226/5784. (Supplier of books and records).

Index

This Index includes brief explanations in brackets of Indian (mainly Sanskrit) words; quotation marks indicate a literal translation. Occasionally the corresponding Indian word is added in brackets to an English headword. Spelling and pronunciation of Indian words are explained on p. viii. As a further guide, compound words are separated in the Index by a hyphen, and the syllable which is usually stressed when speaking English is marked ´. However, since most words of only two syllables are stressed on the first, these have been left unmarked.